A TASTE FOR WINE

A new tasting masterclass for wine lovers

ROSE
MURRAY BROWN MW

MITCHELL BEAZLEY

HOW TO USE THIS BOOK

This book is made up of four sections, with feature spreads and tasting practices interspersed throughout, to equip you with the knowledge you need to hone your wine-tasting skills.

We begin with **Taste Essentials**, looking at what to consider before you start and the factors that influence how a wine tastes. **Understanding Taste** takes you through an A to Z of classic grape varieties and the process from vine to the bottle. In **Exploring Taste**, current popular styles are covered – from orange, pét-nat, natural, biodynamic, vegan and vegetarian, to low- and no-alcohol wines. **Origins of Taste** then guides you around the world's wine countries and regions, offering key facts and recommended producers.

Ten self-guided **Tasting Practices** lead you step-by-step, recommending wines and helping with handy crib sheets. These are specifically designed to be enjoyed at home, with or without friends. Consider each one as a separate lesson, expanding your knowledge first with the relevant information on the preceding pages. If you find it difficult to source the practice wines, look at the alternatives listed – or follow my online suggestions at rosemurraybrown.com.

You will also find six **Feature Spreads** dotted through the book (*italic* in contents opposite) on tinted pages, covering current key topics – from grapes, climate and carbon planning, to wine tourism and urban wineries.

Last but not least, enjoy the journey!

This book is dedicated to my mum, herself a prolific author and writer, who first encouraged me to put pen to paper all those years ago. 'Write about what you know,' she said – so I did.

CONTENTS

INTRODUCTION

When I was first asked to write this book, I hesitated. Yet another book on wine – do we really need it? I checked out my bulging bookshelf of glossy wine bibles and realized that something was missing – and that was the book I needed to write.

So here it is. This book is different in several ways. First and foremost, it is a practical, unpretentious wine book with ten self-guided tasting practices, from full rich reds to sparkling wines, that you can follow in your own home, in your own time – with or without tasting buddies. It's a book that will motivate you to try different styles and help you get the best out of each wine.

But it also goes way beyond that...

A Taste for Wine is also for the adventurous wine-lover. It's the first general wine guide to focus on important taste trends, highlighting indigenous varieties and introducing modern Piwi grapes in detail. There are special two-page features discussing important topics in our changing wine world – from carbon neutral wineries to climatic extremes and future-proof grapes – all looking to what's ahead and how our wine choices will be affected by climate change. These topics need to be aired and discussed, but it's not all doom and gloom: there are opportunities too – for example, look at the recent progress in England, Germany and Canada.

There are accessible chapters on tasting and assessing wine, why wines taste the way they do, where and how grapes grow and how different styles are made. Plus there is plenty of practical information on everything you need at home – from glassware, gadgets and serving temperatures, to spotting wine faults and pairing wine and food – all written by an expert who has been teaching people, like you, about wine for over 25 years.

One of the questions I am asked most frequently when I am teaching is which winery to visit. The detailed origins section takes a tour of 51 wine-producing countries and their regions, covering grapes, styles, top producers and much more. For the wine traveller, there is a directory of recommended wineries to visit, with features on the do's and don'ts when there and an exploration of the rise in urban wineries.

I first fell in love with wine in Italy – in a vineyard. There is no better way to stir passion and interest in wine than to stand on a hillside surrounded by vines, to sample the grapes, inspect a soil pit and learn why manure is buried in cow horns underground, or enter a dark cellar cave to taste the wine in situ, where it was made.

TAKING A LEAP INTO WINE

I wasn't brought up in a wine family or on a vineyard. The only drinks I remember at home were the ones my parents made themselves – nettle beer and elderflower fizz: home-brewing was popular back then in northern England. I recall hearing the odd explosion at night (my bedroom was next to the garage) as they bottled the fizz too warm or had forgotten to 'burp' the bottles – my first lesson in yeasts, sugar and fermentation.

My two light-bulb moments in wine came later – once when I had started working in the wine trade, blowing dust off bottles in the cellars at an auction house. In my first week, I got the chance to taste a venerable old Rhône wine, Hermitage La Chapelle 1961. I had never encountered anything quite like it. Layers of intense flavour dripped with juicy dark fruits, smelling hauntingly of old meat (as Syrah does with age). It took me back to my dad's garage, where he occasionally had an old deer hanging with the nettle beer. Wine can transport you.

My second inspired moment was thanks to my wonderful first boss, the late Patrick Grubb MW, who not only gave me my first wine book but also a taste of pre-French Revolution 1780 Bual Madeira, which, combined with my interest in history, really excited me. How could a wine last that long and still taste so good? I needed to know more.

I feel particularly privileged to have been part of the wine world – and to have watched it progress over the past 40 years. When I first started working, Australian Chardonnay and New Zealand Sauvignon Blanc had only just arrived on UK shores; Argentinian Malbecs were yet to be discovered. Now we have so many exciting artisan wineries – and expansion is heading in a different direction: as polar ice caps recede and climate types shift, our wine world pushes boundaries heading ever closer to the poles.

Science has progressed too. Interestingly scientists still know surprisingly little about smell and taste, but researchers have been working hard to catch up with the world of wine. The existence of the fifth taste, umami, was only globally acknowledged in the 1980s, taste receptors for bitterness only identified in 2000, and for salt as recently as 2010. There will still be more to come, so get your glass ready and join the fun.

Wine has been an incredibly personal sensory journey for me, and I hope it will be for you too.

Rose Murray Brown

Rose Murray Brown MW

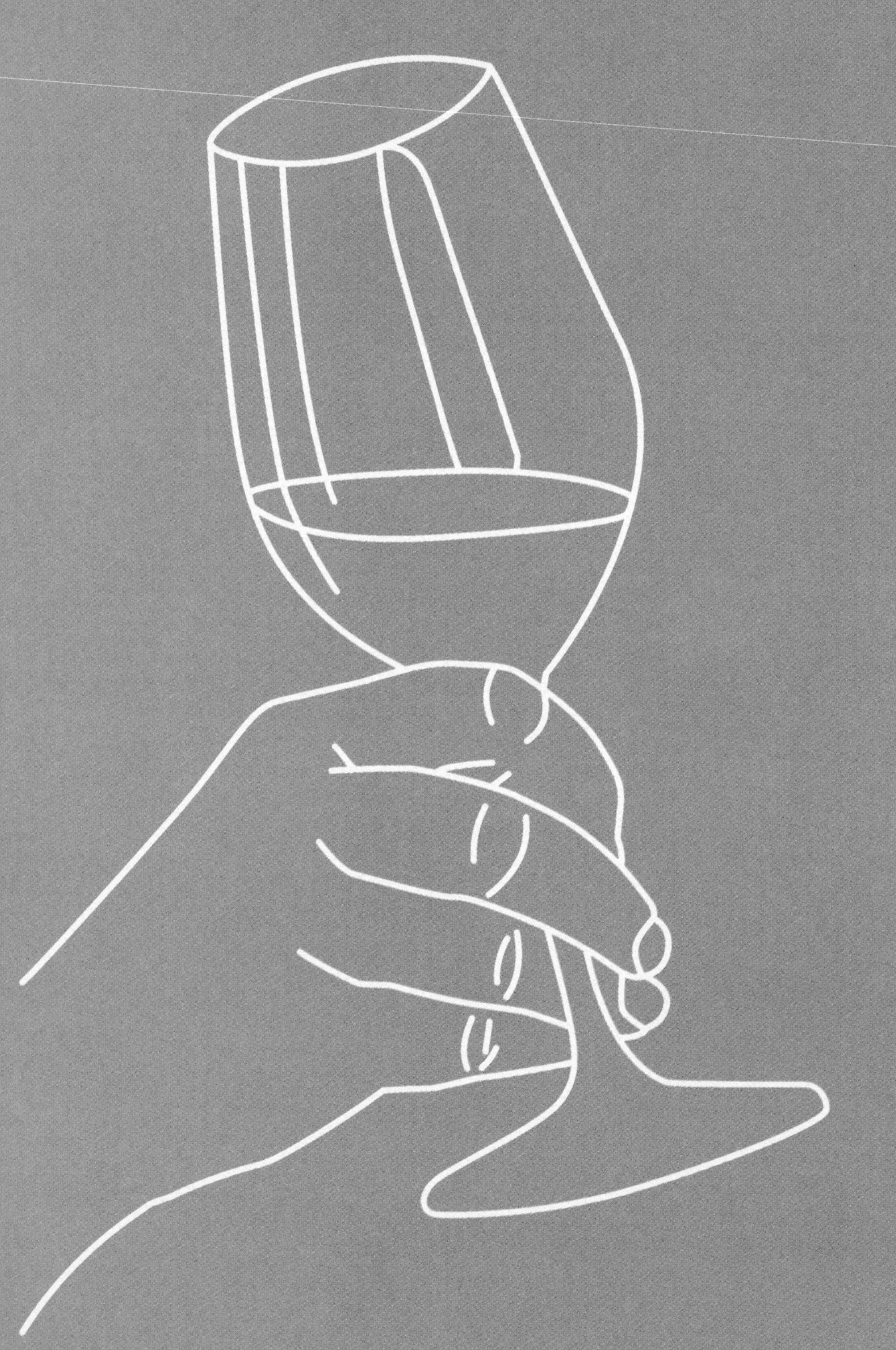

TASTE ESSENTIALS

HOW TO TASTE WINE STEP-BY-STEP GUIDE

① LOOK

Pour a tasting sample, and look down into the wine to assess clarity and depth. Now tilt the glass at an angle so that the wine's gradation of colour is clear against a white background, and note the wine's hue from rim to core.

Sniff the wine without swirling the glass and check its bouquet (*see page* 13), before moving on to the swirl stage.

② SWIRL

Next swirl the glass using a slow, small circular motion and sniff the wine again, noticing that different, heavier smells might now be emanating. The angle and position at which you hold the glass is important.

③ SMELL

Hold the glass around 2.5cm away from your nose, open your mouth just slightly when you sniff and breathe gently. Don't take a huge sniff; short ones are better.

Write down what you initially smell – your first sniff is by far the most important. Once you go back to the wine a few times, you might start to tire or the wine could warm up in the glass, so your perception will start to change. (*See page* 13.)

④ SIP

Take a sip – about a large teaspoonful – into your mouth; pass the wine around your taste buds and, at the same time, draw a little air into your mouth to aerate the wine and help spread the flavours around. Consider the different elements of acidity and alcohol – and tannins in red wines.

Take another sip and think about the balance of the wine; also the structure, mouthfeel and texture. Then the aftertaste and length of time you can still taste the wine.

Savour the wine, and finally spit it out in your spittoon in a long thin neat stream (without dribbling) – it's easy, but it's best to practise with water a few times first. (*See page* 16.)

TASTING & ASSESSING WINE

Wine tasting and drinking are both sensory experiences, but we perform them in different ways. Wine tasting involves slowing down reactions to make time to focus on the different senses: sight, smell, taste and mouthfeel.

Wine tasting is about paying attention to each element of the wine to help build up a bigger picture – a bit like learning the notes in music. This ensures that we get much more from a wine. The act of simply drinking wine, using only our basic sense of taste, is so fast and fleeting that many of the wonderful attributes of the wine can be lost and only a brief sensation is enjoyed. In wine tasting, by closely focusing on each of our senses, the result is so much more rewarding.

STIMULATE THE SENSES

To start, we need to stimulate and tune up our senses and unlock our memories. Our sense of smell, so important in wine tasting, is very emotive because the olfactory-bulb fibres at the top of the nose (which vaporized flavour compounds come into contact with) send smell signals to our brain and memory bank. Humans have an amazing capacity to appreciate smell; scientists have determined that we have 400 olfactory receptors that can detect a trillion different odours.

We don't learn how to smell – it comes naturally, and smells can evoke strong emotions. What we are not so good at is putting words to these smells – and that is what we need to do to help us appreciate wine. Learning to describe each smell we encounter in our everyday life helps us learn to differentiate one wine from another. Start by comparing the colours of everything in your house and try to describe them. Then turn to smells, inside and outside, and try to put a name to each. Repeat this to see if you can still pinpoint and describe the smell. Wine tasting is about repetition, tuning up our senses.

IMPORTANCE OF TEXTURE

When we start learning about wine, the focus is on differentiating smells and flavours, which is important, because much of what we think is taste is actually smell. Our fourth sense, touch or feel, is also key, because we can learn so much about a wine from its tactile sensation – the mouthfeel, structure and length. This is texture, and it's easier to describe than flavour, which is more personal. You can practise this too by tasting different liquids (water, beer, lemon juice, olive oil, milk) alongside each other, thinking about their mouthfeel, viscosity and texture.

We will look at the three stages of wine tasting next – appearance (sense of sight), aroma (sense of smell) and palate (senses of taste and touch).

SEEING

A wine's appearance is important – the clarity, colour and brightness can be very enticing and part of the ritual of enjoying a wine – but the knowledge it relays to us about a wine can be sparse.

In my experience, tasters find this the easiest part. Everyone can tell light from dark and describe colours; they feel confident making a verdict. In fact, visuals are so important in wine that some retailers stock wines on their shelves according to colour, rather than origin. However, while a wine's appearance might give us hints about its grape, origin and maturity, it doesn't tell us much about its quality. There are several factors to consider.

CLARITY

First check that the wine is clear, with no haze or sediment, by looking down into the glass at the wine's depth. Most wines today do have good clarity, so if it's hazy, it should be discarded. If there is a slight cloudiness, this can suggest a natural wine that has not been fined or filtered (*see page* 136), or if fizzy, it could be a pét-nat that might not have been disgorged (*see page* 138).

SEDIMENT

Less likely in whites than reds, sediment in a red might indicate it has not been filtered, since some winemakers feel filtration strips flavour. If small crystal deposits, glass-like shards, appear in a white wine, these are harmless tartrate crystals and indicate that the wine has not been processed with tartrate stabilization or that it has been stored somewhere very cold (-8°C/18°F).

BRIGHTNESS

Important for whites; if high- and low-acid wines are compared, the wine with higher acidity (eg. from grapes on volcanic soil) has greater brightness.

BUBBLES

In a sparkling wine, or Champagne, bubbles are obvious, but it's also possible to have tiny bubbles of carbon dioxide that cling to the glass in pale young light white wine. This effervescence derives from fermentation and can be retained as a deliberate part of the wine's style to give it zip (as in Portugal's Vinho Verde, French Muscadet *sur lie* or Touraine Sauvignon, or Txakolí from Spain's Basque Country). It can also be found in warmer-climate whites, with a little spritz added to the flavour by adjusting carbon dioxide levels just before bottling to convey freshness in low-acid wines.

If a red has distinct bubbles, it might be a sparkling Shiraz or Italian Lambrusco. If it is just a little spritz, it could have residual carbon dioxide at bottling, which helps freshness and gives lift, particularly with lighter reds like Gamay, but this can accentuate tannins.

If the wine is fizzy, smells of yeast and is vinegary and sharp (indicating unwanted secondary fermentation), then it is flawed (*see page* 26).

LEGS / TEARS

The curious thin threads or droplets of wine that form inside the glass when it is swirled are not a sign of quality or a sign of high glycerol. Scientists have established that evaporating alcohol causes this, known as the Gibbs-Marangoni Effect, named after two 19th-century physicists. Legs form with the effect of fluid surface tension; wines with high alcohol (Port) or with high tannins show legs more easily, but the shape and texture of a glass can also have an effect. This can give you an indication of a wine's structure, but not its quality.

COLOUR

It is best to order wines by their basic category (white, red, etc.) and then within that by shade. Colour can give an indication of grape and maturity, but not much about quality (*see page* 12).

WHITE WINE COLOUR

The colour of a white wine varies from almost water-white, to green-gold, through to deep-yellow.

FACTORS AFFECTING COLOUR IN WHITE WINE

Grape type: varies from deeper (Chardonnay) to lighter (Torrontés).
Climate: riper grapes grown in warmer climates give deeper colour.
Fruit intensity: can give deeper colour depending on the style.
Oak: fermentation and maturation in oak deepens colour in white wines.
Winemaking: lees ageing can protect a white wine from deepening in colour, whereas skin contact can have the opposite effect.
Age: white wines go darker with age, becoming gold and amber through oxidation.
Sweetness: some sweet German wines are pale in colour, whereas rich sweet styles of botrytis wine (Sauternes) are golden and darken with age due to caramelized sugars. A golden wine can still be dry (skin-contact orange wine; *see page* 134).

ARE OLDER WINES BETTER?

Some wines are made for early consumption; high-quality wines can improve with age (wine and storage depending); fine wines can need long bottle-ageing before they reach their peak.

RED WINE COLOUR

The pulp inside a red grape is grey-white. The colour of red wine derives from anthocyanin (purple) and tannin (amber) pigments extracted from the skins during fermentation and maceration. Colour is extracted first, while tannins leach out later in the presence of alcohol. The level of colour depends on the length of the fermentation and maceration (*see page* 96). From deep purple (young) through ruby red to brick red, red wines gradually lose colour, developing a tawny rim. As the wine ages, anthocyanins and tannins polymerize (link up) until they eventually drop out as sediment.

FACTORS AFFECTING COLOUR IN RED WINE

Grape type: thicker-skinned grapes have higher levels of anthocyanins, giving deeper colour (Cabernet Sauvignon, Malbec); thinner-skinned grapes (Pinot Noir, Gamay) will be paler.
Climate: riper grapes grown in warmer climates give deeper colour.
Fruit intensity: can give deeper colour.
Oak & winemaking techniques: oak maturation can stabilize colour because of chemical changes, due to oak-derived tannins binding with anthocyanins.
Age: red wines lighten with age.

Above left: Sauvignon Blanc, 14-year gap in age; right shows oldest.

Above right: Pinot Noir, 10-year gap; right shows orange-brick rim of the older wine.

SMELLING

Some tasters have an underdeveloped sense of smell that needs to be trained before they can put words to smells. Others may find this easier.

Wine experts use elaborate vocabulary, but remember it is perfectly possible for anyone to discern between thousands of everyday smells, and it's the same for wine. Time is needed to unlock memory banks and stimulate brains to remember what else is hidden away. It's also important to develop your own sense of smell and build your own personal memory bank, rather than relying on other people's opinions.

It is possible to have aroma blind spots – for example, not being able to smell vanilla or truffle – but most of us have enough olfactory receptors to be able to identify wine-tasting aromas.

The first thing to remember is that wine doesn't normally smell of grapes (as we know them), apart from Muscat (*see page* 42). Grapes often have similar volatile compounds to other fruits (raspberries, blackberries or gooseberries); and wines might have certain smells resulting from the fermentation or maturation process.

Using our sense of smell should become one of the most rewarding parts of the wine-tasting experience. We can tell so much from smelling, because much of what we think is taste is actually smell. All tastes (apart from the basic elements) are actually perceived as aromas by the receptor fibres (epithelium hairs) on the olfactory bulb at the top of our nose.

HOW SMELL WORKS

We smell several times in the act of tasting: initially when we sniff the wine, then when the wine warms up in the mouth and volatile aromas (composed of molecules) linger on the surfaces of the mouth and tongue, before filtering up the back of the mouth, which is known as the retronasal passage. This is why simply drinking (rather than tasting) is different, because without sniffing and enjoying the sensations of the wine through the nose, we do not fully appreciate flavour.

INFLUENCES ON SMELLS

Temperature can make a difference to how a wine smells: if the wine is warm, it vaporizes and gives off more aromas. Swirling and aeration motivate heavier molecules to rise up to your olfactory bulb. The shape and size of the glass can have a big impact too, and manufacturers produce numerous glasses to suit different grapes and styles. Personally, I prefer the universal glass, which works well across the board (*see page* 22). Remember, the first sniff is often the best, because your senses are at their most alert. Sense of smell can tire quickly, so be sure to take a break after several sniffs.

WHERE DO SMELLS COME FROM?

Grapes: The most obvious fruitier aromas (known as primary aromas) emerge from and just beneath the grape skins. White and red varieties vary widely in their aromatics – for example, Gewürztraminer and Sauvignon Blanc are pungently aromatic, while Chardonnay has gentler scents (*see pages 39 to 57*). Aromas from grapes vary from floral fresh fruits and dried fruits, to spice and greener herbal notes. *See* the checklist below for more detail.

Climate: The conditions in which a grape is grown make a big difference to the aromas. Warmer-climate wines (Chenin Blanc in South Africa) give riper, sweeter fruit notes in comparison to cooler-climate wines (Chenin Blanc in Loire, northern France). How the grower tends a vineyard with canopy and yield also makes a difference; excess canopy vegetation gives herby notes, while high-yielding wines have fewer aromas.

Vinification: How the wine is made affects its smell. Fermentation gives complex aromas (dairy-like, yeasty); if carried out in oak it leads to secondary aromas of vanilla and spice, whereas stainless steel retains the primary aromas of the grape.

Maturity: As a wine matures in bottle or cask, tertiary aromas develop. A wine's bouquet can

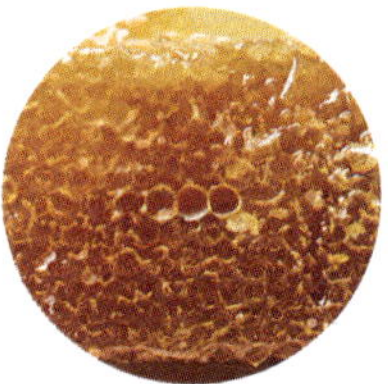

CHECKLIST OF AROMAS & FLAVOURS

Almond – Italian dry whites, Gamay.
Apple – varies from green apple in young whites with high malic acid, to apple blossom in young German Riesling and bruised apple in oxidized wines.
Apricot – Viognier, sweet Loire Chenin Blanc, Tokaji Aszú.
Asparagus – New Zealand Sauvignon Blanc with some age.
Banana – young Beaujolais or other carbonic-macerated reds (*see page* 97), Gewurztraminer.
Biscuity – bottle-aged Pinot Noir-dominant sparkling wine.
Blackcurrant – Cabernet Sauvignon.
Brioche – Champagne, both Chardonnay- and Pinot Noir-dominant.
Bubblegum – young Beaujolais or other carbonic-macerated reds.
Butter – Chardonnay, often caused by the malolactic process (*see page* 90).
Capsicum/bell pepper – New Zealand Sauvignon Blanc of the past.
Caramel – long-aged Tawny Port.
Cherry – red cherry in Pinot Noir, Zweigelt, Sangiovese; black-cherry notes indicate warmer-climate wine.
Cinnamon – ester (a volative compound that creates aroma) in bottle-aged whites like Gewurztraminer or Chardonnay, some Tawny Ports.
Citrus fruit – Chardonnay.
Cloves – emerges from new oak-aged wines, particularly American oak (from the eugenol aroma compound).
Earthy – like petrichor, the smell of soil or undergrowth after rain; often used to describe aged wine.
Elderflower – typical aroma of the Bacchus grape due to methoxypyrazines.
Eucalyptus – typically Australian Cabernet Sauvignon, Shiraz.

change as it ages, as esters form from acids and alcohols. Riesling can develop petrol aromas, Chenin Blanc honeyed aromas; Pinot Noir takes on barnyard notes, and Syrah more gamey, meaty tones, adding to the complexity of the wine.

HOW TO PUT WORDS TO SMELLS

It is best to use a checklist, so that when you sit down to taste a wine you have a list of all the possible smells. This can be an aroma wheel, your own checklist, or the list below. Initially it's much easier to pinpoint a smell this way rather than trying to pluck one out of your memory bank.

PUTTING IT INTO PRACTICE

It is a good idea to smell the wine straight after you have looked at it, without swirling and aerating it. The lighter molecules will rise up first. If you then swirl it and sniff again, you will find heavier molecules emerge and mingle – particularly with more mature wines.

Farmyard – mature Pinot Noir.
Flinty – often used to describe crisp high-acid wines like Chablis or Sancerre.
Floral – typical in young Riesling, Gewurztraminer, Muscat, Torrontés, Moschofilero, or Nebbiolo; they contain terpenes giving aromas of flowers.
Gooseberry – typical in Sauvignon Blanc.
Grapefruit – often in German wines, Scheurebe in particular, occasionally in cool-climate Chardonnay.
Green peppers – Chilean Carmenère, in cooler vintages of Loire Cabernet Franc.
Honey – many sweet wines, including mature dry Riesling and Chenin Blanc.
Leather – some Southern Rhône reds.
Lemon – youthful dry whites.
Lime – good-quality Clare Valley, Eden Valley, Frankland River Rieslings.
Licorice – Cabernet Sauvignon, fortified wines.
Peach – Viognier, Chardonnay.
Pear – young fermented whites.
Pepper – Grüner Veltliner, Northern Rhône Syrah, Southern Rhône red blends.
Petrol – mature Riesling, identified as TDN.
Plum – young Merlot.
Raspberry – Pinot Noir, Gamay or Cabernet Franc.
Spice – Alsace Gewurztraminer, reds aged in American oak.
Toast – Chardonnay-based Champagne, sparkling wine.
Vanilla – typical in new-oak-matured wines.
Violets – Northern Rhône Syrah or Piedmont Nebbiolo.

TASTING

Every part of the tongue is sensitive to all five primary taste elements: sweet, sour, bitter, salt and umami.

It was once thought there were specific areas on the tongue that were more sensitive to each of the taste elements, but scientists have disproved that theory. Taste is perceived by four different types of papillae (little raised bumps) all over the tongue; one filiform type determines texture, while the others are crammed with cells able to differentiate between these basic elements. There are also taste buds in our cheeks, at the back of the throat and on the upper part of the food pipe.

Some of us are more sensitive than others to bitterness, sweetness, sourness and savouriness.

Tastings are a great way to enhance knowledge and compare wines.

This difference, often genetic, explains why we don't all like the same types of wine. Scientists used to think that it was due to the number of papillae, but this has also been disproved and research is ongoing.

YOUR OWN TASTE-BUD MAP

Whatever causes your sensitivity, you need to get to know your own taste-bud map. The two most prominent primary elements in wine tasting are sweet and sour. To find out how these are perceived, it's best to practise first without wine. Sample water, lime juice and sugared water separately to experience where you sense the elements of sweet and sour in your mouth. Then try putting a little lime juice into the sugared water to see how the two elements balance each other out. If plain alcohol (a good brand of unflavoured vodka) is then added to the first three samples, it shows how alcohol spreads around the tongue. Adding a little to the lime-and-sugar-water mix will give the sense of a bland version of wine, while also introducing how the balance of sugar (or fruit), acidity and alcohol become important. To experience tannins, take a sip of oversteeped tea – you will feel the drying sensation across your palate and gums.

ASSESSING A WINE

When wine tasting is put into practice, the initial focus is on these primary elements, or main focal points, and how they are perceived in the wine.

By working through these in the same manner as above, we can start to consider how the sweetness (fruit), acidity, alcohol and tannin in the wine relate to each other when assessing the overall balance of the wine (*see also page* 18).

FEELING

Using our sense of touch, we can explore the tactile sensations of a wine. This could include measuring the bubbles of a fizz to determine the size and aggression of the mousse in a sparkling wine. It can also help us determine if a wine is too cold or too warm, which might affect its flavour, or the weight of a wine, depending on its extract.

TEXTURE

These tactile sensations continue as the wine passes across the tongue, determining the texture of the wine – this is known as mouthfeel. For example, one wine could be soft and silky, another oily; while yet another might be coarse and drying. The texture of a wine can be understood better through the combination of structure, weight and length.

Zalto Balance was the first glass designed to enhance wine structure.

STRUCTURE

The shape, size and type of acidity – often termed acid structure – is a helpful way of explaining the differences between grapes (*see pages* 18, 90). For red wines, the tannin structure is also key, but remember these can vary according to grape type, grape ripeness and wine maturity. By using our sense of touch, we can measure the amount and type of tannin and where you can feel it in the mouth (eg. gums or sides of mouth).

WEIGHT

A wine's weight (or body) is related to extract – the measure of its concentration of flavour. This is dependent on the level of fruit, sweetness and alcohol in the wine, as well as its age. A wine with weight could be either a dry wine with high alcohol and intense fruit, or a lower-alcohol style, such as sweet wine, made from vines with low yields. Red wines usually have a higher extract, due to their higher phenolic content (anthocyanins, tannins and flavour compounds, *see page* 57), and have more weight than white wines. Mature wines tend to have less weight because extract precipitates out over time as sediment (*see page* 25).

LENGTH

Finally, we assess the aftertaste of a wine. Some wines taste 'short', indicating limited flavours reach your throat before they disperse. A finish measures the length of time you can still taste the wine after swallowing or spitting.

High-quality wine has a wide range of persistent tastes and flavours that reach back into the throat and linger. If there is alcohol burn or bitterness on the length, this indicates a less well-balanced wine.

THE LANGUAGE OF WINE

To help understand the elements in wine, each one is considered individually when tasting, and then together to see how they balance with one another.

BALANCE

This term is used to describe the harmony of all the elements in a wine. The alcohol strength, acidity, fruit, tannins and residual sugar meld together to create a seamless whole, with no one element dominating the palate.

ACIDITY

The sourness deriving from the acids present in wine is one of the primary elements sensed by taste buds in the mouth. Grapes have two main acids: tartaric and malic (lactic acid is produced by secondary malolactic fermentation, *see page* 90). Acidity is vitally important in a wine, acting as a backbone or framework to its structure, and is particularly relevant in white wines, which have no tannins. At high levels, acid can be tart and sour, while at low levels it can make a wine taste dull and flabby. Grapes grown in cooler climates have higher acid levels, whereas those from warmer climates are less acidic. (Tartaric acid is often adjusted.) Acidity is important for any wine's balance, stability and preservation, also contributing to finesse.

ALCOHOL

This is created during fermentation, when grape sugars are converted by yeasts to alcohol. Levels are lower in wines produced in cooler climates (Mosel in Germany) and higher in wines from warmer climates (Barossa Valley in Australia). Alcohol helps spread flavours around in the mouth; it tastes hot, warm and sweet and is thick in texture.

RESIDUAL SWEETNESS

Natural grape sugar left after fermentation or any additions made before bottling is measured in grams per litre (g/l). Bone-dry would be 1 to 2g/l; it is rare to have 0g/l because yeasts cannot convert all sugars.

EU regulations stipulate: Dry up to 4g/l (up to 9g/l balanced with suitable acidity); medium-dry 4 to 12g/l; medium-sweet 12 to 45g/l; sweet 45g/l-plus. For sweet wine: Sauternes 125 to 165g/l; Tokaji Aszú 150 to 220g/l-plus; Essencia 450 to 900g/l.

TANNIN

Derived from the skins and pips of red grapes and new oak, tannins leave a dry puckering sensation in the mouth, rather like oversteeped tea. They can vary in strength (higher in thick-skinned Cabernet Sauvignon and lower in thinner-skinned Pinot Noir) and texture (soft, chalky, grippy or coarse) depending on the grape, winemaking decisions and influence of oak.

BITTERNESS

A bitter taste can come from unripe grape tannins, squashed pips and excess oak, and it gives a pricking sensation on the tongue. However, it can also be appealing on the finish of some Italian reds.

SALTY

A taste is rarely found in wine, unless the vineyard is right next to the sea or the soils have a salinity issue.

UMAMI

Few wines have a specific umami-savoury taste (often found in Parmesan cheese or soy sauce), because it mingles with the other primary tastes.

CAN RED WINE EVER BE CHILLED?

Light reds with soft tannins and refreshing acidity (Gamay, Pinot Noir, Frappato, Kadarka, Mencía, Cabernet Franc) can benefit from being served slightly cool. A 20-minute chill in the fridge enhances their fruitiness and makes them more appetizing on a warm evening.

FURTHER TASTING TERMINOLOGY EXPLAINED

Acetic – smells of acetic acid (vinegar); main component of volatile acidity.

Aftertaste – same as a wine's finish.

Aromatic – high level of aromas; can be spicy or floral.

Astringency – dryness caused by tannins; particularly noticeable in skin-contact wines (*see page* 134).

Austere – found in very youthful wines with high tannin that require ageing.

Body – weight on mid-palate; referring to alcohol level and extract.

Concentrated – generous levels of fruit and extract.

Creamy – good-quality wine, either in reds or lees-aged whites; also describes mousse of well-made fizz.

Crisp – refreshing note from high acidity in young dry whites.

Definition – quality-focused wine.

Drying – fading fruit, freshness; mouth left dry.

Extract – derived from winemaking; gives rich concentrated wines that can add to quality – though not if wine has too much tannin.

Fragrant – floral-scented bouquet.

Green – refers to the use of unripe grapes.

Grip – type of tannin found in reds (Malbec or Touriga Nacional).

Intensity – good concentration and depth of fruit.

Jammy – overripeness from a hot climate.

Juicy – delicious mouthwatering sensation; a type of acid.

Leesy – contact with the dead yeast cells after fermentation; a popular method of adding creamy complexity to whites (Muscadet *sur lie*).

Length – mid-palate depth and the length of aftertaste (finish).

Limpid – clear white wines.

Malic – sharp appley acidity; varies with variety and decreases with ripening.

Mature – ready to drink.

Minerally – used to describe aroma, flavour and texture; geologists agree there is no direct connection between flavour of wine and soil or rock minerals.

Mouthfeel – texture.

Oaky – wine fermented and/or aged in oak barrel.

Oily – viscosity; occasionally in Gewurztraminer, Viognier and Sémillon, and some sweet wines.

Palate – how wine feels in mouth.

Racy – higher-acid wines showing energy and refreshment.

Round – soft, broad feeling on the palate.

Short – disappointing aftertaste.

Smooth – ripe, silky tannin texture.

Spritzy – hint of carbon dioxide; a prickle on the tongue.

Steely – sinewy type of high acidity in good-quality white wine.

Struck match – found in young wines produced by free sulphur; swirl the glass to diffuse.

Structure – implies wine with solidity.

Tannic – too much tannin giving astringency.

Typicity – shows authentic character of the grape, region or vintage.

Velvety – smooth silky texture; type of tannin (Pinot Noir).

Volatile – too much acetic acid; sour taste – a flaw (*see page* 26).

Yeasty – bouquet of a traditional-method fizz.

Zesty – fresh youthful white with high acid and juicy ripe fruit (New Zealand whites).

SERVING & STORING

Now that we have learned the basics of tasting, it is time to look more closely at the ideal serving temperature, glassware, storage and any faults we might find, as well as how to interpret labels and bottle shapes.

SERVING TEMPERATURES			
WINE STYLE	TEMP °C	TEMP °F	NOTES
Sparkling wine	4.5 to 8	40 to 46	Serving fizz well chilled keeps the bubbles longer; serving for tasting analysis, use higher end of range
Crisp delicate white	7 to 10	45 to 50	Cool temperatures enliven fruit and freshness; serving for tasting analysis, use higher end of range
Full rich white	8 to 15	46 to 59	Wines like Sauvignon Blanc with higher acidity can be served cooler; fuller-bodied premium Chardonnays can be served in the upper range
Soft juicy red	10 to 15	50 to 59	If you need to cool a red, pop it into the fridge for 20 minutes; medium-bodied reds can be 12.5 to 15°C (54.5 to 59°F)
Full rich red	15 to 18	59 to 64	Never put the bottle near a heat source to warm up; bring to appropriate temperature slowly
Light delicate rosé	7 to 10	45 to 50	Provence, Loire
Full rich rosé	11 to 13	52 to 55	Tavel, Cerasuolo d'Abruzzo, Navarra
Orange wine (light)	10 to 12	50 to 54	England, Romania
Orange wine (medium and full)	14 to 15	57 to 59	Languedoc, Greece, Georgia
Medium-sweet and sweet wine	6 to 8	43 to 46	A cooler temperature makes sweetness seem less cloying
Fino Sherry	5 to 7	41 to 45	Same for Manzanilla Sherry
Oloroso Sherry	11 to 14	52 to 57	Same for Amontillado and Palo Cortado
Tawny Port	11 to 14	52 to 57	Same for Sercial and Verdelho Madeira
LBV / Vintage Port	16 to 18	61 to 64	Same for Bual and Malmsey Madeira

TEMPERATURE & OPENING

To enjoy wine at its best, you need to serve it at its ideal temperature. Serving too cold can reduce aromas and kill flavours, but it can make a less palatable wine seem more refreshing. Served too warm, the wine can lack definition and freshness.

GETTING THE RIGHT TEMPERATURE
The key is to get it just right, but you don't need a temperature gauge; it's mostly common sense. You can feel the bottle in your hand to check if it is cool or warm enough. It's always best to start cooler; you can warm the wine by cupping your hands around the glass for a few seconds once poured. And remember that 'room temperature' is now meaningless, since it is usually cooler than many centrally heated homes.

USEFUL COOLING AIDS
Fridge: slower, but effective.
Ice bucket with ice: quicker and works best if cold water is added.
Rapid Ice sleeve: quicker than the fridge or ice bucket; maintains temperature during serving.

RECOMMENDED CORKSCREWS
Laguiole ①, Pulltap, Screwpull.
For opening multiple bottles: use a lever corkscrew or electric wine opener (these can be a bit noisy and need batteries recharged).
For opening an old wine with a crumbling cork: use a two-pronged cork retriever, called a Butler's Thief ②.

SERVING QUANTITIES
1 x 75cl bottle gives 6 glasses or 15 tasting samples.

SERVING ORDER
White before red, light before heavy, young before old, dry before sweet.

THE UNIVERSAL GLASS

There is a proliferation of glass manufacturers bringing out ever more exotically shaped and expensive glasses to suit and flatter every wine style. However there is nothing more useful for the wine-lover than one fine glass that fits all.

I am a big fan of what is known today as the universal glass. This is a glass designed to flatter all the wine styles – white, rosé, red, sparkling, sweet and fortified. There are all kinds of claims from glass manufacturers that their product can enhance a wine – but who has room in their cupboards, or budget, to buy a glass for every grape variety or wine style?

HISTORY

Glassmaking dates back to ancient civilizations, but glassware suitable for wine with a bowl, stem and base started to emerge in Venice in the 1400s. In the 19th and early 20th centuries it went through a decorative phase; beautiful glasses for collecting and displaying, but not appropriate for analysing wine.

The pioneer of modern wine glassware was Riedel (established in 1756) in Austria, which developed the first machine-made glass, based on different grape varieties, in the mid-1980s. Now Riedel has plenty of competition.

FUNCTIONAL & VERSATILE

All you need is one glass. It should be a plain (clear, not coloured), stemmed glass that is not too thick and weighty, large enough to enable you to swirl the wine and with a tapering bowl to concentrate aromas. My preferred all-rounder for large tasting events is Riedel Restaurant Riesling/Zinfandel. The ISO glass, which was scientifically designed in 1970 to suit all wine styles, is too small, making it difficult to nose and to direct wine onto the palate.

When tasting at home, I use more sophisticated alternatives that do a better job as a universal glass – my current favourites are Jancis Robinson x Richard Brendon Original and Gabriel-Glas StandArt (*see* opposite). There is no doubt that the size and shape of the bowl affect how the bouquet is perceived – though a universal glass that fits one person might not suit another. There are plenty on the market to choose from. Just remember that if you're comparing wines against each other, it's a good idea to use the same glass.

SETTING THE TABLE

Many people like to set their dinner tables with smaller white and larger red glasses. This is fine – Zalto White Wine and Zalto Burgundy work well and look the part. When it comes to serving sparkling wine, the flute might be aesthetically pleasing with the rise of bubbles, but the best glass option is Riedel's Veritas Champagne (*see* opposite).

CLEANING & CARE

I recommend handwashing these universal glasses, particularly finer ones, in warm water with a mild detergent (although manufacturers state they are dishwasher-friendly). To remove red stains, use a cleaning brush – and invest in a dedicated microfibre glass-cleaning cloth for polishing (Riedel or Richard Brendon).

THE TASTE TEST

To assess this glassware, I conducted a blind tasting (blindfolded), sampling four wines in all of the glasses seen opposite – Chilean Sauvignon Blanc, South African Cabernet Franc, Oloroso Sherry and Non-Vintage Champagne. The following notes describe the results.

① **Riedel Restaurant Riesling/Zinfandel:** Machine-blown and sturdy; enhanced fruity aromas in the white and red, but the finish was not as long; the fizz and the Sherry showed better.

② **Jancis Robinson x Richard Brendon Precision:** Machine-blown with heavier feel than the Original; robust, but still attractive with a fine rim and tulip-shaped bowl; good for everyday use.

③ **Jancis Robinson x Richard Brendon Original:** Mouth-blown, feather-light, fine, delicate rim; quite fragile for everyday use; best with the white wine and fizz – but strong contender for the best universal choice.

④ **Zalto Denk Art Universal:** Mouth-blown, angular, deep-bowled; looks the part, but the aromas are slightly muted in comparison to the other glasses; better on the palate, enhancing the fruit and concentration; good for fuller wines.

⑤ **Gabriel-Glas StandArt:** Machine-blown, very shapely bowl, designed to enhance the aromas and flatter the palate; worked well with all the wine styles; also try Gabriel's exquisite mouth-blown Gold Edition.

⑥ **Riedel Veritas Champagne:** Machine-blown; the bowl is more egg-shaped than a normal flute, which enhances the wine's complexity.

HOW LONG TO KEEP WINE

Most wines are made for early drinking and are best drunk within one or two years of the vintage to enjoy their fruity freshness.

A GENERAL GUIDE TO LONGEVITY

Sparkling wine: drink young.
Premium sparkling wine & Champagne: can improve with two to three years' bottle-age.
Rosé: drink young; few are made for ageing.
Crisp delicate whites: drink young.
Aromatic whites: mostly at best drunk young, but Riesling (particularly German, with its fine acidity) and Alsace Gewurztraminer and Pinot Gris can benefit from bottle maturity.
Full rich whites: premium Loire Chenin Blanc, white Burgundies (particularly Grand Cru Chablis), oaked white Bordeaux, Hunter Valley Semillon and most white Rhône (except Condrieu, which is best young) will benefit from age. Generally, the more expensive the wine, the longer it should last (ten years for Premier Cru or Grand Cru white Burgundy).
Soft juicy reds: usually best drunk young (Frappato, Gamay, Kadarka); top Beaujolais crus, premium Pinot Noir and Merlot can age.
Full rich reds: more robust, so can last (Cabernet Sauvignon, Syrah, Nebbiolo, Saperavi, Malbec).
Premium full rich reds: often sold to the customer before they are ready to drink or have reached their peak (Classed Growth Bordeaux, Barolo, Chianti Classico, top Hermitage, Côte-Rôtie or Châteauneuf-du-Pape), so will benefit from long bottle-age (10 years plus). This will depend on the vintage however.
Sweet wines: many late-harvest wines are best drunk young, but botrytized dessert wines (Sauternes, Barsac, Tokaji) and premium Loire sweet wines can age well, thanks to their acidity.
Port: all Tawnies and LBV Ruby are ready to drink when bottled; Vintage Port is made for longer bottle-ageing (20 years plus, vintage depending).
Sherry: Fino and Manzanilla should be drunk young, whereas premium Amontillado, Oloroso and Pedro Ximénez can age well.
Madeira: most are ready to drink when bottled (and can last months once the bottle is open). Due to its high acidity, premium (vintage) Madeira is capable of great longevity.

MONITORING TIP

If you buy a case of wine, you can monitor how the wine is evolving, but bear in mind that it goes through different stages in its development. Initially attractively forward, it can then go into a dumb phase (sometimes a decade for Classed Growth Bordeaux) before reaching its peak.

STORING TIPS

- A cool dark place (not too dry) with no artificial light since it can damage a wine (*see lightstrike, page* 26). Temperature-wise, it should be constant (7 to 14°C/45 to 57°F) without any variations of hot and cold, because this will prematurely age a wine.
- Store bottles with corks horizontally to keep the cork moist, but screwcapped wines can be stored upright.
- Store Madeira upright (the wine outlives the cork).
- For premium wines, you need an appropriate place to store them. A humidity-controlled cellar or a temperature, and humidity-controlled wine fridge are best – or rent space in a merchant's warehouse. If you only have a few bottles, use a simple wood or metal winerack.
- Buy magnums for longer ageing.

WHAT HAPPENS WHEN WINE AGES?

Acidity and tannin are the two important elements that enable a wine to age. Some wines are at their best after long ageing, but it is also a question of personal taste. Often British drinkers enjoy their wines more mature than French or American wine-lovers.

As a wine ages, chemical changes occur – for red wines colour lightens to a brick red with a tawny rim; tannins link together and fall as red/brown sediment, which softens the texture, making it appear less angular. Flavour compounds react to develop a more evolved bouquet with a wider spectrum of aromas, as esters form from alcohols that react with the acid molecules in the wine.

For white wines, colour slowly darkens due to oxidation; dry white wines lose freshness but gain evolved aromas from esters. Both high-acid and premium oak-fermented whites tend to last longer. Sweet botrytis-affected wines are likely to last the longest due to their high sugar level and acidity, developing darker colour, more dried fruit, honey, nutty and caramel notes, and eventually tasting slightly drier. As premium sparkling wine ages it loses fruity freshness, darkens slightly in colour, the mousse softens and nutty biscuity notes develop.

The rate of ageing is also dependent on the bottle size. With a different ratio of wine to surface, half-bottles age quicker than standard bottles, but larger formats (magnums etc.) allow for a slower and more even maturation.

Below: Two examples of Barsac (sweet white Bordeaux) from two vintages – 2016 and 1995 – the right-hand glass shows the darker colour of the older wine.

WINE FLAWS

The technology of winemaking and closures has progressed so far that wine faults are rare these days – but wine is a living product so problems can occur. There is more discussion about wine flaws today, due to an increasing number of wines being made without the protection of sulphur (*see pages* 84, 136, 138).

THEY MIGHT LOOK LIKE FLAWS – BUT THEY ARE NOT

Cloudiness: might occur in whites due to suspended dead yeasts in unfiltered wines, or zero disgorgement in pét-nats (*see page* 138); it's harmless. In reds, it could be stirred up sediment, so just let it settle.

Slight spritz: often carbon dioxide is added to liven up young whites.

White glass-like deposits: (aka tartrate crystals) indicates lack of stabilization.

THE BAD FLAWS

Problems can occur at any stage during winemaking, from vine to bottle. The most common flaws are cork taint and oxidation. Here are some you might encounter.

Cork taint: caused by organic compound TCA (2,4,6-trichloroanisole); wine smells musty or mouldy and of damp cardboard; has stripped flavours and dull fruit.

Oxidation: caused by excess oxygen; whites darken, lose fresh fruit and taste stale. Fruit in reds becomes raisin-like.

Volatile: indicates presence of acetic acid; smells of vinegar and gives a sour taste.

Excess sulphur: too much sulphur dioxide used as preservative; smells like a struck-match, with a prickly feeling.

Reduction: wine starved of oxygen can take on cabbage smells.

Mouse cages: randomly found in zero-sulphur wines; mousy aftertaste (*see page* 138).

Brett: caused by *Brettanomyces* yeast creating volatile phenols; smells of barnyards and tastes metallic.

Premature oxidation: most likely to affect whites; cause could be overripe grapes, vinification or variable cork quality, so many Burgundy producers now choose Diam corks (*see page* 29).

Lightstrike: caused by UVA and blue lighting, this affects wine in clear glass bottles, triggering irreversible damage to amino acids. This strips the wine's character and reduces colour intensity, causing loss of fruit and cabbage aromas. Most prone are white, rosé and sparkling wines.

Lightstrike can affect white and rosé wines in clear glass bottles.

PRESERVING WINE

Once a bottle is open, oxygen will rapidly start to change the wine inside it – and the clock is then ticking. If an unfinished bottle needs to be kept for days, weeks or even months, it is essential to use a preservation system to stop the wine from oxidizing and losing flavour.

Oxidation depends on the wine: inexpensive white, rosé, sparkling and older wines are most prone, whereas high-quality white and red wines can benefit from aeration in a decanter and often taste better the next day.

Just putting the cork or screwcap back on the bottle and popping it in the fridge will not keep it fresh for more than a day, but there are plenty of helpful gadgets on the market. Preservation systems are either vacuum-based or use inert gas; the latter is best for keeping wine fresh.

Coravin (on bottle) allows wine to be sampled without opening.

Vacuum-sealer Vacu Vin is the most affordable option; it removes oxygen from the bottle by a small pump and stopper system, preventing oxygen getting to the wine by sucking it out. It slows down oxidation, but only for two to three days, and wines can be dull; it's best to keep whites in the fridge. The Pulltex AntiOx with built-in activated carbon filter is also inexpensive; for sparkling wines the Vacu Vin Champagne stopper is the cheapest way to protect fizz for a day.

Wine preservation was revolutionized by Coravin. Invented in 2011 by wine-loving nuclear engineer Greg Lambrecht, it is a smart tool. (I use Timeless for still wines.) You don't remove the cork but can keep taking samples over weeks and months from the bottle – perfect for practising tasting skills. Coravin is based on an argon-gas blanket system that prevents (rather than slows) oxidation; it extracts wine through the cork (or Coravin stopper for screwcapped wines) using a thin needle, which replaces extracted wine with argon gas. Downsides are the cost of needle and gas replacements. The company's latest invention is for sparkling wine; after popping the cork, a stopper and hand-held charger go onto the bottle to preserve the fizz with pure carbon dioxide. It can keep sparkling wine intact for two weeks.

DECANTERS

Traditionally used for pouring older wine off sediment or to improve bouquet and texture with rapid oxidation, today decanters are more often simply for aesthetics. When decanting, a funnel and a light source close by avoids mess and mistakes; filter off sediment with filter paper or a pair of tights (it works well!). Double-decanting is when the wine is poured back into the original (cleaned) bottle.

BOTTLE SHAPES

Perplexed by the range of wine bottle shapes? No need to worry. There are no hard and fast rules, but there is a traditional format. Generally, the shape has a connection to the grape, relating to where it was originally grown in Europe.

Bottle shapes do all have something in common; they are designed so that they can be laid on their sides to keep corks moist and prevent oxidation. There are three main bottle shapes.

① BURGUNDY
A classic smooth-shouldered bottle is used for white and red Burgundy, and by almost all Chardonnay and Pinot Noir producers worldwide. It is also used in the Loire for white (Chenin Blanc, Sauvignon Blanc) and red (Cabernet Franc), and in the Rhône for white (Viognier, Roussanne, Marsanne) and red (Grenache/Syrah blends) – and all equivalents worldwide.

② BORDEAUX
A classic high-shouldered bottle is used for Bordeaux and Bordeaux-style reds (Cabernet Sauvignon/Merlot blends) worldwide. It is also used in paler glass for Bordeaux-style whites (Sauvignon Blanc/Sémillon blends).

③ GERMANIC FLUTE
Both Germany and Alsace use slim, long-necked, flute-shaped bottles: Mosel's are traditionally green, Rhine's are browner; green Alsace flutes are slightly slimmer and taller. Many producers of Riesling and aromatic grape varieties use this bottle shape as an identifier of the wine style.

④ VINTAGE PORT
A dark glass bottle prevents lightstrike, with a slight bulge (not shown here) to allow the passage of air over the Port as it is poured. This helps release the bouquet during decanting.

⑤ BOCKSBEUTEL
A short-necked, pot-bellied, flask-like bottle is used in Franken and parts of Baden in Germany; also used in Greece, Italy and Portugal. Tricky to fit into the wine rack!

⑥ REGIONAL OR APPELLATION BOTTLES
These are used in Châteauneuf-du-Pape in the Rhône and Muscadet in the Loire; also Szekszárd and Tokaji (dry and Aszú) in Hungary.

⑦ CLAVELIN
Jura's 62cl squat bottle is specifically used for Vin Jaune – the exception to the standard-size rule.

CHAMPAGNE BOTTLE
A heavy glass bottle is needed to withstand five to six atmospheres of pressure, and this is used widely for sparkling wines. Most have deep indentations (punts) in the base to help strengthen the glass. Dark-green glass is used to protect from lightstrike.

PROVENCE SKITTLE
This clear curvy bottle is not so fashionable or commonly used these days.

STANDARD BOTTLE SIZES
37.5cl for a half-bottle and 75cl for a bottle; 50cl is also used for sweet and fortified wines.

For more information on lightstrike, turn to page 26.
For more information on lightweight bottles and alternative packaging, turn to page 128.

CLOSURES

① **Sparkling-wine cork**
② **Natural cork:** most important and widely used.
③ **Cork agglomerate:** made from carefully selected glued cork remnants, and treated with supercritical carbon to remove TCA. Diam is the best-known brand and increasingly popular; the numbers 2, 3, 5, 10, 30 on a Diam cork refer to how long it is guaranteed for.
④ **Plastic cork:** used for cheaper wines.
⑤ **Screwcap:** popular for aromatic whites and everyday wines.
⑥ **Cork stopper:** used for some fortified wines.
⑦ **Vinolok:** glass stopper with vinyl seal.

WINE LABELS

Although wine labels should be an invaluable guide to the wine inside the bottle, often they aren't. The link between the winemaker and the customer, a wine label is an effective marketing tool. It can tell a story, explain a philosophy, highlight green credentials, encourage loyalty, or make an emotional connection with the wine-lover.

The best wine labels are distinctive, appealing, eye-catching, easy to read and informative. Styles that are graphic, modern or humorous are often used for new wines in order to catch attention, whereas more stylized or traditional labels are often used for established revered wineries, or for wines from classic regions.

Front labels are best kept simple; the back label is where the detail should be – but so often isn't. Surely this is the place to introduce us to the winemaker, vineyard and winemaking information, explaining philosophies, adding a website or QR code, or simply telling a story about the artisan family estate – rather than a dull description of the wine. There is a whole wine-label industry, focused on creating the next-best labels to entice new customers or create a loyal following. Château Mouton Rothschild commissions artist-designed labels reflecting each vintage; Champagne Veuve Clicquot uses its golden-yellow background label colour as part of its brand awareness, while Penfolds highlights its brand through red lettering.

TIPS ON READING A WINE LABEL

It would be much easier for everyone if labels followed the same format, but they don't and never will, because wine-producing countries have different laws and requirements. However, there is a certain amount of information that has to be on the label (depending on the country). These include:

- designation – red wine, sparkling wine
- grape – not allowed in some French appellations
- country of origin
- producer/winery/bottler – name and address should be included; can be shortened or coded
- vintage – unless it's non-vintage
- appellation – in some countries
- lot mark
- bottle volume
- alcoholic strength – wine's actual alcohol can vary significantly from what is on the label; some countries are allowed 1.5% leeway
- compulsory health warning, allergen and ingredient information – contains sulphites, etc.

The following can also be found on labels:

- green credentials (*see page* 88)
- wine competitions/award stickers – there tends to be a surfeit of these
- meaningless terms – Barrel Select, Old Vines (Vieilles Vignes), Winemaker's Selection, etc.

On Champagne labels, look for two-letter codes indicating the origin of what is in the bottle:

- RM is from a grower using grapes from its own vineyards;
- NM is from bought-in grower's grapes;
- CM is made by a co-op.

WHAT IS AN APPELLATION?

An appellation is a legally defined and protected geographical wine-growing area, which can vary in rules and restrictions according to the country – for example, French AOC/AOP, Italian DOC(G), Spanish DO(P) or American AVA.

WHITE FROM RED?

It is possible to make white wine from red grapes. The skins are separated from the juice immediately, prior to any contact with skins at the beginning of the winemaking process (Blanc de Noirs Champagne). Fizz-makers like to use darker-skinned grapes (Pinot Noir) to give body, texture and red-fruit flavours to cuvées, while retaining freshness.

HOW TO ORGANIZE A WINE TASTING AT HOME

Spread throughout the book are ten tasting practices covering Crisp Delicate Whites, Full Rich Whites and Classic Whites; Soft Juicy Reds, Full Rich Reds and Classic Reds; Sparkling, Sweet and Fortified; and Taste Trends.

The intention is to give a clear representation of styles and grape varieties that are available around the world. Each tasting focuses on comparing and contrasting four different wines, looking at specific elements of the wines, and offering advice on basic tasting techniques and what to look for as you progress through each tasting.

Every practice includes guidance on the method for tasting the wines, followed by a crib sheet to check the information you have gathered and to assist with learning. There is a huge number of variables involved for each wine, but the tasting practices help by zooming in to discuss specific important elements, like acidity, tannin, fruit intensity and structure. What we have covered so far in the book has given some background and prepared you for tasting; the instructions below will help you get the best out of each practice.

WHAT YOU NEED

- Well-lit room with natural or good artificial light and no external aromas
- Four clear, tulip-shaped, stemmed wine-tasting glasses ①
- Foil cutter ②
- Corkscrew ③
- Spittoon (one per person if possible) ④
- Access to fridge/ice bucket
- White tasting mat
- Tasting sheets
- Glass of water
- Drop-stop pourers ⑤
- Coravin or Vacu Vin (*see page* 27)
- Dry crackers or dry bread

Remember to avoid spicy food before you taste and to ensure no smoking or strong scents.

HOW TO USE THE TASTING PRACTICES

Read through the tasting practice before you start. Then, while doing the tasting, try not to refer to the book too much, so that you can compile your own impressions of each wine and make your own notes. Once you have finished, check the tasting practice again alongside the crib sheet to see if your notes match up. If you find there are differences, go back over the wines with the guidance and cribsheet.

The tasting can be done on your own or with a group of four to eight friends to save cost and encourage an exchange of ideas. Make sure everyone has four glasses positioned on a white tasting mat, numbered one to four following the wine order. If you are tasting on your own, use a Coravin or Vacu Vin gadget to enable you to preserve the wine and repeat the tasting over several days or weeks.

Repetition is an effective way of understanding and learning levels of acidity, grape characteristics and different wine structures. Once you have done the tasting several times, number the glasses with a sticker under the base of each and switch their order to see if you can still identify the wines.

MAKING NOTES

Always try to make notes as you taste. This might seem hard work to start with, but it is an essential learning discipline. Most importantly, write down your own impressions of the wine. If you are tasting with friends, enjoy the engagement and discussions, but always note your own thoughts, as this will help you learn from your own mistakes, because we often perceive wines differently. You will then be able to refer to your notes again to

①
②
③
④
⑤

assist your learning – it is amazing how quickly you can forget the details of each wine. Try also to create a note-taking shorthand, since this will help if you are ever at a large walkaround tasting, balancing a notebook with a tasting glass, and with multiple wines to taste in a short space of time.

For each tasting practice, create a tasting sheet for every wine with headings: Sight, Smell, Taste, Fruit Intensity, Texture/structure and Conclusion.

BUYING SUGGESTIONS & ALTERNATIVES

Wine recommendations, with regards to price and producer, are given in the tasting practices. If it is not possible to find these, there are suggestions for alternatives on the crib sheets; or choose from the producers listed in the chapters on grapes (*see pages* 39 to 57) or countries (*see pages* 162 to 217).

For white wines remember to try to find the most recent vintages available. Finally, choose the best wines you can afford, since the cheaper examples might not show such good grape typicity.

WHEN TO TASTE

The best time for tasting is when your senses are at their most alert – normally at around 10 or 11am. This might not be convenient, so the next best option is early evening. Don't do the tasting after a heavy meal, particularly a spicy curry, as it will affect your taste buds and how you taste.

SERVING TEMPERATURE

Each tasting practice details the exact serving temperature for the wines. Fridge, ice bucket or Rapid Ice sleeve is suggested for whites, rosés and sparkling wines. For the reds, just keep them at room temperature, not in front of open fires or heaters. (*See also page* 20.)

POURING

It is important to keep to the order of serving for each tasting practice. You should have the four glasses positioned on your tasting mat clearly marked one to four. Once the wines are at the required temperature, pour around 2.5cm of each into the appropriate glasses. Make sure to pour all four wines for the tasting so that you can compare and contrast them against each other.

WINE PRICES

Symbols (£, ££ and £££) alongside wines (and also on the crib sheets) indicate approximate costs for each, but prices fluctuate, so use your judgement where necessary.

HOW TO LOOK FOR VALUE WINES

Value depends on a variety of factors, including where the wine is produced (price of land and production costs), yield, grape selection and fashion. It can also depend on the drinker's disposable income and personal preference.

Classic regions, such as Burgundy, Pomerol or Barolo, that are in high demand fetch eye-watering prices; better-value Pinot Noirs are found in Alsace or Germany, better-value Merlots in Chile and better-value Nebbiolos in Italy. Some regions, such as Napa in California, are expensive because they have an affluent local market willing to pay high prices. In Greece, Santorini's land costs, low yields and scarcity push up the price of Assyrtiko. While in England, cost of production, size of vineyards, tiny volumes and a variable climate push prices higher.

Good value can be found in lesser-known emerging countries and regions. Look to Spain (Navarra, Calatayud), Portugal (Bairrada, Dão), Italy (Puglia, Basilicata), Hungary, Bulgaria, Georgia, Slovenia, Croatia, Moldova, Chile and South Africa; and the best bargain of all is in Jerez, Spain – Sherry!

For more information on countries, regions and producers, turn to pages 162 to 217.

DOES A PUNT IN THE BOTTLE INDICATE QUALITY?

A deep indentation (punt) at the bottom of a bottle does not contribute to wine quality, but it is often used for Champagne and sparkling-wine bottles to help strengthen the glass. It can also aid in pouring the wine.

TASTING TIPS

HOW TO JUDGE WINE QUALITY

I often notice when teaching people about wine that they find it easier to work out if they personally like the wine, as opposed to whether the wine is good quality. Assessing wine quality is not about personal preference but about analysing certain parts of the wine and focusing on specific elements of its structure.

Wide spectrum of aromas: depending on the wine style.

Balance of alcohol, acid & tannin: with none of these elements dominating.

Good level of complexity and fruit concentration

Stand-out features: does the wine have a certain energy, harmony, delicacy or finesse?

Long-lasting finish: one of the biggest keys to assessing wine quality.

The finish is measured from the time the wine is spat or swallowed – from a few seconds to several minutes. The flavours of a quality wine can linger for minutes in the mouth, long after the liquid has left; this is called a long length of flavour. A simple wine will have a short finish, dying quickly within a few seconds.

When tasting more generally, take into account where the wine is being enjoyed, because ambience and ritual – listening to a beautiful piece of music in your home or reclining on a warm sunny terrace in the wine's region of origin – can assist in the appreciation of a wine.

THE QUALITY TEST

Buy two wines – one cheaper and the other more expensive – and ask someone to serve them to you 'blind', so that you can assess them. Another way of learning about quality is to buy three different quality levels from within one region – generic, Village and Premier Cru Burgundy or Supérieur, Cru Bourgeois and Classed Growth Bordeaux. Taste the wines against each other, and try to put them into the correct order, then use a Coravin (*see page* 28) to preserve the wine and repeat the exercise every day until you get it right.

BLIND TASTING

This is the assessment of a wine with the identity hidden from view; some enjoy it as a fun supper game, but it is an important part of wine exams. It is a good way to hone your tasting skills and learn to assess quality; you quickly learn to build up a tasting memory bank.

In my own experience, the key to becoming a good blind taster is knowledge and repetition. I approached my Master of Wine practical exam in the same way I approached the theory exam: learning and methodical analysis, using a detailed card index system. Here are my helpful tips for preparing your tasting to exam standard.

Create the blindfold: invest in numbered bags, or empty, clean and number six bottles. Then ask someone to bag up the wines or decant wines into the numbered bottles.

Learn the theory first: knowledge of grapes, styles, regions, etc. is *very* important.

Record everything you taste: learn by your own mistakes, and practise the ones that confuse you repeatedly until you get them right.

Choose a time limit: ten minutes per wine, including writing the answer, is ideal. Do the easy ones first, then move on to the tricky ones.

Learn your classics: the tastings on pages 46 and 58 focus on classic styles. This knowledge should help you hone assessment of quality too.

Check the order: when you start the tasting, smell all the wines first to work out dry to sweet, because they might be out of order, to trip you up.

Focus on the structure: assess aromas and colour quickly, then move to the body, assessing acidity and tannin.

Continually taste wines that are easily confused: the cribsheet for each tasting practice in this book gives common blind-tasting mix-ups for each wine.

Write a checklist: practice writing a list of prepared grapes and regions as a helpful checklist.

Organize regular blind tastings: do this in the exam format, and stick to time allowed.

Taste widely: and good luck!

UNDERSTANDING TASTE

GRAPES OF THE WORLD

There are an estimated 10,000 grape varieties on our planet, but only a few dominate world plantings. According to grape-variety expert, Dr José Vouillamoz, a mere 13 grape varieties cover more than one-third of the world's vineyard area – and only 33 varieties account for 50 per cent.

'Over the next decades, we expect a return of old forgotten indigenous varieties and an increase in recently bred resistant-hybrid plantings. However, this will not drastically change the world statistics, as long as the traditional regions and the customers will want to stick to the well-known, comforting grape varieties,' says Vouillamoz.

The list of 180 grapes over the next few pages reflects this renewed focus on indigenous varieties – native to regions or countries – and those able to cope with our warming climate. These increasingly popular and often underappreciated native grapes, with distinct personalities, include favourites Assyrtiko, Arinto, Pecorino and Treixadura for whites and Frappato, Kadarka, Saperavi and Xinomavro for reds. Some countries have more indigenous grapes than others – Georgia has 525 native grapes (six covered here), Italy has around 380 (33 covered here) and Portugal has over 250 (15 covered here). Our list also highlights classic grapes – many from France, the birth place of fine wine. Today, these are also referred to as 'international grapes', as they are grown worldwide.

TASTE THE DIFFERENCE

Some grapes, like Nebbiolo, Tempranillo, Blaufränkisch and Malbec, have a variety of synonyms – and to confuse the issue, synonyms can refer to local clones that growers consider as separate varieties, as they develop different characteristics in varying climates and soils.

In this list, a cross refers to two varieties within the same species (*Vitis vinifera*) that might be ancient wild crosses or specifically bred; whereas a hybrid cross is from different species.

Remember that the grape variety is the most important factor in determining the taste of a wine. There might be differences in climate, ripeness, soil or winemaking, but in order to learn more about wine, it is important to familiarize yourself with the grapes – starting with the classics.

Taste them against each other to explore their similarities and differences (using the Tasting Practices), then taste examples of the same grape grown in different climates and soils to build up an understanding of what each grape is capable of.

This directory gives an indication of what to expect from the grape's style, where it is grown and recommended producers *(in italics)*.

For more information on resistant hybrids, turn to page 62.
For more information on how grapes can cope with climate warming, turn to page 68.

Seyval Blanc is an early-ripening hybrid popular in England, Canada and New York State – seen here in Godstone Vineyard, England.

WHITE GRAPES DIRECTORY

PRIMARY FLAVOURS FOR WHITE WINE

FLORAL
Riesling, Malagousia, Roussanne, Torrontés

FRUIT
Chardonnay, Sémillon, Albariño, Chenin Blanc

HERBACEOUS
Sauvignon Blanc, Rkatsiteli, Grüner Veltliner, Carricante

STYLE ICONS

CD = Crisp delicate ***FR*** = Full rich ***** = Classic white

ALBARIÑO: Galicia's fashionable grape with piercing fruit purity, zippy freshness, high acidity and rich texture. In Rías Baixas, northwest Spain, it is usually fresh and unoaked, but can be minerally, and tangy with marine notes and a saline edge in coastal Salnes; responds well to lees, oak and bottle-age *(Maior de Mendoza, Zarate)*. In Portugal's Vinho Verde, it is known as Alvarinho and is often blended with Loureiro and Treixadura. It is best as a varietal in Monção e Melgaço *(Soalheiro)*, with rich weight, white peach and lime zest. Shows promise in Uruguay *(Garzon)*. ***CD***

ALIGOTÉ: French thin-skinned grape with tart high acidity; lively, aromatic, chiselled dry Burgundian whites; weightier citric styles in Bouzeron in warm vintages *(Domaine de Villaine)*. ***CD***

ALTESSE: Indigenous to France's Savoie (where it is also known as Roussette); floral, crisp, high-acid, stone-fruited dry whites with nutty undertones. ***CD***

ARINTO: Back in fashion. Ancient Portuguese grape popular in Lisbon, Tejo, Bairrada, Douro and Vinho Verde for light, tropical-fruit, high-acid styles; age-worthy and waxy in Lisbon's subzone Bucelas. ***CD***

ARNEIS: Italy's aromatic, light-textured Piedmontese grape; white-flower scents, baked apple and almond notes at best in Roero hills. Nicknamed 'little rascal' as difficult to grow; becoming popular in Australia, New Zealand, Uruguay, California, Oregon. ***CD***

ASSYRTIKO: High-quality, hardy Greek variety; at best in homeland Santorini, with pungent, intense, saline, minerally styles from volcanic soils *(Argyros)*. Classic combination of ripeness of fruit, natural acid and ability to express terroir. Popular on mainland Halkidiki and across Macedonia; also in Australia *(Jim Barry)*. ***FR***

AUXERROIS: Low-acid, peach-scented grape; best in cooler England, Luxembourg, Germany and France's northern Alsace, where it adds weight to Pinot Blanc in Crémant d'Alsace blend. ***CD***

BACCHUS: Zesty German cross (Silvaner x Riesling crossed with Müller-Thurgau), needs to be fully ripe. Popular in England, with grassy scents, green-apple and herbal flavours in Sauvignon Blanc style *(New Hall, Camel Valley)*. ***CD***

BICAL: Known as 'fly droppings' in Dão in Portugal; up-and-coming in Bairrada *(Filipa Pato)* and Beiras. In warm vintages, more tropical flavours but with crisp acidity and ages well. ***FR***

BOURBOULENC: Thick-skinned with good acidity and zesty citrus aromas. Popular in France's Rhône (Châteauneuf-du-Pape, Tavel), Provence (Bandol) and Languedoc (La Clape) alongside Clairette or Grenache Blanc; also Paso Robles, US. ***FR***

CARRICANTE: Italy's impressive Sicilian grape often lost in blends. Varietals show promise, with fresh acidity, lemon and honey; herby and aniseed-flavoured Etna Bianco *(Benanti)*. ***FR***

CATARRATTO: Sicily's most planted and Italy's second most planted grape, used in Marsala. As varietal *(Calatrasi)* can be attractively citrus, peachy, herby and nutty, similar to Viognier. ***CD***

CHARDONNAY:** World's greatest non-aromatic white. Subtle aromas, pure citrus, fine acidity and broad mouthfeel with potential for longevity in best examples. Adaptable variety stylistically; almost all dry. Good yields in different climates and soils, with ability to show terroir; oak fermentation and lees work can also enhance subtle flavours. Crisp, unoaked to intense, richly oaked in homeland Burgundy – from sleek Chablis and dense, oaked Côte de Beaune, to lighter, softer Chalonnaise and Mâconnais. Bigger and bolder in California *(Au Bon Climat, Ramey)*; intense fruit in Australia *(Mount Mary, Tolpuddle, Vasse Felix)* and Chile *(Tabalí)*; elegant in South Africa *(Crystallum, Hamilton Russell)*, Canada *(Bachelder)* and Oregon *(Walter Scott)*; citrus-steely in New Zealand *(Kumeu River)* and England *(Danbury Ridge)*. Part of the Champagne grape trio with Pinot Noir and Pinot Meunier; Blanc de Blancs is 100% Chardonnay, with refreshing chalky focus *(Pierre Gimonnet)*. ***FR

CHASSELAS: Herby, nutty, known as Fendant in Swiss Vaud and Valais (*Henri Cruchon*). Also in Baden, Germany; Alsace and Pouilly-sur-Loire, France. ***FR***

CHENIN BLANC:** Exceptionally versatile with naturally high acid; makes fine sparkling from Saumur to Vouvray, and refined bone-dry still Savennières along the Loire in France. This thin-skinned grape with high natural sugar content makes medium-sweet to dense, rich botrytis-affected sweet wines south of the Loire in Coteaux du Layon's Quarts de Chaume and Bonnezeaux *(Château de Fesles)*. Widely planted in South Africa (where it is known an Steen), now taken seriously in Stellenbosch and Swartland *(Careme, David & Nadia)*. ***FR

CLAIRETTE: 'Light one', one of the oldest grapes in France's Midi; floral scents and moderate acid. Also popular in Tavel, Rhône and Clairette du Languedoc; and in Châteauneuf-du-Pape blends. ***CD***

CORTESE: Soft, dry and neutral with good acidity; best known in Italy as Piedmont's still and sparkling Gavi grape *(La Mesma)*; in Lombardy and Veneto too. ***CD***

ENCRUZADO: High-quality, fine-fruited, high-acid Portuguese grape; best in Dão, with flinty minerality, richness and structure; tricky to grow *(Quinta dos Roques)*. ***FR***

EZERJÓ: High acid, vibrant, versatile, citrus-fruited; best in Mór, northwest Hungary *(Csetvei)*, also in Kunság and Neszmély; mainly dry. ***FR***

FALANGHINA: Popular medium-bodied Italian grape, in Campania and Puglia, still and sparkling; floral, peach, almond flavours from Falanghina Beneventano and Falanghina Flegrea. ***CD***

FERNÃO PIRES: Aromatic, light, fresh and grapey, grown extensively across Portugal; best in Tejo and Bairrada (as Maria Gomes). ***CD***

FETEASCĂ ALBĂ: Aromatic, rich citrus and apricot fruits; originated in Moldova, popular in Romania, Bulgaria and Ukraine. ***CD***

FETEASCĂ REGALĂ: Delicate, sleek and aromatic; honeysuckle, elderflower aromas; passion-fruit, peach flavours; in Romania. ***CD***

FIANO: Italy's robust, honeyed, waxy ancient Campanian grape (as Fiano di Avellino); note not the same as Puglia's Fiano Minutolo. Drought resistant, popular in Australia. ***FR***

FRIULANO: Aromatic, herbal, nutty grape; an old variety from Gironde in southwest France (as Sauvignonasse), no relation to Sauvignon Blanc; introduced to Friuli NE Italy (*Vignai da Duline*) where it became known as (Tocai) Friulano. ***CD***

FURMINT: High-quality, versatile, high-acid Hungarian grape, dominant in Tokaj, stylish sparkling *(Demeter Zoltán)*, minerally dry white *(Szepsy)* and botrytized sweet Aszú *(Royal Tokaji)*. ***FR***

GARGANEGA: High-acid, medium-bodied, lean and dry, with apricot, honey and baked-apple notes. Best known as Italy's Soave grape, making dry and sweet wines *(Pieropan)*. ***CD***

GARNACHA BLANCA: Rich, oily, high-extract, popular in *vins secs* and Vin Doux Naturel (VDN) in France's Roussillon (as Grenache Blanc; Maury), Rhône (Châteauneuf-du-Pape). Also in Spain's Catalonia and Aragón; California. ***FR***

GARNACHA GRIS: Herbal, fresh, pink-skinned, making full-bodied varietals and blends in France's Roussillon (as Grenache Gris; *Château de L'Ou)* and Rhône's Rasteau; also in Spain's Catalonia. ***FR***

GEWURZTRAMINER:** Famously spicy (as a result of terpenes found in the skins). This is a pink-skinned grape, tricky to grow in warm climates as optimum sugar levels are reached before flavour develops; at best in cool climates picked ripe – otherwise it is just faintly floral and bland. Most exotically complex with lychees, mango, sweet spice and ginger notes from clay soils in Alsace's Haut-Rhin *(Hugel)* in France. It is frequently off-dry in style and also makes late-harvest and honeyed, spicy botrytis-affected Sélection de Grains Nobles; bottle-age is essential for dry and sweet. It shows potential in Germany's Pfalz, Italy's Alto Adige, New Zealand's South Island and Chile's Bío-Bío. ***FR

GLERA: Uninspiring neutral Italian grape ideal for early-drinking still and tank-fermented sparkling; originally called Prosecco, renamed in 2010 to protect the popular sparkling DOC. ***CD***

GODELLO: High-quality Galician grape; minerally age-worthy whites in Spain's Valdeorras, Ribeiro, Ribeira Sacra, Monterrei; blends with Treixadura in Bierzo. In Portugal it is known as Gouveio. ***FR***

GRECO: Aromatic, herby, apricot-scented; possibly imported by the Greeks to Italy *c.*800 BCE, at best in Campania (as Greco di Tufo); note not the same as Grechetto or Greco Bianco. ***CD***

GRILLO: Italian, floral, tropical fruit, touch of spice; makes increasingly interesting whites across Sicily; historically top grape in Marsala fortified blend. ***CD***

GRÜNER VELTLINER: Austria's flagship, with fresh, spicy to intense, minerally styles and penetrating peppery notes in Wachau *(Pichler-Krutzler)* and Kamptal *(Bründlmayer)*. Also in Adelaide Hills, Australia *(Hahndorf Hill)* and Central Otago, New Zealand *(Quartz Reef)*. ***CD***

HÁRSLEVELŰ: High-quality Hungarian grape; white peach, honey and a spicy, fruity, salty character; adds exotic perfume and softness to Tokaji blend and increasingly as dry varietal *(Kikelet)*. ***FR***

HONDARRIBI ZURI: Main grape of Txakolí in Spain's Basque Country; light, spritzy, citrusy, with moderate alcohol and high acid *(Gorrondona)*; genetically the same as Courbu Blanc, Crouchen and hybrid Noah. ***CD***

IRSAI OLIVÉR: Popular aromatic 1930s cross, at best in cooler Mátra and Etyek-Buda in northern Hungary and in Slovakia. ***CD***

JACQUÈRE: Zippy, fresh, floral-scented Alpine grape, light in alcohol with sappy acidity and mountain freshness in France's Savoie. ***CD***

JUHFARK: Austere, steely Hungarian grape grown mainly on Somló's basalt soil *(Kolonics)*; requires bottle-age to tame fierce acidity. ***FR***

KÉKNYELŰ: Quality, aromatic, medium-bodied, savoury Hungarian grape; enjoying renaissance in Badascony *(Szeremley)*. ***FR***

KERNER: Popular German cross (Schiava Grossa x Riesling); good acidity, tangerine fruits and leafy herbal notes, at best in Franken; also in Italy's Alto Adige *(Pacher Hof)*. ***CD***

KHIKHVI: Honeyed, soft, succulent Georgian white enjoying revival in Kakheti *(Mildiani)*. ***CD***

KISI: Apricot-scented, peppery, broad-textured; one of Georgia's best native grapes, suited to traditional *qvevri* winemaking *(Dakishvili)*. ***FR***

LOUREIRO: Potentially fine, aromatic Portuguese grape in the right hands *(Quinta do Ameal)*; popular in Vinho Verde blends for honeysuckle and orange-blossom scents, green apple and peach. ***CD***

MACABEO: Floral, aromatic; most planted in north Spain; important in Cava blends in Catalonia (as Viura), mainstay of white Rioja. In France (as Maccabeu), makes age-worthy Roussillon. ***CD***

MALAGOUSIA: High-quality, versatile Greek grape revived in 1970s; ranges from lean, minty, lightly floral and fresh, green pepper notes to richer, oakier styles *(Gerovassiliou)*. ***CD***

MALVASIA BIANCA: With its grapey scents and full body, this versatile variety is popular in Piedmont, Abruzzo and Basilicata in Italy. Also in Spain, France, California. ***FR***

MALVASIA FINA: One of Madeira's classic grapes (as Boal/Bual); also grown on mainland Portugal; part of Malvasia family *(Henriques & Henriques)*. ***FR***

MARSANNE: Quince and honeysuckle scent; bold, full-bodied, rich, nutty, age-worthy. As varietal or blended with Roussanne across Rhône in France *(Chapoutier)*. Also in Australia *(Tahbilk)* and California *(Tablas Creek)*. ***FR***

MELON DE BOURGOGNE: Crisp and citric, best with lees ageing. In France, originally from Burgundy; mainstay of Muscadet in Loire since 16th century *(Domaine de l'Ecu)*. ***CD***

MOSCHOFILERO: Aromatic, fresh, high-acid, light-bodied, pink-tinged Greek grape (as Fileri); best in Peloponnese on high-altitude Mantinia plateau *(Novus)*. ***CD***

MÜLLER-THURGAU: Can be dull, but with low yields gives light, aromatic, appley whites; best in Germany's Nahe, Austria's Weinviertel and Italy's Alto Adige and Trentino. ***CD***

MUSCADELLE: Popular blender with Sémillon and Sauvignon Blanc in Bergerac (Monbazillac) in France. Makes decadently sweet Topaque fortifieds in Australia's Rutherglen *(Stanton & Killeen)*. ***FR***

MUSCAT OF ALEXANDRIA: Ancient aromatic grape, with orange-zest aromas. Popular for dry and sweet in South Africa, for dry and fortified in France's Rivesaltes (Roussillon) and for sweet passito *(Donnafugata)* in Pantelleria, Sicily (as Zibibbo). ***CD***

MUSCAT BLANC À PETITS GRAINS: Fragrant, intensely fruity; best in France as dry white Alsace, plus Rhône's Clairette de Die fizz and lightly fortified sweet Muscat de Beaumes de Venise. ***CD***

PALOMINO FINO: Sherry's base grape, written off as dull and neutral, now enjoying revival as unfortified, still, saline dry white from specific Jerez terroirs *(Cota 45, Luis Perez)*; also elsewhere in Spain (as Listán). ***FR***

PARELLADA: Distinctive floral aroma; delicate body. In Spain, important part of Cava trio, softening Xarel·lo; popular for dry whites in Catalonia. ***CD***

PECORINO: Indigenous central Italian grape rescued from obscurity; fresh, nutty, lemony styles in Abruzzo and savoury, minerally, age-worthy in Offida, Marches *(Tenuta Santori)*. ***CD***

PEDRO XIMÉNEZ: Indigenous Spanish grape with high sugar level, traditionally sun-dried; in Andalusia's Montilla-Moriles, Málaga and Jerez makes unfortified and fortified styles *(Ximenez-Spinola)*; also in Australia, Chile. ***FR***

PETIT MANSENG: With high sugar and high acid, produces sensationally fresh, delicate dry and sweet wines in Southwest France's Jurançon *(Cauhape)* and Pacherenc du Vic-Bilh. ***CD***

PINOT BLANC: Like a mild Chardonnay with citrus fruit and medium body; best are creamy, textural examples in Alsace, France; sleek and lean in Friuli and Alto Adige in Italy (as Pinot Bianco) and Germany (as Weissburgunder). ***FR***

PINOT GRIS:** Tricky to pin down; from opulently spicy to plain and bland. Numerous synonyms: Pinot Gris (France), Pinot Grigio (Italy), Grauburgunder or Rulander (Austria, Germany). At best in Alsace with rich, spicy, opulent dry and off-dry styles with honey, ginger and quince *(Zind-Humbrecht)*. Often lacks intensity and concentration in Veneto and Trentino, better in Friuli *(Lis Neris)* and Alto Adige *(Lageder)*. Grows well in Baden and Pfalz. Also in New Zealand as weighty, oily Alsatian styles in Martinborough *(Dry River)*, Marlborough, Central Otago; emerging in England *(Artelium)*. ***FR

PIQUEPOUL BLANC: Aka 'lip stinger' due to high acidity; currently fashionable in France's Languedoc for zippy, citrus, dry Picpoul de Pinet. ***CD***

RIBOLLA GIALLA: Unusual historic variety (as Rebula), with punchy citrus aromas, high acidity and savoury balsamic in Friuli Venezia Giulia, northeast Italy *(Jermann, Gravner)* and Brda in Slovenia *(Marjan Simčič)*. ***FR***

RIESLING:** My favourite grape makes the world's most exciting racy whites with spine-tingling acidity from dry to sweet styles. Renowned for its fragrance, vertical acidity and moderate alcohol, this hardy vine thrives in cool climates, producing floral, linear, juicy, salty to rich, honeyed, succulent styles. Dry German Riesling is back in vogue with thrilling taut Saar *(Zilliken)* and Ruwer *(Maximin Grunhaus)*, minerally, delicate Mosel *(Clemens Busch, JJ Prum)*; richer in Nahe *(Donnhoff)*, Rheinhessen, Rheingau, Pfalz. France offers superb dry terroir expressions on limestone and granite in Alsace *(Weinbach, Trimbach, Zind-Humbrecht)*. Austria gives rich intensity in Wachau *(Hirtzberger)* and Kamptal *(Bründlmayer)*. Elegance in Hungary *(Gilvesy)*, New York's Finger Lakes *(Hermann Wiemer)*, Washington State *(Eroica)*, coastal Chile *(Casa Marín)*. It is best in Australia's Clare Valley *(Grosset)*, Eden Valley *(Powell)*, Frankland River *(Frankland)* and in New Zealand's Central Otago *(Prophet's Rock)*. It also leads on Icewine in Ontario, Canada, and fine botrytis dessert wines in Germany and Austria. ***CD

RKATSITELI: Herbal, citrus, savoury; dominant workhorse grape in Kakheti, Georgia, refined by artisans *(Archils, Orgo)*, with skin contact and *qvevri* fermentation adding nuttiness, tannin texture. ***FR***

RODITIS: Revived ancient, pink-tinged grape; varies from light, aromatic, youthful, to rich, citrus, intense styles; best at high altitude near Patras in Greece's Peloponnese *(Papagiannopoulos)*. ***CD***

ROUSSANNE: Pear-skin and herbal-tea scents, with a rich, weighty, nutty palate. Popular in France in Rhône (Châteauneuf-du-Pape blends), and in Lirac, Vacqueyras and St-Péray (with Marsanne); also in Savoie, Australia, South Africa. ***FR***

SAUVIGNON BLANC:** Much-loved aromatic grape; thirst-quenchingly vibrant, high acidity, herbaceous and lean structure; grows vigorously, so low yields essential. Grassy-green flavours derive from methoxypyrazines and passion-fruit from thiols (both flavour compounds). At consistent, zesty, full-throttle best in New Zealand's Wairau Valley in Marlborough *(Greywacke)*; softer in Martinborough and Hawke's Bay; taut and linear-like in Central Otago. Its homeland is east Loire in France, with flinty Sancerre *(Vacheron)*, broader Pouilly-Fumé *(Château de Tracy)*, softer Quincy *(Bruniers)*, Menetou-Salon and Reuilly. In Burgundy, St-Bris, near Chablis, is nettley, peppery, rich *(Goisot)*. In Bordeaux, best with Sémillon in full, rich (oaked) dry Pessac-Léognan *(Domaine de Chevalier)* and as part of the grape trio (with Muscadelle) for sweet Sauternes and Barsac. Also in Austria (South Styria), Italy (Alto Adige, Collio), South Africa (Cape Point, Constantia, Elgin, Stellenbosch) and Australia's Adelaide Hills *(Shaw & Smith)*. ***FR

SAVAGNIN: Signature grape of Jura, eastern France; aromatic, refined; nutty, citrus, sappy flavours. Styles are *ouillé* (made by topping up barrels to minimize oxygen) or dry, oxidative Sherry-like Vin Jaune, made in Château-Chalon *(Stéphane Tissot)*. Also in Switzerland (as Heida). ***FR***

SAVATIANO: Underrated flagship grape of Attika, Greece; at best it is like toasty Sémillon, but with baked apple, quince, herbs, saline notes. It is the main base of Retsina *(Papagiannakos)*. ***FR***

SÉMILLON:** Versatile grape; makes superb dry and sweet wines in France and Australia. What it lacks in aroma, it makes up for with its waxy textured-and-honeyed citrus palate; an ideal blender with crisp lean Sauvignon Blanc. In cooler climates, it's nettley and lemony. In warmer climes, it's rich and nutty, with more lanolin aromas in unoaked varietal Hunter Valley styles *(Tyrrell's)*; bottle-age develops oak-like toasty vanilla notes. Its thin skin makes it prone to botrytis, creating the world's longest-lived, honey-tinged sweet dessert wines in Sauternes *(Suduiraut)* and Barsac, France. ***FR

SCHEUREBE: White pepper and sherbet aromas, with piercing acidity. This is a German Riesling x Bukettrebe cross, with a rare personality, best in the Pfalz *(Müller-Catoir)* and Franken *(Horst Sauer)*. Also makes refined sweets in Burgenland *(Kracher)* in Austria (as Samling 88). ***CD***

SYLVANER: Unsung hero of Alsace, France *(Boeckel)*; discreet floral to rich citrus, textural Grand Cru Zotzenberg; steeliest best in Germany's Franken *(Wirsching)* and Rheinhessen *(Wittmann)*. ***CD***

TORRONTÉS: Various clones in Argentina, best is fresh, floral, pungent Torrontés Riojano in high-altitude Cafayate in Salta; quality varies. ***CD***

TREBBIANO: Part of a family of varieties; most planted in Italy is high-acid neutral Trebbiano Toscano (aka Ugni Blanc). ***CD***

TREIXADURA: Peachy, with moderate acid; blends with Loureiro in Vinho Verde, Portugal (as Trajadura). Flagship grape of Ribeiro and popular northwest Spain blender. ***CD***

TSOLIKOURI: Soft, oily, textured indigenous Georgian grape, flagship of the Imereti district in the west *(Baia's Wine)*. ***CD***

VERDEJO: Bold, fruity, creamy-textured flagship grape of Rueda in Spain's Castilla y León; best are rich, zesty, herby and nutty *(Naia)*. ***FR***

VERDICCHIO: Floral, peachy, high acid, with bitter-almond notes; best known as Verdicchio dei Castelli di Jesi *(Coroncino)* and Verdicchio di Matelica from Italy's Marches; in Veneto (as Trebbiano di Soave); varied styles. ***CD***

VERMENTINO: Zippy lime, almonds, touch of salinity. Potential in Italy in Sardinia, Tuscany, Liguria; and France (as Rolle) in Corsica, Provence. Suits lovers of Sauvignon Blanc or Muscadet. ***CD***

VERNACCIA: Often overlooked; apricot, sage and anise flavours; opulent Italian whites from San Gimignano, Tuscany *(Falchini)*. ***FR***

VIOGNIER:** A white for people who prefer reds. This lush, spicy, succulent, exotically flavoured, sweet-sour, low-acid grape is currently enjoying a renaissance but is difficult to grow as flavour takes time to build during ripening, while acidity plummets. It originates from Condrieu *(André Perret, Georges Vernay)* and Château-Grillet in Northern Rhône in France, and is well travelled across Southern Rhône and Languedoc as a blender. Also in Australia *(Yalumba)*, California *(Alban, Cline)*; best drunk young. ***FR

WELSHRIESLING: Herb, peach and marzipan; lively acid. Best on Balaton's north shore *(Gilvesy, Pálffy, Zelna)*, Hungary (as Olaszrizling) and Collio, Italy. Elegant sweets in Austria's Styria and Burgenland *(Heidi Schrock, Kracher)*. ***CD***

XYNISTERI: The most planted Cypriot grape, with salty minerality high on the Troodos Mountains *(Vouni Panayia)*. ***FR***

GRAPES Q&A

HOW DOES A GROWER CHOOSE WHICH GRAPE TO PLANT?

Appellations dictate which grapes are allowed to be grown to ensure typicity (Chardonnay in Burgundy, Sauvignon Blanc and Sémillon in Bordeaux), but outside appellation restrictions the grower is free to choose. The decision will depend on the suitability of climate and soil to the variety, with the vine's ability to ripen fruit, its flavour and character – and the grower's view of the market. Drought, rain and extreme heat will also influence planting decisions in the future, with more indigenous local grapes chosen over international varieties.

WHEN ARE ROOTSTOCKS REQUIRED?

Most vineyards today are planted with *Vitis vinifera* varieties grafted onto a selected American rootstock (used to resist phylloxera), and are chosen to enhance vigour, match soil type, or for drought tolerance. Some vines are planted on their own roots (without rootstocks) in isolated regions or on specific soil types free of phylloxera (Chile, Santorini, Sicily, Colares).

WHEN WILL THE VINE BEAR FRUIT READY FOR WINEMAKING?

It takes three years for a newly planted vine to produce fruit suitable for winemaking. As the roots delve deeper into the soil over time, fruit quality gradually increases.

WHAT HAPPENS WHEN A GRAPE RIPENS?

As a grape starts to ripen during veraison, it changes colour, plumps and softens. Sugar and water increase in the berry, while acidity levels drop. There are also chemical changes happening in the skins as the grape's colour progresses and as it softens – but this might not happen all at the same time for each berry in the bunch.

In hotter climates, this process is faster, and acidity might be too low when the berry is ripe, with malic acid decreasing faster than tartaric acid; this can be adjusted by the addition of acid during vinification. Conversely, in cold climates the berries might have too much malic acid at picking time, but this can be adjusted with malolactic fermentation (*see page* 90).

WHY IS ACIDITY IMPORTANT?

Acidity is the backbone of all wine – an essential element ensuring freshness, vibrancy, balance and longevity. It can vary in type, from zesty to powerful, and in its level, from low to high. Examples of high-acid white grapes include Aligoté, Assyrtiko, Chenin Blanc, Furmint and Riesling, whereas lower-acid white grapes include Gewurztraminer, Sémillon and Viognier.

HOW CAN FRESHNESS BE ACHIEVED IN WHITE WINES MADE IN A WARM CLIMATE?

Freshness is controlled by picking earlier, avoiding excessive ripeness and ensuring higher acidity. However, this might result in a loss of flavour, which will not have had sufficient time to build up in the grapes. For example, Viognier has naturally low acidity levels and is prone to sunburn, shrivelling easily on the vine in the heat, but it takes its time to build flavour during ripening – making it difficult to choose the picking date.

TASTING PRACTICE CLASSIC WHITES

Understanding and learning the classics is a great foundation for your wine knowledge. This self-guided tasting practice focuses on four classic wine styles from different regions around the world. You will learn about grape characteristics, levels of acidity and the overall flavour intensity and structure of the wines.

WINES TO BUY (IN ORDER OF SERVING):
① Dry Riesling (Germany) **££**
② Chablis (France) **££**
③ Sauvignon Blanc (New Zealand) **££**
④ White Rioja (Spain) **££**

Preparation: *See page* 32.

Buying & alternatives: Try to find recent vintages with similar price levels for all wines. The Riesling should be dry; if you cannot find a Nahe one, choose an alternative from another region. If finding replacements for the others, note the Chablis (Chardonnay) and Sauvignon Blanc should both be unoaked, whereas the white Rioja (Viura blend) should be oaked.

Serving temperature: 8 to 12°C (46 to 54°F); chill wines in the fridge for 2 hours or in an ice bucket with ice and water for 20 minutes.

Method: Pour the same amount into each of your four glasses, and sample them side by side.

Look: First check the wines for clarity and brightness, noting the colours of all four wines. For each wine, tilt the glass against a white background to make sure you can see the wine colour clearly, and write down what you can see. Then pick up two glasses to compare them against each other; do this for all of the wines. You will find the colour tones are relatively similar, but there are small differences: Wine 1 is lighter and Wine 4 is darker (due to oak and some bottle-age).

Smell: Without swirling the glasses, sniff each wine and write down your initial reaction in terms of what you can smell. Give the glasses another swirl and repeat the process, considering each wine's profile. Wine 1 is aromatic with light floral hints, whereas Wine 2 smells richer with citric notes. Wine 3 is exuberantly aromatic with ripe green fruit and melon notes, and Wine 4 is less fruity, more smoky and savoury.

Taste: Sample each wine individually, trying to slow down your reactions and concentrate on what you can taste. You should take about a teaspoonful of wine into your mouth each time you taste, and swirl it around your taste buds, drawing in a little air to spread the flavour around.

Think about the acidity level of each wine, initially comparing Wines 1 and 2. You will notice both have high acidity – typical cool-climate classics – but the acidity is different. In Wine 1 the acidity is more vertical, whereas in Wine 2 it is quite linear, forming more of a fine backbone from start to finish on the palate as you taste the wine. Wine 3 has moderately good acidity alongside exuberant ripe fruit, making it very zesty, and Wine 4 has the lowest acidity of all the wines.

Now taste the wines again and think carefully about the structure and fruit intensity of each. Try not to compare them initially, but think of them on their own merits – and then do a tasting comparison between Wines 1 and 2, then 3 and 4. Wine 1 has a taut structure compared with Wine 2, which has a softer, rounder texture. Wines 3 and 4 have more intensity and fruit ripeness because they come from warmer climates. Wine 4 is the only oaked wine in the tasting – with smoky, nutty characters muting the fruit.

Finish: As you swallow each wine in turn, notice the sensation of the wine's finish and the length of time you can still taste the wine. Repeat the process, but this time spit out the samples.

Conclusion: In this exercise you will have discovered the characteristics of four classic wines made from different grapes, assessing acidity level, fruit intensity and structure – and comparing unoaked versus oaked wine.

Once you have finished, try it again the following day (and the next) to see if you come to the same conclusions. Repetition is the best way of learning to taste and understanding your own tasting perceptions.

Now check the crib sheet on the next page, and consider trying the tasting again using the alternative wines suggested.

CRIB SHEET: **CLASSIC WHITES**

1. DRY GERMAN RIESLING

REGION: **NAHE**

COUNTRY: **GERMANY**

GRAPE: **RIESLING**

PRICE: **££**

ALCOHOL: **11.5%**

SIGHT: **Very pale light gold flecks**

SMELL: **Floral**

TASTE: **Very high acidity**

FRUIT INTENSITY: **Light limey fruit**

TEXTURE: **Taut, refreshing acidity gives firm structure, slight spritz**

CONCLUSION: **Shows a tightrope of acid and fruit on the palate, with great precision; crisp, dry finish**

COMMON BLIND TASTING MIX-UPS: **Unoaked Loire Chenin Blanc**

ALTERNATIVES TO TRY

German dry Riesling from Mosel or Rheingau; Australian, Austrian or US (Finger Lakes) Riesling

2. CHABLIS

REGION: **BURGUNDY**

COUNTRY: **FRANCE**

GRAPE: **CHARDONNAY**

PRICE: **££**

ALCOHOL: **12.5%**

SIGHT: **Pale gold**

SMELL: **Fuller, citrus**

TASTE: **High acidity**

FRUIT INTENSITY: **Creamy citrus fruit**

TEXTURE: **Rounder mouthfeel like soft satin, broad feeling in mouth**

CONCLUSION: **Shows chalky minerality and lightly creamy, honeyed notes**

COMMON BLIND TASTING MIX-UPS: **Unoaked Loire Chenin Blanc**

ALTERNATIVES TO TRY

Unoaked Burgundy (Chalonnaise or Mâconnais)

3. NEW ZEALAND SAUVIGNON BLANC

REGION: **MARLBOROUGH**

COUNTRY: **NEW ZEALAND**

GRAPE: **SAUVIGNON BLANC**

PRICE: **££**

ALCOHOL: **13.5%**

SIGHT: **Very pale light green flecks**

SMELL: **Pungent green fruits, herby**

TASTE: **Moderately high acidity**

FRUIT INTENSITY: **Full, zesty melon and green fruit**

TEXTURE: **Intense generous mouthfeel, slightly flinty**

CONCLUSION: **Shows typical herbaceous, restrained tropical-fruit style**

COMMON BLIND TASTING MIX-UPS: **Loire Sauvignon Blanc, Melon de Bourgogne**

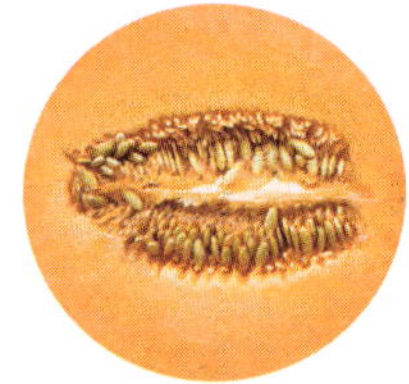

ALTERNATIVES TO TRY
Unoaked Loire (Sancerre, Pouilly-Fumé, Touraine S Blanc); unoaked South African S Blanc

4. WHITE RIOJA

REGION: **RIOJA**

COUNTRY: **SPAIN**

GRAPE: **VIURA**

PRICE: **££**

ALCOHOL: **13.5%**

SIGHT: **Light gold**

SMELL: **Smoky vanilla**

TASTE: **Soft acidity**

FRUIT INTENSITY: **Muted ripe fruit (nutty rather than fruity)**

TEXTURE: **Creamy texture with savoury nutty edge**

CONCLUSION: **Shows barrel-age complexity alongside mineral freshness**

COMMON BLIND TASTING MIX-UPS: **Oaked Chardonnay**

ALTERNATIVES TO TRY
Oaked Southern Rhône white blend; oaked South African Chenin Blanc

RED GRAPES DIRECTORY

PRIMARY FLAVOURS FOR RED WINE

LIGHT RED FRUIT
Pinot Noir, Gamay, Zweigelt, Corvina

DARK FRUIT
Cabernet Sauvignon, Malbec, Merlot, Saperavi

SPICE
Syrah, Grenache, Pinotage, Negroamaro

STYLE ICONS

SJ = Soft Juicy ***FR*** = Full rich ***** = Classic red

AGIORGITIKO: Flagship Greek red; soft to deep spicy richness; best in Nemea, Peloponnese *(Skouras)*; also Macedonia *(Biblia Chora)*. ***FR***

AGLIANICO: Dark, rustic, raisiny, gutsy, tannic Italian; best in Taurasi, Campania *(Mastroberardino)* and Mount Vulture, Basilicata *(D'Angelo)*; surprisingly long-lived. ***FR***

ALEATICO: Central Italian grape, popular in Tuscany, Puglia and Latium for cherry-fruited dry reds; lush, raisiny and sweet in Puglia. ***SJ***

ALFROCHEIRO: Early-ripening grape of Dão, Portugal; deep, dense blackberry fruits *(Quinta dos Carvalhais)*; also in Alentejo, Bairrada, Douro. Related to Trousseau. ***SJ***

ALICANTE BOUSCHET: Late-ripening French cross (Grenache x Petit Bouschet), more popular in Portugal for Alentejo blends than varietals. It is a teinturer grape with red skins and flesh. ***SJ***

ARENI NOIR: Raspberry, cassis, spice, silky-textured with bitter finish; an ancient Armenian grape thriving in Vayots Dzor *(Zorah)*. ***FR***

BAGA: In Portugal, Bairrada's flagship grape; red-berried fruit, leafy notes and tannic grip; now enjoying a revival with its style softened by modern winemaking techniques *(Filipa Pato, Luis Pato)*. ***SJ***

BARBERA: Plush dark plum and cherry, bright acidity, hint of pepper; a prolific Italian grape in homeland Piedmont *(Fontana)*. Also in Argentina *(Vallisto)*, Australia *(Alpha Box & Dice)*, California *(Terra d'Oro)*. ***SJ***

BLAUFRÄNKISCH: Minerally, cherry-fruited Central European grape. In Burgenland, Austria *(Moric, Prieler)*. In Hungary (as Kékfrankos), silky textured in Szekszárd *(Heimann, Takler)*; also in Szekszárd's Bikavér blend *(Sebestyen)* and Eger's Egri Bikavér *(Tibor Gál)*. In Württemberg, Germany and Washington State (as Lemberger). ***SJ***

BOBAL: Name derives from *bovale* (bull's head), reflecting the shape of the grape cluster. Spicy, velvet-smooth, prolific in Spain, best in Utiel-Requena *(Fuenteseca)*, Valencia. ***SJ***

BONARDA PIEDMONTESE: A rare Italian grape, once supported Nebbiolo in Gattinara and Ghemme in northern Piedmont. Note it is not the same as Bonarda in Argentina. ***SJ***

BONARDA ARGENTINA: Soft, low-tannin, low-acid grape, with black-cherry fruit, originally from Savoie, France (as Douce Noir); the second most important Argentinian red *(Nieto Senetiner, Zuccardi)*. ***SJ***

CABERNET SAUVIGNON:** The world's most planted grape; originally a Cabernet Franc x Sauvignon Blanc cross. The hero of Bordeaux, with distinctive dry tannin and freshness, achieving complexity and depth with age in the left-bank communes of Pauillac and St-Julien. Popular worldwide both in Bordeaux-style blends and as a varietal, promising blackcurrant, cassis, violets and cedary savouriness. Fresh ripeness in Tuscany, Italy; bright fruit and structure in Australia's Coonawarra *(Majella, Riddoch)*; fruit-forward soft tannin in Margaret River *(Cullen, Fraser Gallop)*; a ripe, dense, sweet phenomenon in California's Napa *(Cain Five, Spottswoode)*; finesse and herby fynbos in Stellenbosch, South Africa *(Rustenberg, Rust en Vrede)*; herbal soft tannins in Maipo and Colchagua, Chile *(Clos Apalta)*; powerful, super-ripe in Mendoza, Argentina *(Catena, Weinert, Zuccardi)*. ***FR

CABERNET FRANC:** Parent of Cabernet Sauvignon, Carmenère and Merlot. A popular blender, back in fashion as a varietal; shows aromatic brightness, freshness and definition at high alcohol. In France, highly rated as a Loire varietal (as Breton) in Bourgueil, Chinon *(Bernard Baudry)*, Saumur-Champigny and St Nicolas de Bourgueil *(Yannick Amirault)*; in Bordeaux (as Bouchet) used as a blender in Pomerol and St-Émilion. Also in Villány, Hungary *(Heumann, Sauska)*, US, Chile *(Echeverria)*, South Africa *(Damascene)*, Argentina *(Catena)*. ***FR

CAMARATE: The second most planted red in Bairrada, Portugal; dark, tannic, high acid. ***FR***

CARIGNAN: A popular blender adding colour, acidity, tannin and spice in Minervois, Fitou and Corbières in France, in Italy's Sardinia, in Spain's Penedès and Priorat (as Samsó) and Rioja (as Mazuelo); also Chile and California. ***FR***

CARMENÈRE: Originally from Bordeaux (France) now quintessentially Chilean; late ripener thrives in heat and drought; confused with Merlot in Chile until 1990s; spicy savoury (*Casa Silva, Maturana*). ***FR***

CASTELÃO: Portuguese grape (as Periquita) losing popularity, but potentially good with careful handling; best in Setúbal for raspberry-toned, elegant reds ageing with leathery complexity. ***SJ***

CASTETS: Never heard of it? You soon will. One of six new grapes authorized in Bordeaux, France; dark, high in alcohol, acid and spice. One of five reds of Spain's Rioja (as Maturana Tinta de Navarrete). ***SJ***

CÉSAR: Ancient north Burgundy grape in Irancy, Auxerrois; adds colour and tannin to Pinot Noir blends. Also in Chile (as Romano). ***SJ***

CINSAULT: Pale, floral strawberry-fruited, peppery; popular for Tavel rosé in France's Rhône. Thrives in hot dry Lebanon, South Africa *(AA Badenhorst, Sadie Family Wines)*, California. ***SJ***

CORVINA: Fragrant Italian grape, part of Valpolicella blend *(Allegrini, Masi, Quintarelli)* with Molinara and Rondinella; in standard Valpolicella, dry Amarone, sweet Recioto and off-dry Ripasso; lighter in Bardolino. ***SJ***

COUNOISE: Plummy, spicy, high acid; successful blender with Syrah, Grenache and Mourvèdre in France's Châteauneuf-du-Pape, Provence and Languedoc; similarly in California. ***SJ***

CRIOLLA: Grape family enjoying renaissance across South America. The original Criollas include Listán Prieto (as País) in Chile *(Bouchon, Torres)*; Criolla Chica in Argentina *(Catena, Michelini)*; Mollar Cano and Negra Criolla in Peru, and Missionera in Bolivia. ***SJ***

DOLCETTO: Sour-cherry, licorice, herbs, with low acidity; one of three main grapes in Piedmont, northwest Italy; low yields essential *(Bruno Giacosa)*; not sweet, despite its name. ***SJ***

DORNFELDER: Medium-bodied and savoury; Germany's third red grape, in Pfalz *(Knipser)* and Rheinhessen. Also in England. ***SJ***

DURIF: Dense, full, tannic, age-worthy Syrah x Peloursin natural cross from France. Popular from San Joaquin to Sonoma *(Ridge)* in California (as Petite Sirah) and Australia's Riverina and Rutherglen. ***FR***

FRAPPATO: Italian; Sicily's best-kept secret; fragrant, with juicy cranberry fruit, tangy acidity, silky smooth tannins; blends with Nero d'Avola in Cerasuolo di Vittoria, increasing as a varietal *(Donnafugata, Planeta)*. ***SJ***

FREISA: Derived from Latin for strawberry; ancient grape from northwest Italy, related to Nebbiolo; pale ruby, crunchy freshness, high tannin, ageing potential; sweet, dry, fizzy in Piedmont's Langhe *(Vajra)*. ***SJ***

FRÜHBURGUNDER: Elegant, early-ripening Pinot Noir mutation (aka Pinot Noir Précoce); blends in Germany's Franken *(Furst)*, England *(Roebuck)*. ***SJ***

GAGLIOPPO: Ancient, soft, spicy south Italian; possibly related to Sangiovese and Nerello Mascalese; at altitude in mountainous Ciro, Calabria *(Santa Venere)*. ***SJ***

GAMAY:** Ancient natural French cross of Pinot Noir x Gouais Blanc. The renowned Beaujolais grape grows well on granite in a range of styles from youthful, fresh bubblegum-scented, to crunchy, peppery red fruit and high acid; gentle sweetness to minerally intensity in Morgon and Moulin-à-Vent (the most age-worthy; almost Pinot Noir-like) of ten Beaujolais Crus *(Godard, Liger-Belair, Thivin)*. Also in the US: California, Oregon and Washington State *(Syncline)*. ***SJ

GRACIANO: Underrated grape, rich, fragrant, high acid and spicy; popular pre-phylloxera. Used in Spain's Rioja blends *(Contino)* and in Jerez (as Tintilla de Rota; *Luis Perez*). Also in Sardinia, Italy (as Bovale Sardo) and Portugal (asTinta Miuda). ***FR***

GRENACHE:** Enjoying a renaissance as its soft approachability suits a desire for less-structured, fresher, sappier reds. Expect a strawberry, dark-plum, herby, white pepper, rich and generous mouthfeel, with sweet alcohol. Currently France's second most planted grape after Merlot, with almost half of all Rhône's vines: Châteauneuf-du-Pape's main grape, with 80 per cent of plantings *(Beaucastel, Pegau)*, Gigondas, Vacqueyras and popular for VDN in Rasteau. Highly prized for aged Banyuls *(Rectorie)* in Roussillon. Important in Calatayud *(El Escocés Volante)*, Navarra *(Zorzal)* and Rioja *(Artadi)* in Spain; also in Sardinia (as Cannonau), Italy and in Australia's Barossa *(Alkina, Powell)* and McLaren Vale *(Bondar, Thistledown)*, plus South Africa *(David & Nadia)* and California. ***SJ

GROLLEAU NOIR: The French 'black crow' is Loire's third most planted red, mainstay of aromatic light Rosé d'Anjou and dry Touraine, including fizz. ***SJ***

KADARKA: Elegant when made well, with floral fresh cherry, spice and pepper; light-bodied with bright acidity. Hungary's equivalent to Pinot Noir, best in Szekszárd (*Heimann, Peter Vida, Sebestyen*); also Bulgaria (as Gamza). ***SJ***

KALECIK KARASI: Light red fruits, velvet smooth, early drinking; best-known central Turkish red *(Kavaklidere)*. ***SJ***

LAGREIN: Crunchy, fresh, bitter-cherry fruit, violets, balsamic and herbs; this underrated ancient grape is back in fashion. Alpine freshness at home in Italy's high-altitude Alto Adige *(Untermoserhof)*. ***SJ***

LAMBRUSCO: Family of north-Italian grapes. Lambrusco Salomino is most prolific; *labrusca* means wild vine. Cherry-red frothy fizz in Emilia-Romagna; best is *secco* with a cork *(Coccapane)*. ***SJ***

LIMNIONA: Central Greek variety, back in fashion; deep purple, herby, elegant, with strawberry and pepper *(Zafeirakis)*. Note: different from Limnio. ***SJ***

LISTÁN NEGRO
Vivid spicy redcurrant and cherry-fruited juicy native of Spain's Canary Islands, particularly in northern Tenerife *(Tajinaste)*; not related to Listán Prieto. ***SJ***

MALBEC:** Currently in fashion; its inky-dark fruit, sweet-plum and licorice flavours and smoky finish appeal to lovers of big bold reds. In France's Bordeaux, Cahors (as Auxerrois) and Loire (as Cot), it shows tight-knit austerity – popular in blends, but it is Argentina that has created the recent hype. First planted in 1852, and until recently made as mainly succulent sweet fruit-bombs; now serious clonal and terroir research has improved quality in Mendoza *(Catena, Mendel, Weinert, Zuccardi)*. ***FR

MANDILARIA: Originally from Crete, also on Paros and Rhodes (as Amorghiano) in Greece; deep colour, firm tannin, high acid, light body, licorice, plum; a popular blender. ***SJ***

MARSELAN: Aromatic supple Cabernet Sauvignon x Grenache cross. Potential flagship for China: rich and spicy in Ningxia *(Renyiyuan, Silver Heights)* and Xinjiang, light and soft in Shandong. ***SJ***

MARZEMINO: Native grape of Trentino in Italy; fragrant, sour-cherry fruit and herbiness, with velvety texture. In Veneto's Conegliano passito and Lombardy and Emilia-Romagna blends. ***SJ***

MAVRODAPHNE: Traditional Greek grape from northwest Peloponnese and Ionian islands, now in Macedonia: superb tannic dry versions emerging *(Gentilini, Parparoussis)* and sweet PDOs in Patras and Cephalonia. ***FR***

MAVROTRAGANO: Promising dark Greek grape, with elegant tannins; on islands Santorini and Tinos *(T-Oinos)*, and in Macedonia *(Gerovassiliou)*. ***FR***

MAVRUD: Dark and plummy, with licorice and bright acidity; robust flagship grape of Bulgaria; rustic if not handled well *(Bratanov, Rumelia, Villa Melnik)*. ***FR***

MENCÍA: Fashionable aromatic grape from Castilla y León, Spain; best from higher-altitude Bierzo (either unoaked or aged in large neutral oak), with violets, cherries and herby, meaty notes *(Raul Perez)*; also in Dão, Portugal (as Jaen). Similar freshness to Cabernet Franc or Gamay. ***SJ***

MERLOT:** With its sweet plummy fruits and luscious velvet-smooth palate, this grape is a popular softener for blends in France. In Bordeaux, its early ripening is an insurance against late-ripening Cabernet Sauvignon; greatest on Bordeaux's right bank in Pomerol *(Trotanoy, Vieux Château Certan)*. In Italy, it's popular in Friuli and Tuscany's Maremma. It can be opulent in California, often in Cabernet blends and as a varietal in Napa *(Duckhorn, Shafer)*. Polished lushness in Chile *(Casa Lapostelle, Montes)*. ***SJ

MOLINARA: Bright cherry-fruited light red; part of Valpolicella's grape trio with Corvina and Rondinella in Veneto, Italy. ***SJ***

MONASTRELL:** Big, hearty, blackcurrant-scented red, widely planted in Spain's Castilla-La Mancha, Murcia and Valencia. In southern France (as Mourvèdre), it reaches great expression in Provence's Bandol *(Tempier)* and adds weighty structure to Rhône's Châteauneuf-du-Pape blends; also in Languedoc-Roussillon; in Australian (as Mataro) Grenache, Syrah and Mourvèdre blends *(Henschke, Torbreck)*. ***FR

MONDEUSE: Dark, spicy, tannic Alpine grape; related to Syrah; famous in Savoie *(Jean-Francois Quenard)*, Bugey and Isère in eastern France; also in Switzerland and Australia. ***FR***

MONTEPULCIANO: Italy's second most planted grape; in Abruzzo, Marches, Molise and Puglia; medium-bodied, soft tannins, fleshy fruits; not to be confused with the town Montepulciano,Tuscany. ***SJ***

NEBBIOLO:** Best known as the grape of Barolo and Barbaresco in Italy's Piedmont; perfumed, elegant, age-worthy *(Aldo Conterno, Gaja)*. Licorice, violets, tar and roses are typical aroma descriptors, while on the palate it is all about acid and tannin – dry, savoury and earthy; some blends are softened with Bonarda. Also grown in northeast Piedmont (as Spanna), in Gattinara and Ghemme and in Lombardy (as Chiavennasca), in Valtellina with fine elegant Alpine styles *(Barbacan)* and Franciacorta. Also in Australia *(Crittenden)*. ***FR

NÉGRETTE: A sappy, aromatic, softly tannic, spicy grape grown in Fronton *(Bellevue La Forêt)*, north of Toulouse, southwest France. ***SJ***

NEGROAMARO: Rich, sweet, robust, bitter twist, aka 'black bitter' in eastern Salento in Puglia, Italy *(San Marzano)*; best drunk young. ***FR***

NERELLO MASCALESE: Important native Sicilian originating from Mount Etna's volcanic slopes with astounding ability to reflect its Italian terroir *(Benanti, Cornelissen, Terre Nerre)*. Pale, high alcohol, high acid, moderately soft tannins, with ageing potential; often blended with softer Nerello Cappuccio; also in Calabria. ***FR***

NERO D'AVOLA: In Italy, Sicily's prolific red (as Calabrese); dark, sweet plums and pomegranate; robust tannins. Blended with Frappato in Cerasuolo di Vittoria *(COS, Planeta)*, in Erice and Riesi; varietal in Menfi and Vittoria. Also in Australia *(Coriole, Grosset)*. ***FR***

NERO DI TROIA: Puglia's dark horse, ancient Italian grape packs a punch; black cherries, cocoa, spice and velvety tannins; some growers leave bunches on vine to partially dry, enhancing texture *(Diomede)*. ***FR***

PETIT VERDOT: 'Small green' refers to this grape's past ripening difficulties; now with warming temperatures it's popular in Bordeaux blends, adding dense colour, spice, tannin. Bordeaux-style blends in Italy (Tuscany), Australia, California, Chile. ***FR***

PINOTAGE: Much-maligned versatile grape (Pinot Noir x Cinsault). South Africa's flagship, from simple and fruity to serious, structured and site-expressive; best are sweet, brambly, savoury, earthy and muscular *(Beeslaar, Kanonkop)*. ***FR***

PINOT NOIR:** Much-loved grape achieving precise perfumed elegance and velvet-smooth tannins in the right hands. Best in French homeland of Burgundy, with softer, fruitier Côte de Beaune and structured, higher-acid Côte de Nuits, achieving greatness in Grand Crus. Important in Champagne's Montagne de Reims *(André Clouet, Pierre Paillard)* and southerly Aube. Alsace is enjoying a Pinot renaissance with lush-fruited styles *(Albert Mann, Weinbach)*. The US is the world's second-largest grower: Sonoma's Russian River *(Merry Edwards)*, Santa Barbara *(Au Bon Climat)* and Oregon's Willamette *(Eyrie)*. Third largest is Germany (as Spätburgunder), best in Europe outside Burgundy from Ahr (*Meyer-Näkel*), Baden *(Bernhard Huber)*, Pfalz and Rheinhessen. Cherry fruit and higher alcohol in New Zealand's Marlborough, Martinborough *(Dry River)*, Waipara; richer tannins in Central Otago *(Felton Road)*. ***SJ

PINOT MEUNIER: In France, a key Champagne grape, particularly in frost-prone Vallée de la Marne; adds fruity softness to youthful blends alongside Pinot Noir and Chardonnay; limited varietals *(Egly-Ouriet, Gosset)*. Gaining popularity in England for still wines and fizz; makes similar-styled red to Pinot Noir. ***SJ***

PORTUGIESER: Germany's third most planted red in Ahr, Rheinhessen, Pfalz; light, low acid. Also in Austria's Thermenregion, Weinviertel; Hungary's Eger, Villány; also in Italy, Croatia, Czechia, Slovenia and Romania. ***SJ***

POULSARD: In France's Jura (as Ploussard), blending with Trousseau and Pinot Noir; juicy, high acid, flavourful in warm vintages; looks like a dark rosé *(Pignier)*. Also in Bugey Cerdon. ***SJ***

REFOSCO: Family of ancient varieties from northeast Italy; in Veneto, Friuli Venezia Giulia, Piedmont; sappy, floral, cherry, raspberry, high acid. Also in Slovenia and Croatia (as Refošk). ***SJ***

RUBIN: Dark-skinned Bulgarian cross (Nebbiolo x Syrah); sweet spice, tannic, high alcohol, can be jammy *(Haralambievi)*. ***FR***

SAGRANTINO: Very dark and very tannic Italian grape; makes dry and sweet Port-like passito reds from semi-dried grapes; in Montefalco Sagrantino, Umbria. Also in Hungary, Australia and California. ***FR***

SANGIOVESE:** Brunello, Calabrese, Morellino, Nielluccio and Prugnolo Gentile are synonyms for this major central Italian grape. Best known as the main grape of Chianti *(Fontodi)*, Brunello di Montalcino *(Barbi)*, Vino Nobile de Montepulciano *(Avignonesi)* and Super Tuscans. With aromatic complexity, high acidity, chalky tannins and the ability to show its terroir, it is revered in Tuscany. Its heritage is half-Tuscan, half-Calabrian; it's widely planted across Emilia-Romagna, Marches and Umbria. Some found in the US (California), Argentina and Australia. ***FR

SAPERAVI: Georgia's most planted red has a dark inky colour and a name that means 'dye'. This robust, fruity, spicy, versatile teinturier (red skin and juice) grape originates from Kakheti *(Casreli, Lukasi, Orgo)* and is often *qvevri*-fermented. Terroir-sensitive and age-worthy, it tastes like ripe Syrah. Also in Ukraine, Moldova, New York's Finger Lakes, Australia. ***FR***

SCHIAVA: The most planted of the Schiava family is light, perfumed and nutty Schiava Grossa, originally from Trentino-Alto Adige in Italy. Popular in Germany's Württemberg (as Trollinger). ***SJ***

SCHIOPPETTINO: Fragrant, peppery, elegant, ancient Italian variety, back in fashion *(Bressan, Ronchi di Cialla)* in Friuli Colli Orientali and Friuli Isonzo (as Ribolla Nera). ***SJ***

SCIACCARELLO: In France, popular in Corsica's Ajaccio and Sartène *(Clos Venturi);* dark, fragrant and herbal. Italian roots, from Tuscany (as Mammolo); in Chianti and Vino Nobile di Montepulciano blends. ***SJ***

SHAVKAPITO: Rediscovered ancient grape with plum, cherry, herby spice; indigenous to Kartli, Georgia *(Mukhrani, Tiko)*. ***SJ***

ST-LAURENT: Succulent, sappy red, revived in Burgenland and Thermenregion, Austria *(Pittnauer)*. Also in Germany's Baden, Pfalz and Rheinhessen (*Knipser*); in Czechia and Slovakia – its second most planted red. Note no connection to Pinot St Laurent. ***SJ***

SUSUMANIELLO: 'Little donkey', in Salento dialect, refers to this ancient vine's obstinacy; unusual blueberry, rhubarb, white pepper, full-bodied herby notes; indigenous to Puglia, Italy *(Vallone)*. ***FR***

SYRAH:** The only red grape allowed in Northern Rhône crus, and second most planted grape in Southern Rhône, France. It originated as a natural cross (Mondeuse Blanche x Dureza) in the Rhône-Alpes. In the north, Côte-Rôtie *(Guigal, Jasmin)* and Hermitage (*Jaboulet, JL Chave*) offer blackcurrant, black pepper and a taut structure with incredible finesse and longevity. In the south, it adds colour, structure and acidity to blends *(Beaucastel, Pégau)*. Also hugely popular in Australia (as Shiraz), with big assertive styles; best from old vines in Barossa *(Penfolds, Powell)*, Clare *(Jim Barry)* and Eden *(Henschke)*. Potential in California *(DuMol)*, Washington State *(L'Ecole No 41)*, South Africa *(Boekenhoutskloof)*, Chile, New Zealand. ***FR

TANNAT: Uruguay's most planted red in two styles; bright and fruity *(Viña Edén, Garzón)* or structured and powerful *(Bouza, Deicas)*. Its homeland is Gascony, southwest France, with dark, earthy, high-tannin, age-worthy styles in Madiran and Irouléguy. ***FR***

TARRANGO: A light, refreshing, fruit-forward Australian cross (Sultaniye x Touriga Nacional) for hot inland Murray-Darling *(Brown Brothers)*. ***SJ***

TEMPRANILLO:** Spain's champion variety; black cherry, red plum, moderate acidity; capable of great finesse and sophistication. The dominant grape of Rioja, blending with Garnacha *(La Rioja Alta, López de Heredia, Muga)*, and as a varietal *(Finca Allende, Roda)*. Higher-altitude Ribera del Duero (as Tinto Fino) dominates as a varietal with structure and high acidity *(Pingus)*; robust, gutsy Toro (as Tinta de Toro); soft, light Valdepeñas and La Mancha (as Cencibel). In northern Portugal (as Tinta Roriz) and in the south (as Aragonêz). In the US: California, Oregon, Washington State. Also in South Australia *(SC Pannell)*. ***FR

TEROLDEGO: Rediscovered late-ripening variety from Trentino-Alto Adige, northeastern Italy, with its own DOC Teroldego Rotaliano *(Foradori)*; deep-coloured, lush fruit, bright acidity. ***SJ***

TINTA BARROCA: Aromatic, plummy, softly tannic grape popular in the Douro, Portugal, for young Port blends, rarely as varietal wines. Also in South Africa *(AA Badenhorst)* and in Riverland, Australia. ***SJ***

TOURIGA FRANCA: Most widely planted red in the Douro (as Touriga Francesa), Portugal – common in Port blends and occasionally as varietal table wines *(Quinta de la Rosa)*; also in Dão. It is best from warm sites; floral and elegant. ***SJ***

TOURIGA NACIONAL:** Portugal's star grape. Perfumed, rich, dense blackberry and plum fruits, heavy tannins, spicy; capable of complexity and longevity, with affinity to oak. Key role in Douro Port blends and table wines, with some varietals *(Quintas dos Carvalhais, do Noval)*. Its homeland is Dão *(Quinta dos Roques)*; also in Alentejo, Algarve, Lisbon, Setúbal and Tejo, with less consistent, jammier flavours. In California, Australia and South Africa. One of four reds approved for Bordeaux. ***FR

TRINCADEIRA: Spicy, full-bodied Portuguese grape (as Tinta Amarela); popular blender in Alentejo *(Cortes de Cima)*, Dão, Douro, Lisbon and Tejo. ***FR***

TROUSSEAU: In France, blackberry, spice, high sugar and high acid; one of Jura's three reds *(Stéphane Tissot, Pignier)*. Planted more widely in Portugal (as Bastardo). Also California and Oregon *(Eyrie)*. ***SJ***

VRANAC: Quality Balkan 'black stallion' grape; in Croatia, Kosovo, Montenegro, North Macedonia, Serbia; full, tannic, high alcohol. ***FR***

XINOMAVRO: Greece's noble diva. Site selection, low yields and gentle handling are crucial; best in Macedonia and Naoussa (*Thymiopoulos*); similar dry tannins, high acid and age-worthiness as Nebbiolo. Lighter in Amynteo, Goumenissa and Rapsani. Versatile: red, rosé, fizz *(Karanika)* in Amynteo. ***FR***

ZINFANDEL:** Same as Primitivo in Italy, but originally from Croatia and called Tribidrag (or Crljenak Kaštelanski). Versatile for dry and sweet, red, rosé, sparkling. Much loved, full-bodied, sweet and raisiny, with high alcohol, licorice and firm tannins as Primitivo in Puglia *(Morella)*. In California, tannins are softer but still with characteristic sweetness. Best are old vine, dry farmed from Lodi, Napa, Sierra Foothills, Sonoma *(Bedrock, Ridge, Seghesio)*. ***FR

ZWEIGELT: A 1920s Blaufränkisch x St-Laurent cross; voluptuous cherry fruits; popular in Austria for blends and varietals; light and bland to dense, peppery and age-worthy *(Umathum)*. Also in Czechia, Hungary, Germany. ***SJ***

GRAPES Q&A

WHEN IS THE RIGHT TIME TO PICK?
Grapes are picked when they have turned from green and hard to soft and ripe, with the right balance of acid, sugar and tannin. The grape needs a certain level of sugar build-up, balanced with good acidity. This can be measured, but the best way is to taste the grapes and chew the seeds and skins to assess the phenolic ripeness. The picking time is crucial, but it might also depend on when the harvest team or machine harvester is available – or on the weather.

WHAT IS PHENOLIC RIPENESS IN RED GRAPES?
Also known as physiological ripeness, phenolic ripeness depends on the quality, ripeness and finesse of the tannins, build-up of colour pigments (anthocyanins) and aromatic characteristics developed in the skins. Tannins are chemical compounds (also known as polyphenols) that affect the structure and character of wine; they come primarily from the skins, plus seeds and stems. Different wines show varying types and levels of tannin (high for thick-skinned Cabernet Sauvignon, low for thinner-skinned Pinot Noir). The challenge for the grower is to achieve ripeness at the same time as the best acid and sugar balance. This is tricky, and leaf plucking, carefully timed drip irrigation, altering fruit exposure and crop thinning are just a few of the methods they use.

CAN A WINE LABEL INDICATE RIPENESS?
The best way to tell grape ripeness is to check the alcohol level, as riper grapes tend to make stronger wine (14% or over), unless it's sweet or fortified and crafted to that particular style.

DOES GRAPE BERRY SIZE VARY?
Yes, the smaller the fruit, the higher the phenolic content. You tend to get more concentrated flavours and higher colour intensity from smaller berries (Cabernet Sauvignon and Graciano). If a variety has a Petit or Gros version, it will be the Petit that is best quality (Petit Manseng versus Gros Manseng, for example).

WHY IS THE SIZE OF THE YIELD IMPORTANT?
The yield is the amount of grapes produced from an area of a vineyard; this varies according to the pruning method, grape type, terroir and health of the vine. It is normally measured in tons per hectare, but this will depend on the density of planting. Generally, the higher the quantity, the lower the quality and more dilute the wine. So, low yields are best.

WHAT IS A *VITIS VINIFERA* GRAPE?
This is one of many *Vitis* grapevines around the world. It is believed to have originated from the South Caucasus and the Middle East, spreading to the Mediterranean and on to the New World. It includes all main wine-grape varieties (Chardonnay, Merlot, Pinot Noir). It is different from *Vitis rupestris, Vitis riparia* (used for developing American rootstocks), *Vitis berlandieri* and *Vitis labrusca*, native to the US (Concord). Two varieties of the same species can be crossed to create a new variety (Pinotage, created from Pinot Noir x Cinsault). A crossing of two or more *Vitis* species is known as a hybrid – for example, between vinifera and a disease-resistant *Vitis* species from the US (such as Seyval Blanc, *see also page* 63).

TASTING PRACTICE: **CLASSIC REDS**

Four of the world's classic reds are highlighted here. Three are blends, but with a dominant grape variety: Tempranillo in Rioja, Merlot in right-bank Bordeaux and Cabernet Sauvignon in Napa. The fourth is Barolo, a varietal Nebbiolo. More noticeable than individual grape characteristics here are the flavours from each particular terroir (*see page* 70), that make each one so distinctive.

This tasting also offers an oak-ageing comparison. The first two wines compare American and French oak, looking at flavour and texture. The second two contrast large cask neutral old oak for tannic Nebbiolo with smaller oak (a little new) for the lusher Cabernet Sauvignon (*see page* 122).

Once you have completed the tasting, then try the wines with artisanal cheeses to enhance fruitiness: Rioja with Manchego, Bordeaux with aged Gouda, Barolo with Pecorino or Grana Padano, and Napa Cabernet with English Cheddar. (For more on food and wine, *see page* 146.)

WINES TO BUY (IN ORDER OF SERVING):

① Rioja (Spain) **£££**
② Bordeaux (France) **£££**
③ Barolo (Italy) **£££**
④ Napa Cabernet Sauvignon (US) **£££**

Preparation: *See page 32.*

Buying & alternatives: If you cannot find the Rioja, choose an alternative from the same region; the wine should have been aged in American oak. For the Bordeaux, look for right-bank Merlot-dominant blends at a similar price; for the Nebbiolo pick another reputable producer; replace the Cabernet with the same grape from another Napa estate.

Serving temperature: 15 to 18°C (59 to 64°F).

Method: Pour the same amount into each of your four glasses, and sample them side by side.

Look: For each wine, tilt the glass against the white background. Compare Wines 1 and 2 against each other, noticing the lighter hue and tawny rim of Wine 1. Then Wines 3 and 4. Wine 3 has a much lighter colour (typical of Nebbiolo) in comparison to Wine 4's dark intensity (typical of Cabernet).

Smell: Now smell all four wines one after the other. Wines 1 and 3 have some similarity: Wine 1 is dominated by bitter cherry, spice and cedar, and Wine 3 with red fruit, but heavier spice than Wine 1. Wines 2 and 4 offer a riper fruit note – black cherry for the Bordeaux compared to blackberry, almost mocha-like, for the Napa Cabernet.

Taste: First compare the textures and structure of Wines 1 and 2; you will be comparing American oak ageing with French oak ageing. Wine 1 (Rioja) is matured in large neutral American oak for four years, giving it an open generous feel, with cinnamon and vanilla undertones. There is also a tight structure alongside deep chewy fruits, typical of this single vineyard, indicating further ageing potential. Wine 2 (Bordeaux) is matured in 100 per cent new French-oak barriques, giving it a glossy, silky, lush texture with cedary undertones. Note the high alcohol (15%), which gives the Merlot blend a raisiny fruit-cake sweetness.

Wine 3 (Barolo) was matured in large, 25-hectolitre old wood casks to tame Nebbiolo's very high levels of tannins. You do not notice the oak, but it has mellowed and softened the grape tannins alongside the deep powerful fruits typical of Serralunga. Wine 4 (Napa Cabernet) in comparison is full of succulent creamy oak notes, from part-new French-oak ageing, alongside ripe blackberry, iron-rich minerality and earthy tones typical of the terroir.

Finish: Notice the dry finish of Wines 1 and 3 in comparison to the softer, lusher finish of Wines 2 and 4. Think carefully about how long you can savour the flavours after you have swallowed or spat out, as they are all high-quality wines.

Conclusion: You have tasted four classic reds noting flavours that derive from their terroir and specific oak ageing. During the tasting, you should have written down details as you analysed each wine; now go over these and try to write a complete tasting note for each of the classic wines. This is a helpful discipline because it enables you to focus again on the distinctive characteristics of each wine.

Now check the crib sheet on the next page, and consider trying the tasting again using the alternative wines suggested.

CRIB SHEET: **CLASSIC REDS**

1. RIOJA

REGION: **RIOJA**

COUNTRY: **SPAIN**

GRAPE: **70% TEMPRANILLO, 20% GARNACHA, 5% MAZUELO, 5% GRACIANO**

PRICE: **£££**

ALCOHOL: **13%**

SIGHT: **Mid-ruby with tawny edge**

SMELL: **Bitter cherry, cinnamon, vanilla, leather**

TASTE: **Moderate**

FRUIT INTENSITY: **Ripe black-cherry fruit, indicating a warm Rioja vintage**

TEXTURE: **Open generous palate with slight tightness of structure and chewy fruit**

CONCLUSION: **Shows mature American-oaked Rioja's broad open flavours with good structure**

COMMON BLIND TASTING MIX-UPS: **Rhône Syrah**

ALTERNATIVES TO TRY
Spanish Tempranillo (Rioja or Ribera del Duero, American oak-aged)

2. BORDEAUX

REGION: **BORDEAUX**

COUNTRY: **FRANCE**

GRAPE: **95% MERLOT, 5% CABERNET FRANC**

PRICE: **£££**

ALCOHOL: **15%**

SIGHT: **Deep dark ruby**

SMELL: **Sweet, ripe, rich black cherries, sweet licorice**

TASTE: **High acidity**

FRUIT INTENSITY: **Lavish dark fruit, bitter cherry**

TEXTURE: **Soft, velvety, sturdy sweet tannins, silky**

CONCLUSION: **Shows ripe vintage with new French oak: sweet spice, lush texture, dark chocolate**

COMMON BLIND TASTING MIX-UPS: **Mencía, Cabernet Sauvignon blend**

ALTERNATIVES TO TRY
Merlot-dominant Bordeaux (Lalande de Pomerol, St-Émilion or Francs-Côtes de Bordeaux)

3. BAROLO

REGION: **PIEDMONT**

COUNTRY: **ITALY**

GRAPE: **NEBBIOLO**

PRICE: **£££**

ALCOHOL: **14.5%**

SIGHT: **Garnet with pale rim**

SMELL: **Spicy red fruit with heavy spice undertones**

TASTE: **Moderate to high acidity**

FRUIT INTENSITY: **Fruit dominated by spice**

TEXTURE: **Dry tannin and expansive, grainy mouthfeel**

CONCLUSION: **Typical tannic Barolo; spicy, earthy undertones**

COMMON BLIND TASTING MIX-UPS: **Nerello Mascalese, Sangiovese**

ALTERNATIVES TO TRY

Italian Nebbiolo (Barolo Serralunga d'Alba, Langhe), Sangiovese (Chianti Classico, Tuscany), Aglianico (Basilicata)

4. NAPA CABERNET SAUVIGNON

REGION: **CALIFORNIA**

COUNTRY: **UNITED STATES**

GRAPE: **90% CABERNET SAUVIGNON, 10% CABERNET FRANC**

PRICE: **£££**

ALCOHOL: **14.5%**

SIGHT: **Deep dark ruby**

SMELL: **Blackberry and mocha**

TASTE: **Moderate acidity**

FRUIT INTENSITY: **Very ripe fruits, with cedary earthy undertones**

TEXTURE: **Velvety soft smooth structure**

CONCLUSION: **Ripe intensity of Cabernet fruit from top terroir with French oak, rich and expansive**

COMMON BLIND TASTING MIX-UPS: **California Merlot**

ALTERNATIVES TO TRY

Napa (Rutherford or Oakville) Cabernet Sauvignon, Argentinian Cabernet Sauvignon blend

HERE COME THE PIWIS...

Floreal, Souvignier Gris, Cabernet Cortis and Rondo are just a few of the unusual grape names starting to appear on wine labels. These are the Piwis – a new family of hybrid grapes now becoming popular worldwide.

High humidity and excess rainfall have been challenging for winemakers across the world in recent years, a consequence of our changing climate. This has brought increased risk of disease, requiring constant vigilance and treatment. However, there is now a more sustainable solution for the future, one that could help reduce the carbon footprint of wine – the Piwi grape.

WHAT IS A PIWI?

These grapes are naturally disease-resistant, specifically developed to require less treatment and still produce a decent yield in tricky mildew-affected years. The name is short for the German *Pilzwiderstandsfähige* – a bit of a mouthful – basically meaning fungus resistant. Today, Piwis are being bred not just for fungal resistance, but also to cope with increasing temperatures, as later-ripening grapes with resistance to sunburn.

PIWIS VERSUS CLASSIC GRAPES

A Piwi grape is an interspecific 'resistant hybrid variety' (white or red) that has resulted from crossing *Vitis vinifera* with another *Vitis* genus (American or Asian). Widely planted classic grapes like Sauvignon Blanc, Chardonnay and Cabernet Sauvignon are pure *Vitis vinifera*. Robust thick-skinned late-ripening vinifera Cabernet Sauvignon is a popular parent in a Piwi cross (Cabernet Blanc, Cabernet Cortis). Piwis are beginning to taste higher quality; they tend to have moderate alcohol and can offer great value.

A PIWI HISTORY

'Hybrid varieties with some non-vinifera parentage have been around since 1840, when powdery and downy mildew became problematic,' says English viticulturist Stephen Skelton MW. 'The old hybrids almost disappeared, until 1967 when Regent was

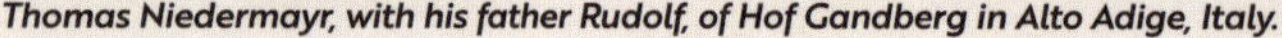

Thomas Niedermayr, with his father Rudolf, of Hof Gandberg in Alto Adige, Italy.

Cabernet Cortis (Cabernet Sauvignon x Solaris).

bred by Professor Alleweldt at the Geilweilerhof institute in Germany. This led to new hybrids with more complicated breeding lines helped by gene editing – what we now call Piwis, which are allowed in EU quality-wine schemes.'

It can actually take 20 years for a new grape cross to be approved, but new Piwis coming on-stream do have an advantage. Not only are they sustainable, requiring little plant protection, but crucially they have improved in taste and flavour.

WHO GROWS PIWIS?

Piwis are popular with German growers (4,000 hectares in 2023) and in Italy, Austria, Switzerland, Scandinavia, Poland, France and England. (In 2024 the UK had 283 hectares of Piwis and 119 hectares of hybrids.) The trend is now spreading to America.

In Italy's South Tyrol, the Niedermayr family of Hof Gandberg were early adopters, switching entirely to Piwis in the early 1990s. They now have some of the oldest Solaris, Bronner and Souvignier Gris plantings and breed their own resistant varieties adapted to their soil.

The largest French Piwi grower is Vincent Pugibet of Domaine La Colombette in Languedoc. He was encouraged to try them 18 years ago, to protect the health of workers and his surrounding population by reducing chemical use. He now grows 40 Piwi varieties across 160 hectares (60 per cent of his vineyard).

'Some Piwis don't need any spraying at all, and others just once or twice a year,' says Pugibet. 'This is nothing compared to what is accepted in organic methods.' By adjusting his vineyard canopy, using single mid-height cordon and spur pruning, he is able to achieve high yields and small berries; his winemaking is no different from that used for other grapes. However, some breeders comment that modern Piwis need to be treated three to four times a year if they start to lose their resistance.

At Château Thieuley in Bordeaux, Marie and Sylvie Courselle have had success with Cabernet Cortis and Sauvignac. The latter grape has been allowed into Bordeaux and Bordeaux Supérieur appellations along with Souvignier Gris, Floreal and Vidoc Noir. However, Cabernet Cortis has to be labelled Vin de France, as it is yet to be accepted.

WHITE PIWIS: CRISP & DELICATE

CABERNET BLANC: Late ripener *(Cabernet Sauvignon x Regent: 1991)* by acclaimed Swiss breeder Valentin Blattner; deep gold, apricot notes, rich weighty, moderate alcohol, good freshness – similar to Pinot Gris or Sauvignon Blanc; popular in Germany *(Mosbacher)*.

SOUVIGNIER GRIS: Early ripener *(Seyval Blanc x Zähringer: 1983)* by Norbert Becker; neutral aroma, but dense, rich extract – reminiscent of Pinot Gris; popular in Austria's Steiermark, Denmark and England *(Blackbook)*.

SOLARIS: Early ripener *(Merzling x Gm 6493 [Zarya Severa x Muscat Ottonel]: 1975)* by Norbert Becker; stone fruits, nutty, essentially acids are ripe; particularly popular in Germany, England, Poland and Scandinavia *(Kullaberg)*.

SEYVAL BLANC: Officially classified as a hybrid rather than a modern Piwi; early ripener *(Seibel 5656 x Rayon d'Or)*; citrus fruit, high acid, good fizz base; popular in Canada, New York State and England *(Breaky Bottom)*.

BRONNER: Mid to late ripener *(Merzling x Gm 6494 [Zarya Severa x Sankt Laurent]: 1975)* by Norbert Becker; light aromatics, apple flavour; grown in Belgium, Germany, Switzerland and Italy *(Niedermayr)*.

FLOREAL: *(Villaris x Mtp 3159-2-12: 2002)* aromatic, peach and apricot notes, medium acidity – similar to unoaked Chardonnay; popular in the Loire *(Lacheteau)*.

RED PIWIS: SMOOTH & JUICY

CABERNET CORTIS: Early ripener *(Cabernet Sauvignon x Solaris: 1982)* by Norbert Becker; inky dark, herbal notes, soft, juicy, smooth texture – similar to a ripe Beaujolais *(Thieuley)*.

CABERNET NOIR: Early ripener *(Cabernet Sauvignon x unknown: 1991)* by Valentin Blattner; dark and mouth-staining, blackcurrant fruit, soft and supple texture – similar to Cabernet Franc *(Domaine La Colombette; Blackbook)*.

RONDO: Early ripener *(Sankt Laurent x Zarya Severa: 1964)* by Professor Vilém Kraus in former Czechoslovakia; moderate acidity and tannin; popular in Germany, Scandinavia, Wales and England *(Winbirri)*.

THE VINEYARD

When choosing to grow vines, the two most important factors affecting a grower's decision – that will influence the style and quality of the wine – are the grape variety and the climate in which it is grown. These are the fundamentals, after which aspect, altitude, soil structure and types of viticulture will all have a more subtle impact on the resultant wine.

CHOOSING THE GRAPE

A grower first needs to select the grape most suited to the style of wine they want to make, but even more important, it must be suited to the climate. To make quality wine, grapes need specific conditions to grow – enough summer sun to ripen, but a cool enough winter to allow dormancy. They are generally grown between latitudes of 30 to 50 degrees on both sides of the equator, beyond which it is too cold or too hot and humid. However conditions such as proximity to oceans, coastlines, micro-climate, climate change and more also have an influence.

Grapes vary in their ripening cycles: some are more suited to continental climates with shorter growing seasons, some thrive better in temperate longer growing seasons; others can cope better in extreme drought and temperature. 'With the ongoing climatic changes, we need to do a better job of matching varieties to the climate... we tend to focus too much on the top ten or so varieties,' explains wine climatologist Dr Gregory Jones.

Currently, growers are actively researching and planting grapes that are most suited to coping with the extreme conditions within their different regions to ensure quality wine can continue to be made (*see page* 80).

Broadly speaking, grapes grown in warmer climates produce riper fruit, higher alcohol, softer acidity and softer, riper tannins, making bolder, brasher, more powerful styles. Grapes grown in cooler climates have lighter fruit, lower alcohol and refreshing, crisp, tangy acidity, giving subtle elegant styles.

Steep south-facing Kirchberg vineyard in Mosel, Germany; horizontally and vertically trained Riesling vines benefit from good sun exposure.

Thick-skinned, small-berried, drought-resistant Palomino grapes thrive in the warm Jerez region of Andalusia, southern Spain.

Vineyards in Lavaux, in Switzerland's Vaud region, benefit from a proximity to Lake Geneva, which helps reflect sunlight and moderates climate.

CLIMATE CONTROL

Climate is of paramount importance because it has a huge impact on the yield (crop level), style and quality of the wine, making it viable to grow the grape in the first place. Localized day-to-day atmospheric conditions (weather) are also important in determining how the grape is grown. Temperature, sunlight and water are key considerations for grape-growers. All these parameters are created by climate, but weather events can change them.

TEMPERATURE

For a vine to thrive, the annual mean temperature needs to be 10°C (50°F). Ideally, the average summer temperature should be 19°C (66°F) or above, but it can vary between 13 and 21°C (55 and 70°F). The mean average winter temperature should not be less than -1°C (30°F). Cold winters help vines sleep and kill off unwanted viruses or fungi, but there is a minimum winter temperature of -5 to -20°C (23 to -4°F), below which plant tissue can be damaged. Vines are buried under soil in winter in northeast China to protect them.

During the growing season, the more constant the temperature, the better, as both heat spikes and severe frosts can be devastating for yield and quality. Diurnal temperatures (difference between day and night) can be beneficial if within the desired range – cooler night-time temperatures preserve grape acidity, ensuring fresher wines (*see also pages* 67 to 69).

SUNLIGHT

Sunlight is essential for photosynthesis. A vine requires at least 1,250 hours of sunshine in the growing season, and the average growing season should be around 150 to 190 days from when the vine buds to when the grapes are ready to harvest.

WATER

Water is crucial for the vine's survival and success. Ideally, there should be at least 500mm of rainfall per annum, spread through spring, summer and autumn, which is enough for photosynthesis in temperate climates. If the climate is warm, more will be required (750mm). This depends on the grape variety however, so carefully controlled irrigation is used. In certain conditions where there is no summer rainfall (or rivers) – for example, on the island of Santorini – vines are weaved into basket shapes (*koulouras*) to capture any moisture and avoid drought-stress. Conversely, heavy rain is undesirable, because it can majorly impact quality by splitting grapes, encouraging fungal disease and causing erosion.

OTHER CLIMATE INFLUENCES

Humidity and wind are also important factors that can influence a vine. Excess humidity in moist tropical climates encourages mildew, so vines must be trained to give high open canopies with good air movement. In wet Rías Baixas in northwest Spain, Albariño vines are trained on the parral (pergola) system 2m above ground.

In various parts of the world – from Mendoza in Argentina, to Provence, Bordeaux and Burgundy in France – localized hail can be devastating for yields. Fierce winds can also cause serious problems, such as cooling or drying out vines, breaking young shoots, delaying ripening and lowering yields. However, wind in moderation can be beneficial in aerating the vine and tempering the heat of the summer (Mistral in Southern Rhône, Tramontane in Roussillon, Poniente in Jerez, Zonda in Argentina).

SITE POSITIONING

Aspect is an important characteristic of a vineyard site. In cool climates, vines are often planted on southern-facing slopes to assist with ripening or to temper weather extremes. Vines on slopes benefit more from the sun in temperate climates due to the angle of the sun. Slopes are also considered ideal because they offer good drainage and better soil structure, away from valley-floor frost traps, flood plains and fertile soils.

Quinta da Manoella in Portugal's Douro has 80- to 100-year-old vines on steep schist terraces; surrounding forest creates a unique micro-climate.

Slopes near bodies of water – oceans, lakes or rivers (for example Germany's Mosel Valley) – can assist ripening as the water acts as a heat reservoir, reflecting sunlight, or offering a moderating influence in more continental climates (such as Hungary's Lake Balaton). The best aspect for sun and drainage is mid-slope, away from the cooler summit exposed to rain and winds. In warm climates, a north-facing slope is preferred to temper heat.

PLANTING AT ALTITUDE

Today, elevation is key in the search for cooler micro-climates to mitigate climate change. Since the mid-1990s, Mendoza's Uco Valley in Argentina (900 to 1,500m above sea level) has expanded from 6,000 to 30,000 hectares, and moves to higher altitudes have transformed the quality of Argentinian Malbec. Growers are also planting high up the Andes – in Peru at 3,300m, in Bolivia at 2,600m and in Chile at 2,200m. The world's highest vineyard is in the Himalayas (at 3,563m) in Tibet. As temperatures warm in Australia, growers in the Adelaide Hills are escaping the heat by planting ever higher – over 650m – in search of cooler, wetter conditions to ensure freshness, elegance and finesse in their Chardonnay.

In the Northern Hemisphere, growers are experimenting with plantings at over 1,200m in the Pyrenees, Gredos and Alpujarras mountains in Spain cutting-edge wineries are being built over 1,100m on the Troodos Mountains in Cyprus and the highest are now at 1,800m in Batroun, northern Lebanon, followed by Tenerife at 1,700m.

When planting at high altitude, a grower needs to bear in mind that for every 100m of elevation above sea level, the temperature drops by 0.6°C (1.08°F) depending on which side of the mountain it is on. However diurnal temperature shifts tend to be greater at elevation, while more ultraviolet radiation aids the quality and development of phenolics, giving more colour, tannin ripeness and flavour development in the grapes.

Vineyards in Uco Valley, Mendoza, Argentina at high altitude benefit from high daytime temperatures combined with cool nights.

CLIMATIC EXTREMES

Polar ice caps are shrinking, climate types are shifting and our temperate Mediterranean zones – where many vines are grown – are getting hotter and drier. For the grower, this has created both challenges and opportunities.

'In general, the overall wine style that a region produces is a result of the baseline climate, while climate variability determines vintage yield and quality differences,' explains climatologist Dr Gregory Jones. 'Climatic changes, which influence both variability and average conditions, therefore have the potential to bring about changes in wine production and wine styles... For grapevines, changes in growth events have resulted in earlier bud-break, bloom, veraison and harvest dates occurring in the majority of regions worldwide.'

Many of our wine regions are in a narrow geographical and climatic range, and within that there are grapes that can only thrive in small niche areas. Some scientists believe the mean annual global temperature in Europe could be more than 2.5°C (4.5°F) higher by the end of the 21st century (above the Paris Agreement's 1.5°C/2.7°F threshold). This is very concerning for growers looking to the future on where and what to plant, or for those with established vineyards in traditional regions, wondering what the future holds.

Unprecedented flash floods in the Ahr Valley, Germany destroyed wineries and lower vineyards in 2021.

HEAT, DROUGHT & UNPREDICTABILITY

According to Jones, heat and drought are the two main issues. 'Wine regions in humid subtropical climates are experiencing increasing humidity and temperatures, creating disease pressure, while semi-arid regions are getting drier, putting more pressure on water resources to maintain current productivity levels.' Harvests are at least two weeks earlier, with August now the norm in the Northern Hemisphere, putting ripening in a warmer part of the growing season and altering ripening profiles.

There is also unpredictability caused by hydroclimate volatility – sudden large and frequent dry-to-wet weather events (wet December followed by dry January in Southern Hemisphere growing season) caused by the atmosphere as it warms. These whiplashes have now increased in frequency, plus extreme cold-weather events still occur, as vineyards in Canada's British Columbia have experienced. That's because the Arctic is warming at nearly four times the rate of the rest of the planet, causing large-scale pulsing of atmospheric circulation in the Northern Hemisphere.

OPPORTUNITIES & CHALLENGES

There are clearly opportunities for some; increasing temperatures have been hugely beneficial in the Northern Hemisphere, aiding grape ripening in Canada, England and Germany – although 2024 presented serious challenges, with high humidity and disease. There are now vines, albeit polygenic disease-resistant hybrids, planted in Poland and Scandinavia (*see page* 194). In the Southern Hemisphere, in Patagonia, vineyards extend to Chubut in Argentina and Chico in Chile, areas previously thought far too cool and risky.

Meanwhile, there are challenges for other areas. Historic regions like Burgundy, with a small number of grapes, are experiencing shorter growing seasons alongside severe frost, hail and heat-spike events, and even the Rhône had frost in 2020. It seems that Europe – between the cold and warm air masses stirred by the Atlantic – is particularly vulnerable to erratic climate events. In the 2020s, bushfires in California and Australia have devastated vineyards, wineries and homes, while causing smoke-taint issues across regions and destroying surrounding biodiversity. In 2021, in northern Germany, the small Ahr wine region lost several wineries – washed away by devastating flash floods. In 2024, in southern Brazil, dramatic flood events from unexpected rainstorms put the Rio Grande do Sul wine region under water.

Smoke taint can affect grapes between veraison and harvest.

LOOKING TO THE FUTURE

Growers and winemakers are a resilient bunch, but it is the uncertainty of what the future holds that is particularly worrying for them. What is needed is a portfolio of responses, both day-to-day and long-term, to manage this crisis. Growers will have to get better at learning how to mitigate and adapt in the vineyard – for example, by altering canopy management so that leaves can shade the grapes to avoid sunburn, or using shade cloths to protect them; by carefully timing irrigation and/or moving to dry-farming to save water; by changing to row orientation or moving to higher elevations. 'We need to get better at site selection – and we also need to utilize the grape genetic diversity resource that we have available,' says Jones.

For more information on future-proof grapes, turn to page 80.

TERROIR

Once considered a solely French term, terroir derives from the word *terre* – meaning earth. It is at the heart of the appellation system and geographical indications (GI), from the renowned crus of Burgundy to new GIs like Paraje Altamira in Argentina's Uco Valley.

The term has now pervaded our vocabulary in both food and drink around the world to such an extent that it has become commonplace. However without definition or rules and regulations, it is often misunderstood.

When mentioned in the context of wine, it does not only mean soil, but refers to a combination of factors – soil and climate, micro-climate, terrain, biological environment – that influence the character of a wine based on where the vines are grown. Many have attempted to define terroir; some call it a sense of place relating to viticulture (a site-specific wine) and say that only certain grape varieties (Furmint in Tokaji or Chardonnay in Burgundy) can mirror and express it.

Surely terroir goes further than this. In Bordeaux, the wines are blends of different grapes. Fine Vintage Port from selected Douro vineyards are often made from a field blend of grapes. Is terroir not part of the equation here too? If a winemaker adds a specific yeast strain at fermentation rather than using the ambient yeasts of the terroir – which vary every year – does this reduce the impact of terroir?

Sharp limestone ridges of Dentelles de Montmirail form one of the natural boundaries of Gigondas in Southern Rhône, France.

Biodynamically farmed Rippon vineyard in Central Otago, New Zealand, overlooks the Southern Alps on the west shore of Lake Wanaka.

THE HUMAN ELEMENT OF TERROIR

The International Organization of Vine and Wine (OIV) came up with a description for terroir that puts humans at the centre of it all: 'Collective knowledge of the interactions between the identifiable physical and biological environment and applied viti-vinicultural practices develops, providing distinctive characteristics for the products originating from this area. Terroir includes specific soil, topography, climate, landscape characteristics and biodiversity features.'

Dr Jamie Goode points out in his book *The New Viticulture* that there is a human element of terroir, and its expression in wine is an interpretative act – just like a musician playing music (their choice of instrument, skill and application are all important). Goode refers to the influence of the bodega practices in creating Sherry, which have been called 'the second terroir'.

Here Goode is referring to the flor yeast that develops on the surface of wines in barrels, specifically in the micro-climates of Sanlúcar (home of Manzanilla Sherry) and Jerez (where Fino Sherry is made). He argues that surely this is also part of the terroir of the wine.

To learn more about the effects of terroir on wine, try the Classic White and Classic Red Tasting Practices (*see pages* 46 and 58). Also try comparing single-vineyard wines from the same producer: August Kesseler in Rheingau, Germany; Artadi in Rioja, Spain; Aldo Conterno in Piedmont, Italy; Pichler-Krutzler in Wachau, Austria; Grosset in Clare Valley, Australia; Zuccardi in Mendoza, Argentina; Kumeu River in Auckland, New Zealand.

SOIL PITS

Visitors to vineyards today might well be taken to view a soil pit, to see the different layers of soils right down to the bedrock. Some vineyards are littered with them, as digging pits have become one of the recent hallmarks of vineyard exploration (along with electro conductivity mapping, or ECM). Their purpose is to check out the texture and water retention of soils. Viticulturists try to establish in different parts of a vineyard what quality nuances they can bring to a wine by careful zoning. They also advise on how irrigation can best be used, digging deep to get a clear view of how water retentive the soil is, as the root systems can penetrate deep – as much as 7 to 10m in some soils.

SOIL

Vineyard site assessments have become much more precise – with soil profiling, digging pits and vineyard zoning now the norm. It's not just the topsoil that is important as the vine's anchorage, but the subsoil layers too, which the grower must evaluate for texture, structure, drainage, microbial life and heat-retaining capacity.

The most suitable soils for vines have a fine topsoil and penetrable lower layers with good aeration, but harder bedrock can mean less erosion risk, which suits older, deep-rooted vines. Soil's water-retaining capacity is important (clay versus gravel) as it affects the soil temperature. Nutrients (magnesium, calcium and potassium) are crucial to the plant for growth, but scientists agree that vine roots are incapable of absorbing compounds – and that there is no link between soil minerals and flavours in wine.

SOIL TEXTURE

According to leading geomorphologist Professor Mike Summerfield, soil texture is key to growing vines. 'Texture is a fundamental characteristic of

SIX KEY SOILS

Gravel / rolled pebbles: Gravel soils (*grabas de Bourdeus*) found in the Pessac-Léognan appellation in Bordeaux, France, are best suited to red grapes, particularly Cabernet Sauvignon. Gravel allows excellent draining and heat-retaining capacity, which radiates absorbed heat and contributes to grape ripeness.

Clay: The clay soils of Jura in eastern France are cold and compact, with good water retention in comparison to the region's well-drained limestone soils. Clay in Jura is very suitable for growing Savagnin, resulting in wines with lower pH and greater character, compared to limestone.

Loess: Heat-retaining, porous and permeable, silt-sized wind-blown loess is good for root penetration, producing elegant wines in Szekszárd in Hungary (pictured), Wagram in Austria, Walla Walla in Washington State and Shanxi in China.

soil,' he says, 'and is determined by the calibre of soil particles, from clay, silt and sand to cobbles. The calibre and mixture of soil particles play the key role in aeration, along with drainage, and the retention and availability of soil moisture for vine growth. Soil texture also affects heat retention, as fine-grained soils lose energy through evaporation, whereas stony soils, with a high proportion of gravel and cobble-sized material, can retain more heat, aiding grape ripening and reducing the risk of frost damage.'

Summerfield goes on to say, 'Nutrients required for vine growth are both recycled from organic material in the soil and provided by the weathering of mineral particles. Clay minerals also play an important role in retaining nutrients and making them available to vine roots. A vast array of micro-organisms that are present in soils also affect soil structure and the way in which vine roots are able to access nutrients from water in the soil.'

SOIL STUDY – ALSACE RIESLING

Winemaker Olivier Humbrecht MW, from leading estate Domaine Zind-Humbrecht in Alsace, makes Riesling from three different soils and explains the difference in taste.

'**Granite** vineyards are usually steep with solar warm terroirs and poor soils, but their roots go deep; young vines struggle, but old vines do well. Rieslings are bright, vertical and expressive in youth, with crystalline acidity (low malic).

'**Limestone** vineyards have softer slopes because soils are more eroded; the richer soils contain finer elements and are therefore more resistant to drought. Rieslings are broader, less expressive in youth, with citrus fruit and high acidity; they can appear austere in some vintages, but age well.

'**Volcanic or slate** vineyards on steep slopes have harder rock material, like granite, so old vines do much better than young. Rieslings have an exceptional mineral richness, with saline acidity and usually good power.'

Sand: With good aeration, heat retention and drainage, but not so efficient at holding nutrients, sand is believed to be phylloxera-resistant – for example in Colares and Setúbal (pictured) in Portugal and Blewitt Springs in Australia's McLaren Vale.

Limestone: In Jerez in southern Spain, the white *albariza* soil (with 25 to 40 per cent active chalk) is highly porous, with a capacity to retain moisture. Limestone here plays a key role in water supply to the vine.

Slate: Heat and moisture-retaining, radiating warmth at night, slate is particularly useful in cool-climate parts of Germany. Mosel's famous steep slopes between Trier and Zell have blue Devonian slate soils; in other parts of the Mosel, there is iron-infused red slate.

VOLCANIC SOIL

Volcanic wine has become a popular term these days. There is actually no such thing as a volcanic wine – it is a unifying term used to describe a family of wines produced from vineyards located in regions of volcanic rock or sediments, such as lava flows or volcanic ash.

Winemakers have been attracted to volcanic soils for centuries – with good reason. Volcanoes might have a destructive dark side, but they are prized in the wine world for their specific properties and can be rich in potassium, iron and calcium.

Soils deriving from volcanic activity form two groups. Vent-based soil forms from ash (tuff) ejected into the air and cooled before settling and hardening; it might end up being mixed with clay, limestone or rocks. Lava-based soil forms from lava flowing down the volcano's slope or erupting from widely dispersed fissures, rapidly cooling and solidifying, creating basalt, andesite or rhyolite; they can be grey-black or red-brown.

Volcanic wines have an exciting tension and savoury quality, which seems more about the place where they are grown, rather than the grape. Whites tend to be more distinctive, more aromatic, brightly fruited, minerally, savoury, saline and with a pithy long finish; reds are elegant and fresh. Both have mouthwateringly high natural acidity.

THE ADVANTAGES OF VOLCANIC SOIL

Volcanic wine expert John Szabo MS explains why volcanic soils are good for wine. 'Although extremely varied, there are properties shared by many volcanic soils that make them particularly

***Hoyos** pits and semi-circular walls in La Geria in Lanzarote protect dry-grown, low-trained vines from wind and conserve moisture.*

suitable for high-quality wine. Young volcanic "soils" are often more rock than soil, holding little water. Since low water availability is the single most important growing factor to produce quality grapes, this is an advantage. Volcanic ash, sand and tephra [fragments from volcanic eruption] also tend to drain like sieves; and lastly, given that volcanic material is often found on hillsides, gravity helps ensure that water is limited. Despite having generous amounts of the major nutrients required by plants, they are not readily available; they have to be weathered into an available form and then made soluble in water to be taken up by root systems.

'But water, as we've just seen, is in short supply, and young soils/rocks are not ready to give up their nutrients just yet. In the end, vines get a broad and balanced diet but in small quantities (low fertility). Simply put, semi-parched, semi-starved vines produce less fruit, smaller bunches, thicker grape skins, and result in more deeply coloured, concentrated, structured and age-worthy wines with a broad range of flavours.'

To learn more about the effects of volcanic soils, follow the Tasting Practice on the next page.

WINE REGIONS WITH VOLCANIC SOILS

ITALY: Veneto *(Pieropan)*, Campania *(Mastroberardino)*, Sicily *(Benanti, Cornelissen, Donnafugata, Graci, I Vigneri)*.
FRANCE: Côtes d'Auvergne *(Verdier-Logel)*, Alsace *(Zind-Humbrecht)*.
GERMANY: Baden *(KH Johner)*, Pfalz, Nahe, Mosel.
SPAIN: Canary Islands *(Bermejos, El Grifo, Suertes del Marques, Tajinaste)*.
PORTUGAL: Madeira *(Henriques & Henriques)*; Pico, Azores *(Azores Wine Company)*.
HUNGARY: Tokaj *(Demeter Zoltan, Royal Tokaji, Szepsy)*; Somló *(Kolonics, Kreinbacher, Spiegelberg)*; *Badascony (Gilvesy)*.
SLOVAKIA: Nitra *(Pivnica Brhlovce)*.
GREECE: Santorini *(Argyros, Sigalas, Vassaltis)*.
ISRAEL: Golan Heights.
CHILE: Colchagua, Maule, Itata, Malleco.
THE US: Napa *(Diamond Creek)*; Dundee Hills, Oregon *(Domaine Drouhin, Eyrie)*; Finger Lakes.
NW AFRICA: Fogo Island, Cape Verde.
NEW ZEALAND: Mount Taupo.
JAPAN: Yamanashi *(Grace Wine, Mercian)*.

Basalt columns in Somló, Hungary, known for its intense whites.

WHAT'S THE DIFFERENCE?

TUFF: Fine-grained volcanic rock (Tokaj in Hungary; pictured above).
TUFA: Porous calcium-carbonate rock (Noto in Sicily).
TUFFEAU: Marine limestone soil (Loire in France).

TASTING PRACTICE FULL RICH WHITES

In this tasting, you will learn how to identify the characteristics of volcanic wines, including bright aromatics, high acidity, savouriness, minerality and salinity. Dry white wines tend to show volcanic character better than reds.

The first two full-bodied whites in this tasting are made from varieties grown on volcanic soils; both are unoaked. The second two wines are varietal expressions of full, dry whites matured in French oak, but they are not volcanic. Both have less dominant fruit and more secondary flavours, with their texture, mouthfeel and structure enhanced by the use of oak (*see page* 122) during their making. Once you have completed the tasting, experiment by matching the wines with other flavours, as full rich whites pair well with food (*see page* 146).

WINES TO BUY (IN ORDER OF SERVING):

① Furmint (Hungary) **££**
② Assyrtiko (Greece) **£££**
③ Semillon (South Africa) **£££**
④ Viognier (Australia) **£££**

Preparation: *See page* 32.

Buying & alternatives: The Furmint and Assyrtiko demonstrate the typicity of volcanic wine, but other options include Juhfark or Soave. Both the Semillon and Viognier should be oaked; alternatively try an Australian Semillon (varietal not blended), or an oaked Australian Chardonnay for the Viognier.

Serving temperature: 8 to 12°C (46 to 54°F); chill wines in the fridge for 2 hours or in an ice bucket with ice and water for 20 minutes.

Method: Pour the same amount into each of your four glasses, and sample them side by side.

Look: You will notice that Wine 1 is paler than Wine 2, while Wine 3 is very pale. Wine 4 is the darker of the four – almost yellow gold.

Smell: Focus on the first two wines, which give the typical bright aromatics of volcanic wine. Wine 1 is more floral, with ripe pear and a hint of honey; Wine 2 shows richer citrus fruit. Now move to Wines 3 and 4, the two oaked wines. Wine 3 is not overtly fruity but offers honeysuckle and a hint of lemon zest; Wine 4 is very ripe, with apricot and fresh ginger and the sweetest, most concentrated nose of the four.

Taste: Sample Wines 1 and 2, and you will see quickly that the acidity in both is high, acting like a backbone through the wines. The fruit is citrusy in Wine 1, but more melon and thyme in Wine 2.

The mouthfeel of Wine 1 is steely and minerally, smoothed by a creamy texture. Comparatively, Wine 2 is richer, with more cream and spice, held by a weighty, broad-shouldered structure; it's almost as if it has been oaked. Both wines finish with a dry saline edge, which is typical of volcanic wine.

Next turn your attention to Wines 3 and 4; they are not overtly fruity but are textural and structured on the palate. Wine 3 has layers of flavours, with a buttery, almost flinty feel and hints of vanilla, whereas Wine 4 is nutty and earthy, rather than fruity, with a rich texture and lingering salted-caramel note. Both have a long dry finish with some tension, promising further development with bottle-age.

Finish: There is a defined difference here again, with the pithy persistent finish of Wines 1 and 2 in comparison to the dry nuttiness of Wines 3 and 4.

Conclusion: In this tasting, you have discovered the typicity of wines made from grapes grown on volcanic soils, with high acidity, steely notes and distinct salinity. You have also compared two full-bodied whites that show the primary fruit being overtaken by a smoky nuttiness created during their ageing in oak. Also note that all of these wines have ageing potential, as full-bodied whites tend to age better than more delicate whites.

Now check the crib sheet on the next page, and consider trying the tasting again using the alternative wines suggested.

CRIB SHEET: **FULL RICH WHITES**

1. FURMINT

REGION: **TOKAJ**

COUNTRY: **HUNGARY**

GRAPE: **FURMINT**

PRICE: **££**

ALCOHOL: **13.5%**

SIGHT: **Very pale with light-gold flecks**

SMELL: **Floral (white flowers), ripe pears**

TASTE: **Dry, high acidity**

FRUIT INTENSITY: **Full citrus flavours**

TEXTURE: **Steely and minerally, with creamy undertone**

CONCLUSION: **Fiery, steely character, mouthwatering acidity and saline edge**

COMMON BLIND TASTING MIX-UPS: **Unoaked Chardonnay (Chablis)**

ALTERNATIVES TO TRY
Hungarian Furmint or Juhfark (both Somló)

2. ASSYRTIKO

REGION: **SANTORINI**

COUNTRY: **GREECE**

GRAPE: **ASSYRTIKO**

PRICE: **£££**

ALCOHOL: **14%**

SIGHT: **Pale yellow gold**

SMELL: **Richer, fuller, dense core of citrus fruit**

TASTE: **Very dry, high acidity**

FRUIT INTENSITY: **Intense herbal notes, orchard fruit, lemon and lemongrass**

TEXTURE: **Weighty structure; flinty, intense textural palate; rich creamy length**

CONCLUSION: **Powerful, weighty; steely, salty, flinty, showing depth from old vines**

COMMON BLIND TASTING MIX-UPS: **Old-vine Albariño**

ALTERNATIVES TO TRY
Italian Soave Classico

3. SEMILLON

REGION: **FRANSCHHOEK**

COUNTRY: **SOUTH AFRICA**

GRAPE: **SEMILLON (2% MUSCAT OF ALEXANDRIA)**

PRICE: **£££**

ALCOHOL: **13.5%**

SIGHT: **Very pale with yellow-gold flecks**

SMELL: **Honeysuckle, light lemon zest, nutmeg**

TASTE: **Dry, moderate acidity**

FRUIT INTENSITY: **Not overtly fruity white peach and chamomile**

TEXTURE: **Waxy; smoky, vanilla, buttery mouthfeel from oak and concrete ageing**

CONCLUSION: **Layered flavours; great tension indicates further age potential**

COMMON BLIND TASTING MIX-UPS: **Oaked Chardonnay, oaked Chenin Blanc**

ALTERNATIVES TO TRY

Oaked Sémillon from Bordeaux (France) or Barossa Valley (Australia)

4. VIOGNIER

REGION: **EDEN VALLEY**

COUNTRY: **AUSTRALIA**

GRAPE: **VIOGNIER**

PRICE: **£££**

ALCOHOL: **13.5%**

SIGHT: **Yellow gold**

SMELL: **Ripe peach and apricots with fresh ginger**

TASTE: **Dry, moderate acidity**

FRUIT INTENSITY: **Moderate, some ripe peach**

TEXTURE: **Rich textured; nutty undertones from oak ageing, white-pepper finish; well structured with silky, soft mouthfeel**

CONCLUSION: **Weighty and rich; earthy nuttiness overshadowing primary aromas and fruits**

COMMON BLIND TASTING MIX-UPS: **Oaked white Rhône blend, oaked Grenache Blanc**

ALTERNATIVES TO TRY

Viognier from Northern Rhône or Casablanca (Chile); oaked Yarra Valley Chardonnay (Australia)

FUTURE-PROOF GRAPES

One of the main challenges facing wine-growers today is choosing which grapes to plant – those able to withstand climatic challenges. So, what makes a grape future-proof, and who is growing them?

In the past, a wine-grower chose the grape variety with certain criteria in mind – they considered soil type, aspect, elevation, altitude and micro-climate, as well as the style of wine they wanted to make, taking into consideration local appellation requirements. Now they have a much bigger issue to consider; they need to make sure the vine will be able to survive and thrive in the future under increasingly stressful climatic conditions.

DROUGHT & HEAT

The grape they plant needs to be future-proof and able to cope with the two main climatic challenges facing our planet: drought and heat. First, it needs to be drought-resistant and not too thirsty; some grapes like Chardonnay or Sauvignon Blanc require larger amounts of water to thrive than Assyrtiko, Garnacha or Nero d'Avola, with minimal water footprints.

Second, the grape must be heat-tolerant, able to cope with sunburn and heat spikes of 40°C (104°F) and over. When temperatures rise, this shortens the growing season; harvests are getting earlier and earlier. Some grapes do not have time to develop secondary compounds; an imbalance occurs between alcoholic and phenolic maturation, and this affects wine quality. So, ideally, a future-proof grape in these conditions is a late ripener.

With rain at unexpected times of the year or intermittent with heat causing high humidity, diseases like downy mildew become prevalent. The future grape needs to be both disease-resistant and hardy enough to cope with unexpected winter storms or freezes; milder

Garnacha can adapt to hot, dry conditions and is drought-resistant, making it an ideal future-proof grape; it is seen here in Rioja Alta, Spain.

Portuguese varieties Touriga Nacional (left) and Alvarinho (right) are now being trialled in Bordeaux, France.

winters mean that vines find it harder to cope if temperatures suddenly plummet.

MEDITERRANEAN VARIETIES

The question is, do these future-proof, long-cycle grapes actually exist? According to world grape-variety expert Dr José Vouillamoz, 'It depends on the wine regions, but Mediterranean varieties like Garnacha [Grenache] and Mazuelo [Carignan] from Spain, Assyrtiko and Xinomavro from Greece, and Aglianico and Malvasia Bianca from Italy can be used in very dry or extreme conditions; their adaptation will vary from one region to another.'

That's why Assyrtiko is now planted in Clare Valley and Nero d'Avola in McLaren Vale in Australia. In Spain, drought-resistant grapes like Palomino Fino in Jerez, Garnacha Blanca in Catalonia and Albillo Real in Sierra de Gredos are proving popular.

In the early 1980s, winemaker Miguel Torres began researching heritage Catalan grapes, initially to rehabilitate long-forgotten varieties, but he soon realized these grapes take longer to ripen and were ideal as future-proof grapes.

'Ancestral varieties proving to be very resilient and coping well with drought and heat are Moneu, Pirene, Gonfaus [red] and Forcada [white], planted in Penedès,' says Torres. 'Based on our experience, all four achieve phenolic maturation in synchrony with sugar accumulation and demonstrate optimal performance in the drought conditions and high temperatures we have been suffering in the Penedès region for the last three years [2021–23]. Forcada grown at 550m is harvested more than a month later than Chardonnay.'

In Rioja, Professor Juan Carlos Sancha has revived heritage grapes planted at 500 to 700m in Rioja Alta's Najerilla Valley. Sancha champions sustainable viticulture and wants to preserve varietal and genetic diversity, restoring red Monastel de Rioja (Morate) and Maturana Tinta de Navarrete (Castets) and white Maturana Blanca, which all retain acidity and freshness in warmer temperatures; the latter two are now on Rioja's official grape list.

To cope in the future, European appellations will have to adapt. Bordeaux has introduced trials of six new grapes, including Portuguese Alvarinho and Touriga Nacional. In Champagne, polygenic resistant French hybrid Voltis is allowed in up to five per cent of a producer's vineyard. According to Vouillamoz, 'In France, Artaban, Vidoc and Floreal are promising... and Calardis Blanc, Felicia and Villaris show good oenological potential in Germany.' Our vineyards of the future might well look very different.

For more information on hybrid grapes, turn to page 62.

WHAT HAPPENS IN THE VINEYARD?

Careful vineyard work, from planting, pruning and trellising, to grape ripening and harvesting at the right time, are all crucial activities to ensure the best-quality fruit.

Once the site is chosen, there are several decisions to be made by the grower. First is the preferred row orientation for required sunlight (normally north to south) or required shade (east to west) and planting density. If planting on a steep slope, they consider whether terraces are required, allowing movement across contours. Mechanism is an important consideration, as it compacts soil, but horsepower is a labour-intensive option. On very steep slopes in Valtellina, Italy, or Mosel, Germany, everything is done manually, occasionally using pulleys and winches for harvesting and ploughing.

The most appropriate training method is next: the vine is a fast-growing climbing plant; left on its own it sprawls along the ground putting down roots, rather than bearing grapes. Wire-trained trellis (height is important), pergola, individual stakes or individual bush vines are matched to the site, grape and yield. Irrigation pipes also need to be installed (if required or allowed in the appellation). Rootstock (for phylloxera protection) and clone choices depend on the grape variety. Once planted, a vineyard will then take at least three years before its grapes can be used for wine.

THE VINEYARD YEAR

During the vineyard year, pruning is critical, determining the yield and the vine's growth. Many prefer hard pruning (best by hand) during the vine's dormant period for quality control, but some experiment with minimal pruning to increase buds and shoots. The timing of pruning is becoming an issue, with harvests starting earlier and earlier; later pruning can delay bud-break to miss serious frosts. The extent of pruning affects yield, so appellation systems include maximum crop levels.

After bud-break (March to April in Northern Hemisphere; September to October in Southern Hemisphere), shoots and foliage will appear; this is followed by flowering (a vulnerable period),

Tiny caps of petals form as flowering begins, looking like mini grapes.

Grapes begin to swell and ripen, softening and turning red.

These fully ripe grapes are ready to be harvested.

fruit-set and ripening. During the growing season, growers must be vigilant to ensure precise canopy management up to the time of ripening. Leaf plucking was once popular; now reduced leaf trimming keeps shade, and slow ripeness is often preferred to retain acidity and freshness in the wine. Finally, the most important decision for the grower is when to pick (August to October Northern hemisphere/February to March Southern).

BUYING IN GRAPES

Some wine producers do not own vineyards, instead purchasing grapes from growers (Rioja or Champagne). This practice has also become popular with the new winemaking generation (Spain, California, Australia, South Africa), as purchasing, establishing and maintaining a vineyard is very expensive. Often producers buy in grapes with no written contracts, just on a handshake; this works well in abundant vintages but is tricky in poor ones. Some wineries own and tend their own vineyards as they prefer to have control over every aspect of the process – the preferred method for all top wine producers worldwide. Some wineries do both, using their own grapes for top wines and buying growers' grapes for house wines – this is seldom clear from the label.

SUSTAINABILITY

A very loose term, sustainability means, in essence, promoting soil health and biodiversity, minimizing the negative environmental impact of viticulture – it is a move towards organics. Sustainability should also be seen in the context of a business, which needs to be financially viable. It differs from conventional viticulture, which is focused on keeping the vine healthy to produce a good yield by using any available means, including toxic sprays. Many countries now have their own viticulture sustainability programmes, but certification varies widely from country to country and can be very loosely defined. There is an emergence of wineries grouping together with a focus to become carbon neutral (*see page* 88) – for example, International Wineries for Climate Action (Torres, Ridge, Symington, Jackson Family, Cullen and Spottswoode are members).

CLONES

Existing grapevines are grafted onto different rootstocks to create clones and produce a better-quality or disease-resistant vine, but the clone still shares the same genetic family. The choice of clone often depends on the grower's yield intentions. It offers uniformity and more predictability but a lack of genetic diversity, which can make the plant vulnerable to disease. There are localized clones that have evolved over years (such as Tempranillo: Tinto Fino, Tinta de Toro, Tinta del Pais).

FIELD BLENDS

Field blends are a mix of different grape varieties grown, picked and fermented together. Most famous is Austria's Gemischter Satz *(Wieninger)*; also popular in Portugal's Douro *(Niepoort)*; Sonoma, US *(Ridge)*; South Africa *(Sadie)*.

OLD VINES

Gnarly old vines do attract attention; the term (*Vieilles Vignes* in French) is used on labels as an enticement, but there's no legal definition. As a general rule, it refers to vines over 35 years old, which are deemed to give better concentration and complexity, provided they are still healthy. Some old-vine charters have been developed in Australia, South Africa and California, USA: Old Vines (35-plus), Survivor (70-plus), Centenarian (100-plus), Ancestor (125-plus). The oldest Australian vines in Barossa Valley date back to 1843 (*see* oldvineregistry.org).

IRRIGATION VERSUS DRY FARMING

Irrigation is essential for growing vines in hot dry climates, mainly installed as drip or deficit irrigation so that water can be carefully targeted to each vine to avoid water stress. It can also depend on soil types: sand and gravel are less good at water retention, compared to clay. Irrigation is largely practised in warmer New World countries, but it is possible with our warming climate that classic European wine regions might need to use it in the future (emergency irrigation is currently allowed). However, water scarcity can be a big issue. Dry-farmed vines, considered desirable by some New World producers (*Frog's Leap* in California, *De Martino* in Chile), basically rely on rainfall alone.

ORGANIC VITICULTURE

Some winemakers choose to tend their vineyards using organic and biodynamic methods – both of which have certification systems that take at least three years to be granted. With climate challenges, more wine producers are now turning to these methods as the best sustainable option, so they are becoming more mainstream.

Growers, keen to ensure they have an active living soil without chemical contamination, will adopt methods using no synthetic herbicides, fertilizers, pesticides, fungicides or GM products. With soil health and promoting biodiversity at the heart of organic viticulture, only natural fertilizers are used. Sulphur additions are permitted, but at lower levels than for non-organic wines: 100mg/l for red (rather than 150mg/l), 150mg/l for white and rosé (rather than 200mg/l). There is an increasing number of organic certifications worldwide – regulated by government bodies but outsourced to approved agencies (see below).

However, as humidity and excess rain from climate extremes increase, some growers find organic production too challenging and use sustainable viticulture instead, giving them the option to spray if absolutely necessary (particularly useful in England or Germany).

HOW TO FIND ORGANIC WINES

Countries vary with certification systems, so it's best to look at the label. In the EU, look for the leaf logo with government or third-party certifying bodies' badges, including AB and Nature & Progrès (France has six government-approved certification bodies) or Bio-Siegel and EcoVin (Germany). Outside the EU, look for BioGro (New Zealand); NASAA (Australia); Argencert (Argentina); USDA (the US).

RECOMMENDED ORGANIC PRODUCERS

Pago de Tharsys (Spain)
Castello di Volpaia (Italy)
Yannick Amirault (France)
Schloss Vollrads (Germany)
Quinta do Vallado (Portugal)
Ridge (California)
Dog Point (New Zealand)
De Martino (Chile)

BIODYNAMIC VITICULTURE

More of a spiritual movement or philosophy, biodynamic viticulture is an extension of organic – only using grapes grown without the use of man-made chemicals. The ideal is that biodynamic wineries work as closed, self-contained ecosystems, with an emphasis on enhancing soil and vine health. All synthetic products are banned (as for organic), but biodynamic winemakers go further.

They make their own green-waste compost from manure provided by their cows or horses. They also use herbal and mineral treatments (from stinging nettle, chamomile, oak bark or yarrow flowers), administered in homopathetic quantities to help the vine express itself better.

COW HORNS & LUNAR CALENDARS

Vines are treated regularly with nine biodynamic preparations. The best known is the Horn Manure Preparation 500. Cow horns filled with manure are buried under the vines throughout the winter and retrieved after six months, teeming with micro-organisms. The mixture is then diluted, dynamized in a special vortex and sprayed on the vineyard to help root growth and general vine health. Often horses, rather than tractors, are used in the vineyards to reduce soil compaction.

Biodynamic winemakers also follow the lunar calendar for their vineyard activities – pruning on root days, watering on leaf days, harvesting on

Manure-filled cow horns are buried under vines in winter.

fruit days and no treatments on flower days. The result is brighter and more focused wines, but quality depends on the skill of the winemaker.

HOW TO FIND BIODYNAMIC WINES

Look at the wine label: the EU's leaf logo along with a badge from Demeter (largest body), Biodyvin (in France) or Respekt-Biodyn (in Austria, Germany, Italy and Hungary) indicate biodynamic certification. There is a large number of organically certified winemakers who also use some (but not all) biodynamic methods but choose not to be fully certified.

RECOMMENDED BIODYNAMIC PRODUCERS

① *Stéphane Tissot* (Jura, France)
② *Zind-Humbrecht* (Alsace, France)
③ *Felton Road* (New Zealand)
Chapoutier (Rhône, France)
Huet (Loire, France)
Palmer, Pontet-Canet (Bordeaux, France)
Dr Bürklin-Wolf (Germany)
Loimer (Austria)
Ancre Hill (Wales)
Domaine Hugo (England)
Cullen (Australia)
Seña, Emiliana (Chile).

BIODYNAMIC – PUTTING IT INTO PRACTICE

Domaine Zind-Humbrecht in Alsace was an early biodynamic pioneer. Owner and winemaker Olivier Humbrecht MW explains:

'In the late 1980s, we had soil compaction, no biodiversity, soil-inversion issues, mineral deficiencies, a lack of parasite predators, increased resistance to sprays forcing us to increase dosage, and fermentation problems due to a drop in our wild yeast population. We converted to organic and biodynamic at the same time – and all our problems went away. We don't have deficiencies or compaction, soil functions normally with no anaerobic organic fermentations anymore – and we have good predators to parasites etc. Plus, something totally unexpected happened: the acidity went up in our wines, and pH went down, so we can harvest grapes earlier because they ripen physiologically faster. Dare I say that we are beating climate change for the moment? Costs are higher – labour cost per hectare is eight times greater than an average producer in Alsace. In the end, it is most influenced by the quality dedication of the producer. Biodynamic wines reinforce the signature of terroir, and the wines have a certain energy.'

Olivier Humbrecht MW is a vocal champion of biodynamic methods.

REGENERATIVE VITICULTURE

This is a new term for a collection of traditional (and some modern) practices that have a strong focus on living soil. Justin Howard-Sneyd MW, trustee of the Regenerative Viticulture Foundation (regenerativeviticulture.org) explains:

'Regenerative Viticulture [RV] is rooted in science and in close observation and measurement. It prioritizes minimizing soil disturbance and making decisions based on the specific context of each vineyard, rather than following a rule book of what to do, or what not to do. In looking for alternatives to ploughing [cover crops, crimping, mulches etc.] and to copper as a fungicide [RV advocates believe that limited and necessary use of some synthetics can be more targeted and cause less collateral damage than copper], RV practitioners can build soil organic matter incredibly quickly, and can help the vine and the vineyard ecosystem to thrive in a living landscape where most of the nutrient cycling is driven by the active soil biology.

'RV shares many of the objectives of biodynamic viticulture to create a closed-loop, self-sufficient farming system, and both philosophies overlap to a considerable degree. But RV does not encourage farmers to subscribe to a mystical (and at times anti-scientific) belief system. What attracted me to RV was the huge sense of hope that we have, a movement capable of improving the farming of 93 per cent of the world's vineyards that are *not* yet organic [6 per cent] or biodynamic [1 per cent], and in the palpable sense of community and shared purpose felt by adopters of regenerative agriculture. The Regenerative Viticulture Foundation aims to spread the word about regenerative practices in vineyards, so that RV becomes the new normal for viticulture.'

RECOMMENDED RV-CERTIFIED PRODUCERS

Mirabeau (France)
Familia Torres (Spain)
Tablas Creek (California)
Emiliana (Chile)
Domaine Bousquet (Argentina)

HOLISTIC VITICULTURE

There are other forms of viticulture that producers feel give a better balance with nature and an interconnectivity of vines with surrounding biodiversity. A proponent of this natural, spiritual approach is the iconic Vignai da Duline, a small artisan ten-hectare estate in Colli Orientali, northeast Italy, where a combination of biodynamic and holistic viticulture is used. Owners Lorenzo Mocchiutti and Federica Magrini were initially inspired by Japanese farmer Masanobu Fukuoka's book *The One-Straw Revolution*. 'Fukuoka's farming techniques are a radical challenge to global systems, requiring no chemicals, no tilling, no ploughing and little weeding,' says Mocchiutti.

This 'do-nothing' natural-farming ideal has led to great success. Mocchiutti created his own machine to lower impact between vines, moving the organic surface rather than layers of soil. They planted 2,000 trees around the vineyards to encourage biodiversity and protect them from neighbour's sprays; they do no leaf-thinning or green-harvesting, as they feel it keeps their old vines in balance (some believe this is required to concentrate a vine's efforts). Alfalfa is used as a fertilizer to help aerate the soil with its deep roots and to fix nitrogen (their vegetarian 'green cow'). Bees help pollinate cover crops (their 'best workers').

Their unusual viticultural methods and the purity and age-worthiness of their wines has attracted attention from top Burgundy estates.

MASSAL SELECTION

Many leading wine-growers use the massal-selection method of propagation, which involves using individual cuttings from exceptional old vines (sometimes pre-phylloxera) to preserve the clonal variations. Advantages include that the vineyard is then less vulnerable to disease, but one disadvantage is that yields can be unpredictable.

According to Argentinian winemaker Sebastián Zuccardi, 'Massal selection offers more diversity, balance and complexity as the old massal selections are well adapted to our climate conditions and soils selected by generations of viticulturists.'

Other leading producers using this method also believe it gives more complex, terroir-expressive wines: *Gaja* in Piedmont, Italy; *Zind-Humbrecht* in Alsace and *Louis Roederer* in Champagne, France; *Henschke* in Eden Valley, Australia.

Ducks at Vignai da Duline eat insects and slugs, keeping the vineyards clean and healthy.

WINE SUSTAINABILITY – CARBON-NEUTRAL & BEYOND

We all know about the wildfires, droughts, floods and increasing global temperatures, and we know that they are affecting wine producers everywhere. So what are wineries doing to alleviate climate disruption? What can they do to reduce their carbon footprint to become at least carbon-neutral – or even better, climate-positive?

For the wine producer, it's all about decision-making in the vineyard and cellar, and partnering with the right suppliers to reach carbon zero – and beyond. Over half of a winery's carbon emissions relate to logistics and glass packaging.

CARBON-NEUTRAL TARGETS

A carbon-neutral winery has net greenhouse gas emissions equal to zero. This is achieved by reducing emissions and sequestering carbon in the vineyard and winery (*see* right). If this is not enough, then wineries can purchase certified credits to offset emissions, these are effectively carbon swaps, where they can compensate for extra emissions by supporting other carbon-neutral aims.

ENVIRONMENTAL IMPACT

The environmental impact of winemaking can be offset in a number of ways.

In the vineyard by:

- recapturing carbon using special trellis systems and organic/biodynamic/regenerative viticulture, using cover crops, composts and mulching as green cover all year round
- introducing renewable energy sources: wind, solar power, electric or biofuel vehicles, tractors
- reducing sprays and planting trees

In the winery by:

- capturing carbon during fermentation
- lighter-weight bottles and alternative packaging
- working with carbon-neutral suppliers to reduce transport weight

Green cover helps recapture carbon and reduce emissions at Cullen.

Healthy soil at Cullen aids carbon sequestration.

SUSTAINABILITY STUDY: CULLEN WINES

Cullen Wines (pictured) was established in 1971 in Margaret River, Western Australia, but the first plantings were in 1966. At the forefront of environmental issues, it is a leading pioneer in biodynamic viticulture in Australia. Second-generation owner and winemaker Vanya Cullen is now keen to be an authentic pioneer for carbon-neutral, taking her first steps towards this as early as 2006.

'We began with carbon-neutral in Western Australia by planting trees in Yarra Yarra Biodiversity Corridor [a native reforestation project]. We have worked with several bodies, but being one of the first is not easy, as there is no precedent and the goalposts keep changing. We now work with government body Climate Active in Australia, where our emissions are made public and we buy certified ACCUs (Australian Carbon Credit Units) to offset emissions. Since 2006, our emissions have been between 1,200 and 1,400 tons of carbon dioxide, but with all of our recent efforts they are now down to 700 tons in our latest recording; we pay on average AU$25,000 per year to offset our emissions,' reports Cullen.

Vanya's team discusses emission reductions four times a year, including using a new solar power system, lightweight glass and working closely with freight partners. The biggest issue to combat is 'Scope 3 emissions' (those not actually produced by a company itself but as part of its supply chain), as many freight companies state it is too expensive to become carbon-neutral.

For Cullen, however, it all goes back to the vineyard. 'I feel the game-changer for being climate-positive is in proper landcare,' she says, 'and organic/biodynamic is the best way to start. Others feel emissions reduction is more important, but we are an agricultural industry, so land has to be the most important.'

WHITE WINEMAKING

Classic white winemaking differs from red winemaking, as fermentation takes place off the skins. The winemaker's decisions will affect the final style of wine.

HARVESTING

The winemaker's picking decision is fundamental. They assess the balance of sugar, acid and potential aromatic and flavour complexity by tasting the grape and chewing the seeds and skins (*see page* 57). Picking dates are usually dependent on when the grapes are ready, but weather forecasts, picking teams or winery vat space might affect this.

In very warm climates, grapes are picked through the night or in early morning to ensure cool grapes arrive at the winery. Machine-picking is fast and efficient; hand-picking, slower and more targeted. Top wine producers pick by hand into small trays, so grapes arrive in good condition at the winery.

CRUSHING & PRESSING

Grapes are kept chilled prior to processing. Some producers use crusher-destemmers (separating out leaves or stems), then chill and add sulphur before pumping into a pneumatic press. Some use triage tables with optical grape-sorting machines (with or without a destemmer). Then it's decided whether to add whole bunches (for cleaner juice and reduced phenolics) into the press, how much sulphur to use (if any, *see* opposite) to protect fresh primary fruits, and also whether to use skin contact (2 to 24 hours) before pressing. Skin contact gives further flavour and viscosity but can cause astringency (*see page* 19). Gentle pneumatic white-wine presses release juice without harshness and bitterness from skins and pips; the first juice is most prized. Following pressing, decisions include settling (*débourbage*) and clarifying, allowing excess solids to drop down in the tank to leave clear juice. Cool temperatures are essential to prevent fermentation starting, or oxidization.

A hopper-screw feeds Chardonnay grapes in Austria to the crusher-destemmer where leaves and stems are separated from grapes.

FERMENTATION

White-wine fermentation takes place in stainless-steel tank, oak barrel, concrete vat or egg, or clay amphora. Light white wines are fermented at cool temperatures (12 to 17°C/54 to 63°F; lower than reds) in inert vessels and protected from oxygen; richer fuller whites are often fermented in oak at warmer temperatures. Decisions include whether to use cultured yeast (aiding fermentation) or to rely on natural ambient yeast and to acidify (in warm climates) or chapitalize (to neutralize acid in cool climates). Fermentation (conversion of sugar to alcohol and carbon dioxide by the interaction of yeast, *see* opposite) takes one week to one month, after which yeasts tire or are overcome by alcohol.

Now the winemaker decides whether to allow any (partial or full) malolactic fermentation, where bacteria converts sharp malic acid to softer lactic acid, which can add breadth and texture; this can be hindered by temperature, sulphur or filtering. Allowing lees contact means leaving dead yeasts in white wine to add creamy complexity; stirring

Epoxy-free concrete tanks in Bodega Garzón in Uruguay are used for fermenting Albariño and Tannat.

the lees (*bâtonnage*) is regularly done in barrel, enhancing flavour and texture, but it introduces oxygen to the opened vessel. Racking (passing wine from vessel to vessel) is then carried out to draw wine off its lees into another container.

MATURATION

Light white wines are kept in their inert vessels, while richer concentrated whites can benefit from oak fermentation and maturation (with regular topping up and racking); any yeast still present will help oak tannins or aromas to be absorbed and deepen the colour. If the wine has been fermented in tank and then put into oak for maturation, the resulting style can be less well integrated. Blending can also be done at this stage.

FINAL STAGES

Larger wineries use fining, where bentonite or isinglass remove suspended particles, filtration to ensure clarity by removing yeasts and bacteria, and cold stabilization to prevent tartrate crystals forming deposits (*see page* 11). Blending can also take place here, before the final decision – another crucial one – of when to bottle, depending on the style of wine intended by the winemaker.

YEASTS

Yeasts are essential for fermentation to convert sugar to alcohol; these can be natural and ambient, present in vineyard and winery, or they can be cultured to be added by the winemaker. *Saccharomyces cerevisiae* is the strain normally associated with winemaking. In sweet winemaking, more sulphur is required to suppress yeast activity. In Sherry-making, flor yeasts (Fino and Manzanilla) that develop on the wine in cask are film-forming strains that produce a waxy or fatty coating, usually in springtime, that protects the wine from oxidation.

SULPHUR DIOXIDE

Sulphur is used as a preservative throughout the winemaking process on grapes, juice and wines, in storage and just before bottling (to reduce spoilage). It is added as gas or as potassium metabisulphite. The EU's maximum permitted levels for total sulphites vary: for red (150mg/l), dry white and rosé (200mg/l), sparkling (235mg/l) and sweet (250mg/l-plus). This is usually indicated as 'contains sulphites' on the label. Minimal or zero use of sulphur is an important part of natural winemaking.

TASTING PRACTICE
CRISP DELICATE WHITES

Fresh, crisp, unoaked whites from four different grapes and countries are the focus of this tasting. All have been made using cool-fermentation techniques in inert vessels, so they show the grape's primary fruit characteristics clearly. Here you will learn how wines can vary depending on the grape and how to compare different acidity levels. You will also learn about balance in terms of acidity, alcohol and fruit.

WINES TO BUY (IN ORDER OF SERVING):
① Malagousia (Greece) **£**
② Muscadet de Sèvre et Maine *Sur Lie* (France) **£**
③ Albariño (Spain) **££**
④ Grüner Veltliner (Austria) **££**

Preparation: *See page* 32.

Buying & alternatives: If you cannot find these producers, try to find replacements from the same areas at the same price point and from a recent vintage; otherwise try the alternatives overleaf.

Serving temperature: 8 to 12°C (46 to 54°F); chill wines in the fridge for 2 hours or in an ice bucket with ice and water for 20 minutes.

Method: Pour the same amount into each of your four glasses, and sample them side by side.

Look: Check the wines to ensure they are clear and bright; with this style of wine there is often little to distinguish between them as they are all unoaked and youthful. For each wine, tilt the glass against a white background, then pick up two glasses to compare against each other.

Smell: First smell each wine, without swirling. Then give the glasses a swirl and repeat the process, considering each wine's aromatic profile. You will notice Wine 1 is floral (white flowers) compared to Wine 2, which has subtle fruits (green orchard fruits). Wines 3 and 4 are also fruit-driven, with riper fruit notes (peach and pears) than Wine 2; Wine 3 has the most pungent fruit aromas.

Taste: Consider Wine 1 and 2 first and their differences in relation to acidity. Wine 1 has lower acidity than Wine 2, as it comes from a warmer climate. Wine 2 has a build-up of tart (almost sharp) acidity as you swirl it around your mouth – it is very noticeable, typical of a cool-climate wine. Taste Wines 3 and 4; you will find that Wine 3 has higher acidity than Wine 4 but that the acidity in both is lower than Wine 2. Acidity is a little more difficult to assess in Wines 3 and 4 as the fruit is riper than in Wines 1 and 2.

All the wines you are tasting are dry, but their fruit flavour and intensity, texture and structure vary. Wine 1 is lime-flavoured with light fruit intensity, the leanest of all four wines. Wine 2 is fuller in fruit intensity and texture but is still quite firm-structured. Wine 3 is zesty with a more rounded, slightly creamy mouthfeel; and Wine 4 offers a touch more ripeness and exotic fruit, more concentration and softer texture.

Finish: Swallow a little of each wine first, noticing the sensation of the wine's finish and the length of time you can still taste it. Taste again, but spit out the wine this time. Wine 1 has the shortest finish, with its slightly lower alcohol level and lighter concentration, while Wine 4 has the longest finish. Wines 2 and 3 have a saline dry note to finish, and Wine 4, an additional white-pepper element.

Conclusion: You have compared four different grape varieties from different countries, assessing acidity levels, fruit intensity, balance, mouthfeel and structure in these unoaked fresh whites. In blind tastings, Wines 3 and 4 are often confused with each other – try to remember what you found different about each wine.

Repeat the tasting going back over the wines to compare them, and repeat again over a period of days or weeks to teach yourself what to look for specifically with each grape.

Now check the crib sheet on the next page, and consider trying the tasting again using the alternative wines suggested.

CRIB SHEET: **CRISP DELICATE WHITES**

1. MALAGOUSIA

REGION: **PELOPONNESE**

COUNTRY: **GREECE**

GRAPE: **MALAGOUSIA**

PRICE: **£**

ALCOHOL: **11.5%**

SIGHT: **Pale, almost water white with green flecks**

SMELL: **Floral: jasmine and honeysuckle**

TASTE: **Moderate acidity**

FRUIT INTENSITY: **Light lime, grapefruit and lemon zest**

TEXTURE: **Lean structure, light**

CONCLUSION: **Expressive pure floral aromas and light, juicy, citric palate with herbal edge**

COMMON BLIND TASTING MIX-UPS: **Torrontés**

ALTERNATIVES TO TRY

Greek Moschofilero, Roditis, Vidiano

2. MUSCADET DE SÈVRE ET MAINE *SUR LIE*

REGION: **LOIRE**

COUNTRY: **FRANCE**

GRAPE: **MELON DE BOURGOGNE**

PRICE: **£**

ALCOHOL: **12%**

SIGHT: **Very pale with pale gold flecks**

SMELL: **Mild green fruit notes**

TASTE: **Very high acidity**

FRUIT INTENSITY: **Orchard fruit**

TEXTURE: **Tart acidity, light and silky**

CONCLUSION: **Dominated by high acidity, balancing green fruit with hint of saline**

COMMON BLIND TASTING MIX-UPS: **Pouilly-Fumé, Petit Chablis**

ALTERNATIVES TO TRY

French Piquepoul (Picpoul de Pinet), Italian Vermentino

3. ALBARIÑO

REGION: **RÍAS BAIXAS**

COUNTRY: **SPAIN**

GRAPE: **ALBARIÑO**

PRICE: **££**

ALCOHOL: **12.5%**

SIGHT: **Pale with light yellow-gold flecks, green hints**

SMELL: **Pungent ripe fruit**

TASTE: **High acidity**

FRUIT INTENSITY: **Zesty greengage, apricot, peach**

TEXTURE: **Broad mouthfeel underpinned by acidity**

CONCLUSION: **Crisp fruit-forward style with minerality, slight nuttiness and saline finish**

COMMON BLIND TASTING MIX-UPS: **Verdejo, unoaked Loire Chenin Blanc, Grüner Veltliner**

ALTERNATIVES TO TRY
Portuguese Arinto, Loureiro, Treixadura; Spanish Verdejo

4. GRÜNER VELTLINER

REGION: **KAMPTAL**

COUNTRY: **AUSTRIA**

GRAPE: **GRÜNER VELTLINER**

PRICE: **££**

ALCOHOL: **12%**

SIGHT: **Pale with yellow-gold flecks**

SMELL: **Ripe fruits, celery and hay notes**

TASTE: **Moderate to high acidity**

FRUIT INTENSITY: **Full, ripe pear and exotic fruit**

TEXTURE: **Intense fruit concentration**

CONCLUSION: **Well-balanced lively acidity and fruit, distinct white pepper finish**

COMMON BLIND TASTING MIX-UPS: **Dry Riesling**

ALTERNATIVES TO TRY
Italian Greco, Gavi Cortese; Alsace dry Riesling

RED WINEMAKING

Red winemaking concentrates on the use of the grape skins, to add colour, texture and flavour to the wine.

Cut a red grape in half, and you will notice that the pulp is grey-white; only the skin is coloured. Grape skins and pips contain polyphenols that leach out during fermentation and maceration; anthocyanins (colour) come out first, then tannins are drawn out in the presence of alcohol. The key for the winemaker is to have first picked red grapes at their optimum ripe tannin level – and then to know how much to extract them during the process to ensure a balanced wine.

HARVESTING & PRE-FERMENT

For fine red-wine production, grapes are hand-picked into small trays to prevent crushing. In top wineries, arriving grape bunches are put onto a sorting table, as with whites, to be sorted either by hand or optical machine, discarding leaves and stems. The winemaker's first decision is whether to use whole bunches or part-whole bunches.

Hand-sorting grapes at Alkina Wine Estate in Barossa Valley, South Australia.

Keeping some of the stems on at this stage can aid freshness, enhance aromas or add structure – popular for Pinot Noir and Syrah. Alternatively, all the stalks are removed before the grapes are crushed.

The winemaker can then choose to carry out a pre-ferment maceration, holding crushed red-grape must at a cool temperature (5 to 10°C/41 to 50°F) for a few hours to several days before fermentation begins. This extracts even more colour, flavour and aroma from the skins; these will also be extracted during fermentation. Tannins leach out later, in the presence of alcohol.

Techniques such as reverse osmosis can be used to concentrate colour and flavour and remove excess water in wet harvests. But it's an expensive process that some think of as 'manipulation'.

INTO THE FERMENTING VAT

The grape must is pumped into the fermenter; if whole bunches are being used, they go in too. Some winemakers like to 'layer' – alternating must and bunches to enhance texture. Acidification or chaptalization might be done at this stage, and yeast inoculation if preferred (*see page* 90). The red-wine ferment temperature is much higher than for whites (25 to 30°C/77 to 86°F).

The key is to maintain a constant temperature throughout, as stuck or overheated ferments are a nightmare for the winemaker. Carbon dioxide is given off as fermentation gets going, pushing skins to the top of the vat – creating something called a cap. It is essential to plunge the cap back into the vat by either pumping-over or mixing with a wooden paddle up to three times daily (*pigeage*) – often used for Pinotage, Pinot Noir and Syrah.

Fermentation in reds takes one to two weeks; light reds are drawn off skins early, while richer fuller reds macerate for longer to extract flavour and tannins (post-fermentation maceration). The free-run wine is kept apart from press wine (which

A wooden paddle is used to mix fermenting red grapes (pigeage) *to ensure the cap of skins does not dry out, as seen here in Collio in Fruili, Italy.*

is more tannic), though some might be blended carefully back in. Malolactic fermentation (*see page* 90) is standard practice for all reds.

MATURATION

Reds are often oak-aged for as long as 18 to 24 months (*see page* 120). Oak tannins are anti-oxidative, aiding colour and adding complexity and longevity. New oak must be used judiciously; there is great skill in knowing how long to age a wine in oak. Some makers put their red wine into barrel before fermentation completes, to assist the integration of grape and oak tannins. The current trend is for larger oak formats and less new oak, as drinkers now prefer to taste the wine's fruit. Topping up barrels and racking must be done during maturation.

FINAL STAGES

The decisions taken before bottling red wines are similar to those for whites (s*ee page* 91).

For information on how rosé, orange, pét-nat and low- or no-alcohol wines are made, turn to pages 132 to 141.

ALTERNATIVE METHOD: CARBONIC MACERATION

Carbonic maceration is used in Beaujolais and in other parts of the world (including Spain, Australia and the US). It is a type of whole-bunch fermentation often used for Gamay.

For pure carbonic maceration, initial fermentation is carried out under pressure of carbonic gas in an anaerobic (no oxygen) atmosphere. Uncrushed bunches are put into a sealed carbon dioxide-filled vessel. Fermentation takes place within the grape itself, which produces small quantities of alcohol and releases specific aromas. The berries burst with the weight of grapes on top of each other and release carbon dioxide; fermentation then continues normally, making distinctive, bright (or light)-coloured, light-bodied, approachable, fragrantly fruity, low-tannin, moderate-acid wines – often with bubblegum aromas.

Most producers in Beaujolais use a semi-carbonic maceration (*macération traditionnelle*), which combines this method with traditional winemaking techniques.

TASTING PRACTICE
SOFT JUICY REDS

Each wine in this tasting is a single-varietal expression of a thin-skinned red grape. It offers the chance to learn more about the characteristics and distinctive flavours of these red grapes, within the particular climate in which they are grown. Here, the most important element to focus on is structure. Thin-skinned grapes have less prominent tannins, giving the wine a soft, smooth structure and often silky, textural mouthfeel – and the wines are medium-bodied, rather than full-bodied. This style of wine is often popular with those who normally drink white wine or are just starting to explore reds.

These reds are best served with food, rather than as apéritifs. Once you have finished the tasting, try matching lightly chilled Gamay with charcuterie, and refer to the food-pairing recommendations later in the book for Pinot Noir, Cabernet Franc and Grenache (*see page* 146).

WINES TO BUY (IN ORDER OF SERVING):
① Gamay (France) **£**
② Pinot Noir (Germany) **££**
③ Cabernet Franc (Hungary) **££**
④ Grenache (South Africa) **££**

Preparation: *See page* 32.

Buying & alternatives: Replace the Gamay with a Beaujolais Villages or lighter Beaujolais Cru; find a Pinot Noir from another German region and a Loire Cabernet Franc from a ripe vintage; try a Spanish Garnacha or Australian Grenache.

Serving temperature: Wine 1 should be served at a cooler temperature, 12 to 14°C (54 to 57°F); Wines 2 to 4 at 16 to 18°C (61 to 64°F).

Method: Pour the same amount into each of your four glasses, and sample them side by side.

Look: Tilt your glass against a white background to check clarity and colour, paying attention to the base colour and the rim. Compare Wines 1 and 2; Wine 1 has a mid-ruby hue with an almost purple rim, indicating its youth. Wine 2 is mid-crimson, with a pink rim. Repeat with Wines 3 and 4; Wine 3, from a warmer climate, has a deeper ruby rim than the pale ruby pink of Wine 4.

Smell: Without swirling the glass, smell each wine; then swirl each wine and consider their aromatic intensities. Wine 1 has subtle raspberry fruit notes with herbal undertones, compared to Wine 2 with its strong perfume of strawberry and black cherry. Wine 3 smells of darker cherry fruits and leather, with earthy undertones. Wine 4 is dominated by overripe strawberries, with underlying cloves and beeswax adding to its character.

Taste: Focus first on Wines 1 and 2. Both wines are from a cool climate and have good acidity, but Wine 1 has higher, more prominent acidity and is lighter, as it is unoaked. Both wines are dry, but the fruit intensity is different: Wine 1 has cranberry and sour-cherry fruits, while Wine 2 has riper, more developed summer-fruit-compote notes; because it's from a more mature vintage, it displays mellower fruits. Both Wines 1 and 2 are soft and smooth in structure.

Wines 3 and 4 have moderate acidity, which is barely discernible on the palate. The fruit intensity of Wine 3 shows ripe dark cherries, almost prune-like, with leather and dark-chocolate notes indicating its warm origin, while light toast and spice indicate oak ageing. Wine 4 has more ripe strawberry and clove with herb and pepper notes typical of Grenache. Wine 3 has more prominent tannin, giving it a slightly firmer structure, whereas Wine 4, aged in large old oak, has much softer tannins and is a smoother style.

Finish: Swallow each wine first, thinking about the finish and the length of time you can still taste them after you have swallowed. Taste again, but spit out the wines this time.

Conclusion: You have learned to distinguish between four thinner-skinned grape varieties that are often confused with each other in blind tastings. Wine 1 has a bright crunchy fruitiness, with earthy minerality, whereas Wine 2 has more silky rounded fruit, initially rich, finishing dry. Wine 3 is all front-end fruit, followed by toast and spice with an earthy finish. Wine 4 has a strawberry and strong pepper element.

Now check the crib sheet on the next page, and consider trying the tasting again using the alternative wines suggested.

CRIB SHEET: **SOFT JUICY REDS**

1. GAMAY

REGION: **BEAUJOLAIS**

COUNTRY: **FRANCE**

GRAPE: **GAMAY**

PRICE: **£**

ALCOHOL: **13%**

SIGHT **Mid-ruby with purple rim**

SMELL: **Lightly perfumed with raspberry and herbs**

TASTE: **High acidity, succulent and mouthwatering**

FRUIT INTENSITY: **Light; candied raspberry, cranberry, sour-cherry**

TEXTURE: **Smooth, light tannins, soft**

CONCLUSION: **Light- to medium-bodied; fresh crunchy fruit palate; pepper and earthy notes on finish**

COMMON BLIND TASTING MIX-UPS: **Pinot Noir, Grenache**

ALTERNATIVES TO TRY
Beaujolais Villages or light Beaujolais Cru (Fleurie, St-Amour)

2. PINOT NOIR

REGION: **PFALZ**

COUNTRY: **GERMANY**

GRAPE: **PINOT NOIR**

PRICE: **££**

ALCOHOL: **13.5%**

SIGHT: **Mid-crimson**

SMELL: **Fragrant with strawberry and black cherries**

TASTE: **High acidity, less obvious with rich fruit concentration**

FRUIT INTENSITY: **Deep; ripe summer fruits**

TEXTURE: **Silky, rounded, creamy softness**

CONCLUSION: **Cool climate, lightly oaked; showing grape's typical creamy soft structure**

COMMON BLIND TASTING MIX-UPS: **Gamay, Grenache**

ALTERNATIVES TO TRY
Pinot Noir from Germany (Ahr, Rheinhessen, Rheingau) or New Zealand

3. CABERNET FRANC

REGION: **VILLÁNY**

COUNTRY: **HUNGARY**

GRAPE: **CABERNET FRANC**

PRICE: **££**

ALCOHOL: **15%**

SIGHT: **Deep ruby**

SMELL: **Cherry compote with leather and earthy undertones**

TASTE: **Moderate acidity**

FRUIT INTENSITY: **Deep; ripe cherries and prunes, mellowed with age**

TEXTURE: **Tannins more noticeable; firmer structure**

CONCLUSION: **Mature, oaked; from a warm climate; shows freshness despite high alcohol**

COMMON BLIND TASTING MIX-UPS: **Merlot**

ALTERNATIVES TO TRY

Cabernet Franc from Loire or South Africa

4. GRENACHE

REGION: **PIEKENIERSKLOOF**

COUNTRY: **SOUTH AFRICA**

GRAPE: **GRENACHE**

PRICE: **££**

ALCOHOL: **13%**

SIGHT: **Mid-ruby with pale-pink rim**

SMELL: **Overripe strawberries with cloves and a touch of lanolin**

TASTE: **Moderate acidity**

FRUIT INTENSITY: **Medium; ripe red fruits dominate the palate**

TEXTURE: **Soft, rounded tannins, smooth, well-rounded palate**

CONCLUSION: **Medium-bodied, expansive well-rounded structure typical of grape**

COMMON BLIND TASTING MIX-UPS: **Tempranillo, Pinot Noir**

ALTERNATIVES TO TRY

Australian Grenache (McLaren Vale); Spanish Garnacha (Navarra)

SPARKLING WINEMAKING

Sparkling wine was once only drunk for celebrations, but now it's a popular everyday drink with booming sales. Champagne is still considered the hallmark of premium fizz, but there are many rivals to its crown – from England to Australia.

Making fizz is challenging. First, it is essential to start with quality grapes, high in natural acidity, to ensure finesse and elegance. The second challenge is getting the bubble size and pressure right. The basics of making fizz works on the principle that the carbon dioxide formed during fermentation, that normally escapes, is kept dissolved in the wine – trapped as bubbles in the liquid in bottle or tank, only to be released when the bottle is opened.

TRADITIONAL METHOD

This is the premium method for making sparkling wine – compulsory in Champagne (*méthode champenoise*), for Cava in Spain, Franciacorta in Italy and South Africa's Cap Classique. It is also used widely around the world from England to Tasmania.

After a normal first fermentation (in tank or barrel), a range of still wines from different grapes, vineyards or vintages will be assessed and blended. (NV, or Non-Vintage, is a blend of different vintages, while Vintage is from one single year.)

The quality of this base wine is critical to the final wine, which often has old reserve wine added for enrichment. The base wine is bottled with a carefully measured addition of sugar, yeast and yeast nutrients (*liqueur de tirage*), and a second fermentation takes place within the bottle, usually under crown cap. The lees (dead yeasts) are left in contact with the wine (minimum 15 months in Champagne) to enhance complexity and the biscuity, toasty aromas – its autolytic character.

The lees need to be removed from the bottle and are carefully coaxed into the bottle neck. This takes about eight weeks, hand riddling the bottle (*remuage*) a little each day on a *pupitre* (*see picture*, opposite), or eight days mechanically by *gyropallette* – a process invented by Cava producers and used worldwide. The wine can be further aged if preferred, with the bottle inverted on its neck (*sur pointe*). The neck is then put into frozen brine, and the lees cap is ejected under pressure (disgorgement). Final adjustments with base wine, sulphur dioxide or dosage to adjust sweetness (*liqueur d'expedition*) are then done, before corking captures the bubbles – jetting (*see* opposite) can be used here to prevent oxidation.

SPARKLING-WINE STYLES

FRANCE

Champagne: made from Chardonnay, Pinot Noir and Pinot Meunier; for grower Champagne look for RM on the label.
Crémant: eight styles focus on local grapes from Alsace, Loire, Burgundy, Savoie, Jura, Bordeaux, Die and Limoux. A good Champagne alternative.

SPAIN

Cava: made in four Spanish regions (95 per cent in Alt Penedès), mainly from Macabeo, Xarel·lo and Parellada; organic focus.

ITALY

Franciacorta: Lombardy's premium fizz.
Trento: high-quality fizz in Trentino.
Asti: Piedmont's lighter Muscat fizz.
Prosecco: delicate soft Glera-based fizz; DOCG best.

GERMANY

Sekt: best is Winzersekt, traditional method and 100 per cent estate grown.

ENGLAND

English Sparkling Wine: best from Chardonnay and Pinot Noir; Champagne houses already investing.

OTHER COUNTRIES TO WATCH:
Hungary, Austria, Slovenia, Croatia, California, Australia (Tasmania) and New Zealand.

Large-format Champagne bottles on pupitres are hand-riddled each day to encourage dead yeasts into the neck of the bottle, prior to disgorging.

DOSAGE LEVELS

Brut Zero/Non-Dosage/Brut Nature/Ultra Brut: 0 to 2g/l. Extra Brut: 0 to 6g/l. Standard Brut/Brutto: up to 12g/l. Extra Dry/Extra Sec/Trocken: 12 to 17g/l. Sec/Secco/Trocken: 17 to 32g/l. Demi-Sec/Abboccato/Halbtrocken/Semi-Dulce/Riche: 32 to 50g/l. Doux/Dolce/Doce: >50g/l.

Low dosages are now standard with the current trend for drier wines, and fruit is generally riper due to warming temperatures requiring less dosage.

TRANSFER METHOD / BOTTLE FERMENTED

While the second fermentation takes place in bottle, it will not be sold in that bottle. After the fizz has been created, the liquid is transferred into tank under pressure at a cool temperature, where it is clarified and then rebottled, avoiding the expense of riddling and disgorgement. This method is often used for lower-priced New World fizz.

CUVE CLOSE / CHARMAT METHOD

This is a popular bulk method – not necessarily lesser quality, it depends entirely on the quality of the base wine and ageing. Second fermentation takes place in tank rather than bottle. It is often used for more aromatic grapes (such as Riesling) that do not lend themselves to the autolytic aromas from second fermentation in bottle. This method is widely used for Prosecco production.

OTHER METHODS

Ancestrale / Rurale: a historic method, covered more on page 138 (interruption method).
Carbonation: an inexpensive method that injects carbon dioxide. Sophisticated techniques ensure bubble sizes that are as fine as those made from traditional or tank methods.

JETTING

This technique, used in the brewing industry, has been adapted for sparkling-wine production to avoid oxygen uptake after disgorgement and topping-up (and potentially reduce sulphur additions). A micro-pulse jet of sulphited water is injected into the wine, causing the bubbles to rise up and foam, ejecting any air. The cork is inserted just as the foam rises, so timing has to be precise.

TASTING PRACTICE
SPARKLING WINES

In this tasting there is an added challenge – bubbles! This is, of course, the integral part of all sparkling wine, created by carbon dioxide trapped in the wine, which reacts in the glass and with the moisture on our palates. As a result, tasting fizz can be very tricky. (I used to dread the pop of the corks in my wine exams.) You have to assess the pressure and finesse of the mousse, how it integrates into the wine and relates to texture – the silkier the better – and how the wine displays and keeps its effervescence through to the finish.

Bubbles often hide the structure of the wine, so you have to work harder to analyse the wine behind the fizz for all the usual parameters of acidity, sweetness, fruit intensity and length of flavour. If you are up for this fun challenge (this tasting will be popular with your friends), it is time to assess four sparkling wines from around the world made in different climates to see how they differ in style and taste.

WINES TO BUY (IN ORDER OF SERVING):
① Pét-nat (Austria) **£**
② Cava (Spain) **£**
③ English sparkling wine (England) **££**
④ Champagne (France) **£££**

Preparation: *See page* 32.

Buying & alternatives: If you cannot find Austrian pét-nat, try English or Italian Col Fondo; Cava should be Reserva or Gran Reserva, or swap to quality Crémant d'Alsace. English fizz is a distinctive style, and NV Champagne should be at least three times more expensive than the Cava.

Serving temperature: 6 to 8°C (43 to 46°F); chill wines in the fridge for 2 hours or in an ice bucket with ice and water for 20 minutes.

Method: Pour the same amount into each of your four glasses, and sample them side by side.

Look: Check for clarity, brightness, colour and mousse reaction. Wine 1 is the odd one out: it's pale, frothy and slightly cloudy, as this style is made using the ancestral method and is often unfiltered (*see page* 139). Wines 2 to 4 are all pale yellow gold in colour. Mousse reactions are due to the glassware (if there is an imperfection, for example) and might differ according to how the glasses were cleaned and when they were polished (ideally at least four hours prior to tasting). The only way to tell the pressure of the fizz and size of the bubbles is by taste.

Smell: Focus on Wine 1: it has green apple, pear and a herbal floral undertone. Now see how it varies from Wines 2 to 4, which are all made by the traditional method, with second fermentation in bottle (*see page* 102). Wine 2 is toasty and spicy, with pain au raisin and a hint of rubber and butter (typical of this style). Wine 3 is fruitier, with lychees, apples, melons, pear and elderflower. Wine 4 has the most enticing aroma of all: brioche, apricots, mangos, bruised apple, honey, pistachio and roasted almonds.

Taste: Assess each wine individually for acidity and flavour, as well as mousse pressure and texture. Wine 1 has high acidity, herbal notes and a caressing, soft, frothy mousse that gives a light texture typical of pét-nat. Wine 2 has moderate acidity and richer sweeter fruits, indicating a warmer climate, with a soft, rounded texture but more aggressive, rougher bubbles that seem to sit alongside the toastiness rather than integrating.

In comparison, Wine 3 has racy high acidity, a greenness typical of English wine and fruit richness that indicates long ageing (six years in this example). Its texture is also soft and round, with a delicate mousse. Wine 4, again, has it all: high acidity, nutty flavours, good intensity and silky smoothness from its incredible bubble finesse and reserve wine; notice the seamless integration of mousse and fruit.

Finish: Wine 1 is crisp, dry and light, but authentic with moderate alcohol. Wine 2 in comparison is richer, slightly sweeter and long on the finish from its white-fruit blend. Wine 3 has sweet-sour notes, almost sherbet-like, while Wine 4 has an intriguing vanilla note to finish. This comes from the amount of reserve wine used (50 per cent; *see page* 102) and from part of its first ferment being in old Burgundy barrels to help enhance complexity.

Conclusion: You have assessed four sparkling wines and learned how the mousse reacts in each wine, affecting texture. Repeat the tasting to reassess the wines, focusing on structure and flavour. If you have leftovers, use a Champagne stopper, Vacu Vin or sparkling Coravin – and keep bottles chilled. Note: a spoon in the top of the bottle does not preserve fizz.

Now check the crib sheet on the next page, and consider trying the tasting again using the alternative wines suggested.

CRIB SHEET: **SPARKLING WINES**

1. PÉT-NAT

REGION: **KAMPTAL**

COUNTRY: **AUSTRIA**

GRAPE: **70% GRÜNER VELTLINER, 30% GELBER MUSKATELLER**

PRICE: **£**

ALCOHOL: **11%**

SIGHT: **Pale straw**

SMELL: **Ripe apples, pears, herby, floral**

TASTE: **Dry, high acidity**

FRUIT INTENSITY: **Light; citrus fruit**

MOUSSE TEXTURE: **Frothy; light, soft, smooth**

CONCLUSION: **Crisp acidity balances fruits, dry finish; no sulphur used; fresh and bright**

COMMON BLIND TASTING MIX-UPS: **Col Fondo**

ALTERNATIVES TO TRY
English pét-nat;
Italian Col Fondo, Prosecco

2. CAVA

REGION: **PENEDÈS**

COUNTRY: **SPAIN**

GRAPE: **50% XAREL·LO, 35% MACABEO, 15% PARELLADA**

PRICE: **£**

ALCOHOL: **12%**

SIGHT: **Pale yellow gold**

SMELL: **Baked fruit, toast and spice, with buttery rubbery hints**

TASTE: **Dry, moderate acidity**

FRUIT INTENSITY: **Medium; rich, sweet fruit**

MOUSSE TEXTURE: **Aggressive; soft, rounded**

CONCLUSION: **Bubble and toast dominate here – mainly dry from zero dosage, but fruit is baked; long finish from white fruit**

COMMON BLIND TASTING MIX-UPS: **Crémant**

ALTERNATIVES TO TRY
Crémant from Alsace, Loire, Burgundy or Jura

3. ENGLISH SPARKLING WINE

REGION: **SUSSEX**

COUNTRY: **ENGLAND**

GRAPE: **68% PINOT NOIR, 30% CHARDONNAY, 2% PINOT MEUNIER**

PRICE: **££**

ALCOHOL: **11%**

SIGHT: **Pale gold**

SMELL: **Fruity apple, pear, lychees**

TASTE: **Dry, high acidity**

FRUIT INTENSITY: **Bright, crisp**

MOUSSE TEXTURE: **Delicate; soft rounded, smooth to finish**

CONCLUSION: **Long lees-aged, racy acidity, rich fruits, yeastiness, sweet-sour dry finish**

COMMON BLIND TASTING MIX-UPS: **Grower Champagne**

ALTERNATIVES TO TRY

Other English sparkling; New Zealand or Australian (Tasmania) sparkling

4. CHAMPAGNE

REGION: **CHAMPAGNE**

COUNTRY: **FRANCE**

GRAPE: **40% PINOT NOIR, 40% CHARDONNAY, 20% PINOT MEUNIER**

PRICE: **£££**

ALCOHOL: **12%**

SIGHT: **Pale yellow gold**

SMELL: **Brioche, mango, apricot, plums, dried fruits, pistachio, almond**

TASTE: **Dry, high acidity**

FRUIT INTENSITY: **Rich honey, nuts**

MOUSSE TEXTURE: **Fine; silkiness, distinct smoothness from reserve wine**

CONCLUSION: **Beautifully integrated mousse, silky, rich fruit concentration from reserve wine**

COMMON BLIND TASTING MIX-UPS: **Grower Champagne**

ALTERNATIVES TO TRY

Champagne Blanc de Noirs or Blanc de Blancs

SWEET WINEMAKING

Sweet wines, mostly whites, are produced with a perceptible amount of residual sugar. The way they are made and their alcohol strength vary according to style.

One method used is to stop the fermentation by chilling and adding sulphur. This stuns the yeasts into inactivity, and they then stop converting sugar to alcohol; this results in a wine with unconverted, or residual, sugar. Another method used for sweet table-wine styles is to ferment the wine to dryness and then add a sweet reserve (known as *süssreserve* in Germany).

Grapes can also be left longer on the vine to concentrate natural sugars. Once picked – always by hand and often in *tries* (several sweeps through the vineyard, a time-consuming and sticky process) – grapes are pressed and slowly fermented. Yeasts find this sugar overload hard work and will stop naturally in the region of 8 to 15% alcohol. The majority of the world's best sweet wines are made using variations on this method.

LATE PICKING

Grapes picked at least a month after normal harvest are usually quite dehydrated and often have high levels of sugar and acidity. Late-harvested sweet wines are made all over the world, but the best have naturally high levels of acidity to balance sweetness (*JJ Prum Wehlener*

Healthy bunches of grapes are hung up in cellar lofts to concentrate sweetness and flavour, for making Vin Santo dessert wine in Tuscany, Italy.

Sonnenuhr Auslese from Mosel, Germany; *Siefried Sweet Agnes Riesling* from Nelson, New Zealand).

In Jurançon in France, grapes are left to shrivel and dry on the vine (*passerille*), while winemakers in Australia achieve a similar effect through a technique called cut cane, doing just that; this halts water supply to the grape, encouraging shrivelling and concentration (*Mount Horrocks*, Clare Valley, Australia).

DRYING GRAPES

In Jura, healthy bunches of grapes are picked and laid on straw or in trays to dry to make Vin de Paille. This process of partially drying bunches on mats or trays or by hanging them up in cellars is called *appassimento* in Italy, used for Passito, Recioto, Amarone and Vin Santo. Grapes lose water, but sugar, acidity and flavour are concentrated – for Amarone, they are dried for three to four months; Recioto for six. Other countries use a short drying method to add depth.

RESIDUAL-SUGAR LEVELS

Vouvray Moelleux: 40 to 80g/l
Mosel Auslese: 90g/l
Sauternes: 125 to 165g/l
Tokaji Aszú 6 Puttonyos: 150 to 220g/l
Canadian Icewine: 180 to 250g/l
Tokaji Essencia: 450 to 900g/l

THE WORLD'S SWEETEST WINE

Essencia is an extraordinary wine – if it is a wine at all, as it's rarely above 2% alcohol. It is created in Tokaj in northeast Hungary by collecting drips of intense juice from a tap at the bottom of vats full of carefully macerated, dried, botrytis-affected hand-picked aszú berries – usually Furmint and Hárslevelű. This incredibly sweet liquid is stored in glass jars (25 to 100 litres) in cellars for years to slowly ferment (if at all), at which point it is then carefully bottled (such as *Royal Tokaji*). Once savoured by popes and kings as a medication, it is now sold in restaurants at over £100/US$130/€120 per spoonful.

Grapes for Icewine are left on vines into winter in Ontario, Canada.

NOBLE ROT

The world's most famous sweet wines are often made from grapes affected by *Botrytis cinerea* (noble rot). This mould occurs in conditions with an interchange between misty humid mornings (which develop the mould) and sunny afternoons (which concentrate the juices). It attacks white grapes, piercing the skin and dehydrating the grape. Wines are made in this way in Sauternes and Barsac in Bordeaux, Loire, Alsace in France, Austria, Germany, and Tokaj in northeast Hungary.

FROZEN-GRAPE WINES

A speciality of Germany (Eiswein) and Canada (Icewine), these wines are also made in Austria, Luxembourg, Oregon, Moldova and northeast China. Grapes are left on the vine into winter's freezing conditions, down to -10°C (14°F), then frozen bunches are picked at night and pressed immediately, leaving the water crystals behind in the press, resulting in a hugely sweet and concentrated liquid that slowly ferments.

The difference between Canada and Germany is that Eiswein (made from healthy non-botrytis grapes) tends to have lower alcohol (7 to 8%) and more refreshing acidity, while Canadian Icewine (9 to 13%) tastes sweeter. Some winemakers in the US and Japan experiment with freezing picked bunches (a method called cryoextraction).

TASTING PRACTICE COMPARING SWEETNESS

Sweet wines might not be the height of fashion these days, but for those with a sweet tooth (like myself) they offer an almost seductive, hedonistic pleasure. This tasting compares four classic sweet-wine styles from around the world, crafted using late-harvested grapes (either botrytis-affected or frozen) and made with different winemaking methods, all of which affect the final taste.

Sugar levels vary, but you will notice how high acidity alters the taste and freshness of the wine, making it seem less sweet than it actually is. You might find this tasting saturating and tiring on the palate; to help with this, serve a mixed platter of walnuts, dried apricots, blue cheese (Stilton, Roquefort, Fourme d'Ambert), honey, compote, fruit tart or fruit-cake alongside. Notice how salty blue cheese contrasts well with the richness of the wines.

WINES TO BUY (IN ORDER OF SERVING):
① Vouvray Moelleux (France) **££**
② Tokaji Aszú (Hungary) **£££**
③ Barsac (France) **£££**
④ Icewine (Canada) **£££**

Preparation: *See page* 32.

Buying & alternatives: The Vouvray could be interchanged with German Riesling Spatlese. For Tokaji, try 5 Puttonyos or Szamorodni, and swap Barsac for Sauternes or late-harvest Semillon. Try German Eiswein instead of the Icewine.

Serving temperature: Sweet wines benefit from being chilled to ensure freshness, otherwise they will seem too rich and sweet: 6 to 8°C (43 to 46°F). Chill wines in the fridge for 2 hours or in an ice bucket with ice and water for 20 minutes.

Method: Pour the same amount into each of your four glasses, and sample them side by side.

Look: Wine 1 is much lighter compared to the others. Wines 2 and 3 are similar, whereas Wine 4 is the darkest with a deep-golden hue.

Smell: Focus first on Wine 1: the nose is subtle, with light apricot and honey, and barely smells sweet, indicating late-harvested grapes with only a touch of botrytis. Now try Wines 2 and 3: you will find that Wine 2 has an orange-peel, apricot, raisiny, marmalade sweetness compared to Wine 3, which shows brighter citrus fruit. Both wines indicate botrytis notes of honey and ginger. In contrast, Wine 4 has carmelized-orange and grapey aromas; there is no botrytis here, but it still promises sweetness.

Taste: Take a sip of Wine 1. There is a baked-apple sweetness from the late-picked grapes, with a creamy-curd texture, but the sweetness is masked by the high acidity, which leaves the wine very fresh; you could serve this as an apéritif.

Now compare Wines 2 and 3. You find much higher acidity in Wine 2, with a minerality typical of Tokaji made from Furmint grown on volcanic soils. The individually picked aszú berries used to make the Tokaji give it the marmalade sweetness. It has a fabulous balance, with its racy acidity freshening the palate. Wine 3 is densely sweet, but not with such raisiny sweetness; it has elegant notes of honey and butterscotch, with a waxy lanolin feel to the palate.

Wine 4 is made from healthy ripe grapes that are frozen on the vine and picked on a crisp winter night; it is unctuously rich and sweet but not overpoweringly cloying; it has oozing juicy ripe fruit with a smooth, velvety texture.

Finish: Wine 1 has a clean finish, but notice the difference among the other three: Wine 2 is fresher from its naturally high acidity; Wine 3 has a warm alcohol finish typical of its style; and Wine 4 is light and balanced, thanks to its moderate alcohol. Now try Wines 3 and 4 with samples of blue cheese, and notice how the cheese affects the taste of the wine, contrasting saltiness with sweetness, making it seem less sweet and refreshing on the palate.

Conclusion: In this exercise, you have tasted sweet wines made from late-harvest, botrytis-affected and frozen grapes – and have assessed the different sugar, acidity and alcohol levels of sweet wines.

Now check the crib sheet on the next page, and consider trying the tasting again using the alternative wines suggested.

CRIB SHEET: COMPARING SWEETNESS

1. VOUVRAY MOELLEUX

REGION: **LOIRE**

COUNTRY: **FRANCE**

GRAPE: **CHENIN BLANC**

PRICE: **££**

ALCOHOL: **12.5%**

SIGHT: **Pale with gold hints**

SMELL: **Subtle, light apricot and citrus**

TASTE: **High acidity (residual sugar 65g/l)**

FRUIT INTENSITY: **Rich, candied apple; honeyed**

TEXTURE: **Soft, creamy-curd mouthfeel; smooth structure**

CONCLUSION: **Fresh, vibrant late-harvest wine, with high acidity, so sweetness less noticeable**

COMMON BLIND TASTING MIX-UPS: **German Spätlese**

ALTERNATIVES TO TRY
Loire Coteaux du Layon (Village level); German Riesling Spätlese

2. TOKAJI ASZÚ

REGION: **TOKAJ**

COUNTRY: **HUNGARY**

GRAPE: **FURMINT**

PRICE: **£££**

ALCOHOL: **10.5%**

SIGHT: **Rich gold**

SMELL: **Toffee apple and orange peel**

TASTE: **High acidity (residual sugar 189g/l)**

FRUIT INTENSITY: **Rich, dense citrus, marmalade; honeyed**

TEXTURE: **Silky-soft; light, zesty, mineral, fresh, despite its sweetness**

CONCLUSION: **Wonderful balance of sweetness, racy acidity and raisiny botrytis fruit**

COMMON BLIND TASTING MIX-UPS: **Sauternes or Barsac**

ALTERNATIVES TO TRY
Tokaji 5 Puttonyos or Édes Szamorodni

3. BARSAC

REGION: **BORDEAUX**

COUNTRY: **FRANCE**

GRAPE: **75% SÉMILLON, 23% SAUVIGNON BLANC, 2% MUSCADELLE**

PRICE: **£££**

ALCOHOL: **13.5%**

SIGHT: **Rich gold**

SMELL: **Orange grapefruit, pineapple, peach**

TASTE: **Moderate acidity (residual sugar 140 to 150g/l)**

FRUIT INTENSITY: **Rich and juicy, fresh citrus fruit, ginger and butterscotch**

TEXTURE: **Creamy, velvety; viscous, almost oily and waxy**

CONCLUSION: **Elegant, honeyed botrytis dessert wine; warmth on finish from alcohol**

COMMON BLIND TASTING MIX-UPS: **Late-harvest Semillon**

ALTERNATIVES TO TRY
Sauternes; Alsace Riesling, Gewurztraminer or Pinot Gris SGN; late-harvest Semillon (Australia)

4. CANADIAN ICEWINE

REGION: **ONTARIO**

COUNTRY: **CANADA**

GRAPE: **VIDAL**

PRICE: **£££**

ALCOHOL: **11%**

SIGHT: **Dark gold**

SMELL: **Ripe pears, grape juice, carmelized orange**

TASTE: **Moderate acidity (residual sugar 185g/l)**

FRUIT INTENSITY: **More rich tropical fruits (quince, guava) on palate than on nose**

TEXTURE: **Unctuous and rich, smooth mouthfeel, but not cloying; oozes juicy ripe fruit**

CONCLUSION: **Good balance of high sweetness and acidity; dense rich fruits and moderate alcohol leave palate light and fresh**

COMMON BLIND TASTING MIX-UPS: **German Eiswein**

ALTERNATIVES TO TRY
Canadian Riesling Icewine or German Riesling Eiswein

FORTIFIED WINEMAKING

Quite simply, any wine that has been given an alcohol boost with neutral, high-strength grape spirit is known as a fortified wine – in white, red, dry or sweet styles.

These are the wine world's treasures, often underappreciated and great value for money. There are myriad styles to explore – from fresh, fruity semi-sweet Vin Doux Naturel, to tangy, saline dry Fino Sherry; from intensely nutty and sweet Tawny Port and rich, sweet and peppery Ruby Port, to raisiny and very sweet Australian Liqueur Muscat. Alcohol levels vary too, from 15 to 22%, noticeable as heat on the taste and finish, but the alcohol does help spread flavours around the palate.

Vinification methods follow different paths, with alcohol added at different stages.

Early mutage: adds alcohol to grape juice (with or without skins) before fermentation, so styles are sweet (Vin de Liqueurs).

Early fortification: (also called mutage) adds alcohol during fermentation, styles are also sweet (Port, Vin Doux Naturel and Liqueur Muscat).

Late fortification: wine is fermented to dryness with alcohol added afterwards (Sherry).

PORT

Made from native white and red Portuguese grapes grown in the hot arid Douro Valley, inland from Oporto in the north. Whites Malvasia, Viosinho and Gouveio and reds Touriga Nacional, Tinta Roriz, Tinta Barocca and Touriga Franca are almost always blended. The key is to quickly extract colour, tannin and flavour in the short 48-hour fermenting time, by foot-treading in stone *lagares*, robotic treading or in covered autovinifiers. When alcohol reaches 6 to 8%, fortification (using 77% abv grape spirit) halts fermentation, leaving unconverted sugars. Port is always sweet and retains its grapey flavour.

There are two styles of red Port: Ruby (Late Bottled Vintage and Vintage), with short wood ageing and longer bottle maturation, which retains colour, rich damson fruit and tannic grip; and Tawny (aged Tawnies and Colheitas), with long wood ageing, which gives the wines their distinctive oxidative nutty flavours.

Producers to try: *Graham's, Niepoort, Quinta do Noval, Taylor's.*

SHERRY

Now enjoying a revival, with a vibrant group of independent bodegas focusing on making premium styles, Sherry is exciting again.

Palomino is grown on *albariza* chalk (*see page* 73) in hot dry Andalusia in southwest Spain across nine towns including inland Jerez de la Frontera and coastal Sanlúcar de Barrameda. Moscatel and Pedro Ximénez are sun-dried and are either used for sweetening during blending or are made into intensely sweet varietals.

Standard wine fermentation is followed by a series of classifications to determine the eventual style. If flor grows on the wine's surface in barrel, the wines are fortified up to 15% (using 96% abv grape spirit) and aged biologically (under flor) as Fino (Jerez) or Manzanilla (Sanlúcar). Sherries destined for Oloroso are fortified to 18 to 20% and aged oxidatively for years in cask.

Amontillado and Palo Cortado styles feature both biological and oxidative ageing, with alcohol around 17.5%. Maturation for almost all Sherry is done in a solera system (with young wine added to old), and all Sherry is naturally dry, unless a sweetener (such as Pedro Ximénez) is added.

Jerez DO's recent law changes have expanded the number of towns allowed to make Sherry and removed mandatory fortification (if 15% alcohol achieved naturally). Research focus is now on single-vineyard *pagos* and reviving six newly permitted pre-phylloxera grapes.

RESIDUAL-SUGAR LEVELS

Port: 90 to 110g/l
Bual Madeira: 100g/l
Malmsey Madeira: 130g/l
Muscat de Beaumes-de-Venise: 100 to 120g/l
Australian Liqueur Muscat: 200 to 290g/l
Pedro Ximénez Sherry: 220 to 400g/l

Producers to try: *Cota 45, Equipo Navazos, Fernando de Castilla, Luis Pérez, Tradición, Ximénez Spínola.*

MADEIRA

The volcanic soil of this small, remote subtropical Atlantic island gives Madeira its high acidity and ability to age. It is made in four styles (in increasing order of sweetness): Sercial, Verdelho, Bual and Malmsey; the best are made as varietals. Tinta Negra is widely planted, but Terrantez is rare. Fortification (96% abv grape spirit) at different stages depends on the required sweetness, while *estufa* or *canteiro* heating methods replicate the tropical journeys of the founding ships, giving Madeira its caramel oxidative character.
Producers to try: *Barbeito, D'Oliveiras, Henriques & Henriques.*

OTHER FORTIFIEDS

Vins Doux Naturels may undergo mutage (the addition of 96% grape spirit) during fermentation (on or off the skins). These include Rhône's Muscat de Beaumes-de-Venise, Roussillon's Muscat de Rivesaltes and Grenache-based Maury and Banyuls (aged oxidatively in cask and glass *bonbonnes*). Other fortifieds include Liqueur Muscat and Topaque from Rutherglen in Australia (aged oxidatively in cask), as well as Marsala in Sicily and Málaga in Spain.
Producers to try: *Gauby, Mas Amiel, Rectorie (Roussillon), Bernardins (Rhône), Campbells (Australia), Bartoli (Sicily), Málaga Virgen (Spain).*

Glass **bonbonnes** *at Mas Amiel, Roussillon, France are used for ageing Maury* **Rancio** *VDN outside to encourage oxidation.*

TASTING PRACTICE
FORTIFIED WINES

This tasting includes the cornerstone of the fortified-wine family, the trio of Sherry, Port and Madeira. The fourth wine is Australia's unique contribution to the fortified wine world, Rutherglen Muscat. Within these categories there are varying styles from dry to sweet, but the wines selected all have something in common – long oxidative ageing in cask – and can often be confused with one another in blind tastings. This exercise should help you look for markers to identify each one through colour, acidity, alcohol, flavour and texture.

The palate can tire easily tasting high-alcohol wines (these are all 18 to 20%). So, to refresh and add an interesting element to the tasting, serve a selection of charcuterie and cheeses alongside: jamón Ibérico and almonds (for the Sherry), mature Comté, Gruyère or Manchego (for the Madeira); and for those with a sweet tooth, honey-and-almond cake (for the Tawny Port) and dark-chocolate florentines (for the Muscat). Taste through the wines on their own first, then match with the selected foods to see how that changes and enhances the taste.

WINES TO BUY (IN ORDER OF SERVING):
① Oloroso Sherry (Spain) **£££**
② 15-Year-Old Bual Madeira (Portugal) **£££**
③ 20-Year-Old Tawny Port (Portugal) **£££**
④ 12-Year-Old Rutherglen Muscat (Australia) **££**

Preparation: *See page* 32.

Buying & alternatives: The dry Oloroso Sherry could be replaced with dry Amontillado (which also has some oxidative ageing); Bual for a sweeter Malmsey Madeira; 10- instead of 20-year-old Tawny Port; Rutherglen Topaque in place of Muscat.

Serving temperature: All of the wines can be served after a short chill in the fridge, 11 to 14°C (52 to 57°F), known as cellar temperature (although not many of us have cellars today). They lose freshness if served too warm.

Method: Pour the same amount into each of your four glasses, and sample them side by side.

Look: Wine 1 is coppery with burnt-orange notes, in contrast to the dark brown with green flecks of Wine 2. Note the deep-red tinge in the amber tawny of Wine 3, clearly identifying it. Wine 4 is light amber with gold flecks. All colours from copper to amber to tawny indicate long oxidative ageing.

Smell: The distinctive aroma of spice, figs and nuts in Wine 1 is accompanied by an earthy undertone. Wine 2 is more subdued, with green tea, cinnamon and caramel (typical of Madeira). Wine 3 smells more of soft leather, hazelnuts and cinnamon, compared to Wine 4, which has a distinct bouquet of treacle and raisins (typical of Rutherglen Muscat), with coffee-bean and floral undertones.

Taste: There is a glycerol texture to Wine 1; it is dry, with deep citrus and dried-fig flavours, mouthwatering saline savoury notes and a bitter olive twist. Wine 2 is medium-sweet, with a rich, smooth texture, raisiny-toffee flavours and remarkably high acidity keeping the palate fresh (high acidity is typical of Madeira).

Wine 3 tastes sweeter (the residual-sugar level here is similar to Wine 2, but its acidity is lower), and it has a silky and invitingly soft texture, with delicate fruit notes and nuttiness. In comparison, Wine 4 is more viscous in texture, with distinct raisiny sweetness and lingering caramel.

Finish: All of the wines show heat on the finish due to their high alcohol level. Wine 1 is dry through to the finish, with a grippy intensity. Wine 2 is sweeter than Wine 1 but finishes fresh and dry. Wine 3 has a nutty finish compared to the treacley caramel-sweetness of Wine 4.

Conclusion: In this exercise you have compared four fortified wines made using different winemaking methods – but all aged oxidatively in large casks. You have learned to identify the glycerol texture, salinity and savouriness of dry Oloroso, the distinctively high acidity and caramel notes of Madeira, the red colour, silky texture and fruity sweetness of Tawny Port and the sweet, raisiny, caramel notes of Rutherglen Muscat.

Repetition is the best way of learning to taste and understanding your own taste perceptions – so now check the crib sheet on the next page, and consider trying the tasting again using the alternative wines suggested.

①

②

③

④

CRIB SHEET: **FORTIFIED WINES**

1. OLOROSO SHERRY

REGION: **JEREZ**

COUNTRY: **SPAIN**

GRAPE: **PALOMINO**

PRICE: **£££**

ALCOHOL: **20%**

SIGHT: **Copper**

SMELL: **Complex blend of walnuts, spice, orange peel, dried figs; earthy**

TASTE: **Moderate acidity (residual sugar 5g/l)**

FRUIT INTENSITY: **Not fruity, but complex intense palate of dried fruits and spice**

TEXTURE: **Glycerol-like; firm structure**

CONCLUSION: **Complexity; mature, oxidative nuttiness; saline savoury notes; all dry with bitter twist to finish**

COMMON BLIND TASTING MIX-UPS:
Dry Amontillado or Palo Cortado Sherry

ALTERNATIVES TO TRY
Dry Amontillado or Palo Cortado Sherry

2. 15-YEAR-OLD BUAL MADEIRA

REGION: **MADEIRA**

COUNTRY: **PORTUGAL**

GRAPE: **MALVASIA FINA**

PRICE: **£££**

ALCOHOL: **20%**

SIGHT: **Burnt orange**

SMELL: **More subdued; green tea, spice, caramel**

TASTE: **Very high acidity (residual sugar 109g/l)**

FRUIT INTENSITY: **Distinct caramel, cloves and baked fruit**

TEXTURE: **Soft and smooth**

CONCLUSION: **Pungent, medium-sweet, caramel and raisins; Canteiro ageing**

COMMON BLIND TASTING MIX-UPS:
Marsala or Oloroso Sherry

ALTERNATIVES TO TRY
Malmsey Madeira

3. 20-YEAR-OLD TAWNY PORT

REGION: **DOURO**

COUNTRY: **PORTUGAL**

GRAPE: **TOURIGA NACIONAL BLEND**

PRICE: **£££**

ALCOHOL: **20%**

SIGHT: **Dark amber, with light-gold flecks; amber tawny, distinct red notes**

SMELL: **Nutty, soft leather; fruity orange peel**

TASTE: **Moderate acidity (residual sugar 115g/l)**

FRUIT INTENSITY: **More fruit, but delicate**

TEXTURE: **Very soft and silky**

CONCLUSION: **Soft, luscious, sweet, nutty; fruity sweetness on palate**

COMMON BLIND TASTING MIX-UPS: **Sweet Oloroso Sherry, aged white Port**

ALTERNATIVES TO TRY

10-Year-Old Tawny or aged white Port; Tawny style from Australia or South Africa

4. 12-YEAR-OLD RUTHERGLEN MUSCAT

REGION: **VICTORIA**

COUNTRY: **AUSTRALIA**

GRAPE: **MUSCAT ROUGE À PETITS GRAINS**

PRICE: **£££**

ALCOHOL: **18%**

SIGHT: **Medium amber**

SMELL: **Subtle treacley nose, with coffee beans and rose petals**

TASTE: **Moderate acidity (residual sugar 290g/l)**

FRUIT INTENSITY: **Not fruity, but raisiny, figgy**

TEXTURE: **Viscous, dense**

CONCLUSION: **Gorgeous raisin and treacle, with lingering caramel finish; almost decadently sweet, but with crispness**

COMMON BLIND TASTING MIX-UPS: **Pedro Ximénez Sherry**

ALTERNATIVES TO TRY

Australian Rutherglen Topaque

OAK & OTHER VESSELS

Not so long ago, lavish amounts of new oak were considered the height of fashion and quality. Now it's all change; winemakers have realized that a heavy, oaky taste is not so popular, because drinkers today prefer to taste the fruit in the wines. Many producers have gravitated to larger oak formats, to older oak, or have abandoned oak and are experimenting with concrete or clay vessels instead.

Fire in the barrel as seen here at Bodega Muga's cooperage in Rioja, Spain, allows staves to be bent and toasts the oak inside.

The preferred wood for barrels is oak, a durable medium that has been used for centuries. It has a natural affinity with wine, certainly more than chestnut, acacia, beech, or pine and can add colour, aromas and flavours. Oak can also soften texture by exposing wine to a slow oxidation, which also aids flavour complexity. Plus it adds oak tannins, which help stabilize the wine.

SIZE & TOAST MATTERS

Smaller barrels with a greater oak-to-wine ratio obviously give a stronger oaky flavour. The standard barrel size in Bordeaux is 225 litres (*barrique*), in Burgundy it's 228 litres (*pièce*), and in Australasia it's 300 litres (hogshead). Now many winemakers are abandoning barriques for larger 500-litre casks or for *foudres* of 1,000 litres or more. Some wineries like *Weinert* in Argentina never stopped using vast 6,000-litre oak casks for ageing – and these are now coming back into fashion.

The level of toast (light, medium or heavy) can have more impact than the origin of the oak. In barrel-making, coopers use fire to bend the staves into place, but it is the end of this process that gives the toasty taste.

The age of the oak also has an impact on the wine: new oak imparts more flavours, aromas and tannins compared to older oak. Over time, tartrate crystals build up and the vessel becomes inert, which is ideal for the slow ageing of Sherry in Jerez's soleras. Time in oak for fine reds worldwide is around 18 months, but the oaky taste depends on how the barrel ageing is managed – for example, racking (*see page* 90) can aerate and soften the wine – rather than the barrel-ageing time.

GRAPE AFFINITY

Some grapes have more affinity with oak. For whites, fuller-bodied grapes like Chardonnay or Sémillon can handle new French-oak fermentation in small formats, but delicate, floral Riesling cannot. For reds, thin-skinned Pinot Noir is only aged in French oak, whereas thick-skinned, robust Cabernet Sauvignon can withstand American oak, though French is considered more subtle and

Winemakers have a wide variety of sizes and types of oak to choose from; shown here is Château de Chassagne-Montrachet in Burgundy, France.

elegant. Slightly sweeter-flavoured grapes like Zinfandel, Shiraz and Tempranillo are often aged in American oak.

Which brings us to Rioja. It is interesting in an age when oak flavours are becoming less desirable and winemakers are trying to avoid too much oak that Rioja is as popular as ever. Rioja is all about oak and age, but people don't associate toasty oak with Rioja. Today, Rioja is more likely to be aged in subtler French oak, which can reflect terroir well, rather than American. People love Rioja's soft texture and vanilla hints from long oak ageing.

CHIPS & STAVES

If a wine label states 'oaked' (not oak barrels or casks), it might not have been near a barrel. Bags of oak chips or staves are suspended inside the fermenting vat to impart an oaky flavour (but the result lacks the texture imparted by a barrel).

ORIGIN OF OAK

Slower-grown oak trees have tighter grains and are most prized for winemaking.

French: (*Quercus petraea*) The sessile oak is preferred for richness. There are numerous French forests (Tronçais, Nevers, Allier, Vosges), each with their own terroir. High trunks (*la futaie régulière de chêne*) are premium quality from 150- to 250-year-old trees – tight grained, split and air-dried, giving subtle flavours; these are expensive. Winemakers often have preferred coopers (François Frères, Taransaud) rather than forests.

American: (*Quercus alba*) White oak with thick tylose walls is looser grained; sawn and kiln-dried, it gives stronger vanilla-clove notes. It is usually half the price of French oak, as there is less wastage.

Other countries: Austrian and German (*Quercus petraea*); Hungarian (mainly *Quercus petraea*); Slavonian (*Quercus robur*).

OTHER VESSELS

STAINLESS STEEL

Stainless steel is easy to clean, inert and inexpensive, with an option to have an open or closed top and temperature-control technology. This is the winemaker's vessel of choice for cool fermentation to retain primary fruit aromas and flavours in fresh fruity whites.

CONCRETE

Hardwearing, neutral, porous and cheap, concrete is used for fermentation and maturation of whites and reds. Originally based on the amphora shape, egg-shaped concrete vessels have become particularly popular, aiding complexity, texture and improved mouthfeel in whites. These concrete eggs are generally unlined (allowing tiny amounts of oxygen ingress) and treated with tartaric acid. The shape gives a higher level of contact between the wine and its lees, allowing for continuous flow due to convection currents as fermentation heats up, moving the wine around freely. Concrete is a good insulator, so wines can be fresher, but the downside with concrete eggs (which vary in size from 500 to 1,500 litres) is that they are pricey and very heavy.

Winemaker Sebastián Zuccardi comments on why he prefers concrete to oak: 'I prefer concrete for some wines because it doesn't give any taste and flavour to the wines and gives us the chance to show the sense of place in pureness and transparency. With Malbec grown in Mendoza, we prefer less micro-oxygenation during fermentation and ageing. Temperature management is more efficient with concrete and it's a natural material; but obviously like oak it does not guarantee a great wine, as for that the key is the terroir and the viticulture. For us, transparency is essential in our interpretation of the place.'

Armenian karas (clay vessels), seen here at Zorah winery, are only two-thirds buried, creating natural temperature control for fermentation.

Weingut am Stein, in Würzburg in Germany's Franken region, has concrete eggs, as well as five buried qvevri *imported from Georgia.*

GRANITE

The Douro Valley in Portugal is renowned for its granite stone troughs (*lagares*), where the grapes are foot trodden and fermented, while some winemakers in Spain (*Adegas Galegas, Altos de Torona, Torres Penelas* in Rías Baixas) are experimenting with eggs made from granite – the natural bedrock of their region.

CLAY

Historically used for transportation, clay amphorae are now made in a variety of shapes for fermentation and ageing. With the growing popularity of skin-contact wines (*see page* 134), amphorae are used as an oak alternative by wineries worldwide (*De Martino*, Chile).

Countries and regions have different names and sizes for their clay vessels. *Tinaja* (Spain and southern Chile), *talha* (Alentejo, Portugal) and *pithari* (Greece) are all being revived. Local clay is usually used, and most vessels are free-standing in the cellar and treated inside with beeswax.

In Georgia, clay *qvevri* (*see page* 192) are buried underground up to their necks, needing no temperature control for fermentation or maturation, but cleaning and hygiene are a challenge here. The ancient *qvevri* winemaking tradition is now on UNESCO's Intangible Cultural Heritage list. Today's European skin-contact movement was inspired by winemakers such as Josko Gravner, who has 47 underground *qvevri* in his cellar in Italy's Collio.

GLASS

Glass demi-johns (25 to 70 litres) have long been popular for maturation. Called *bonbonnes* in Roussillon in France, they are used for maturing Vins Doux Naturels (*see page* 115) outside for 9 to 12 months before oak maturation.

In Tokaji cellars in Hungary, glass demi-johns are used for the slow fermentation and maturation of Essencia (*see page* 109). Glass globes (25 to 400 litres) made from borosilicate glass are becoming popular for their hygienic, neutral qualities – and for giving purity to wines.

Gravner is now experimenting with maturing in glass containers and has just ordered one of the world's largest, at 7,000 litres.

TASTING PRACTICE
FULL RICH REDS

Big, bold, powerful reds made from thick-skinned grapes are the focus of this tasting – with each wine representing a single-varietal expression. The opportunity here is to learn about grape characteristics and the distinctive flavours that come from the particular climate in which the vines are grown.

Full-bodied reds have a deep colour and high alcohol, particularly from warmer climates. The grapes vary in acidity levels (higher in cool climates, lower in warmer climates), but there is always an intensity of dark-fruit flavours (dark cherry, brambles, blackcurrant). Wines made from full-bodied red grapes can have different tannin textures (fine-grained to rustic) that add to the mouthfeel and the overall structure and breadth of the wine. Once you have done the tasting, try matching the wine with food, such as stews, curries, harder cheeses or red meats (*see page* 146).

WINES TO BUY (IN ORDER OF SERVING):
① Syrah (France) **££**
② Primitivo (Italy) **££**
③ Carmenère (Chile) **££**
④ Malbec (Argentina) **££**

Preparation: *See page* 32.

Buying & alternatives: If you cannot find the options pictured, try to replace with wines from the same grape and area and at the same price point; otherwise try the alternatives overleaf.

Serving temperature: 15 to 18°C (59 to 64°F).

Method: Pour the same amount into each of your four glasses, and sample them side by side.

Look: First, check each wine for clarity, and note the range of colours against the white background, paying particular attention to the base colour and rim. Hold Wines 1 and 2 alongside each other. Wine 1 has a lighter hue than Wine 2. Repeat with Wines 3 and 4. Wine 3 has a lighter depth of colour compared to Wine 4, which has purple hints on the rim, typical of this thick-skinned grape in its youth.

Smell: Without swirling the glasses, sniff each wine and write down your initial thoughts; then swirl the wines considering their aromatic intensity (without taking a sip). You will notice that Wine 1 is aromatic with restrained red fruits and undertones of violets, whereas Wine 2 smells sweeter and riper, with prune and raisin notes. Wine 3 is greener and more herbaceous, rather than fruity, compared to the juicier damson aromas of Wine 4.

Taste: Focus on Wines 1 and 2, comparing acidity levels. There is high acidity in Wine 1, but it's more moderate in Wine 2. Now think about tannin levels and fruit intensity. Wine 1 has refined, fine-grained tannins, with a polished feel to the fruit, a moderately firm palate structure and overall feeling of dryness. Wine 2 has softer tannins, with a velvety texture, lush ripe fruits and hints of vanilla and licorice from American oak, with an overall feeling of sweetness. Note that the high alcohol of Wine 2 adds to its weight and mouthfeel.

Now move to Wines 3 and 4. Consider the acidity: it is higher in Wine 3 than in Wine 4. Note the grainy texture of the tannins in Wine 3 compared to the firmer tannins in Wine 4. There is a graphite (almost mineral) note in Wine 3, a herbaceousness; it has a softer texture overall than Wine 4, despite its higher acidity. The robust, sweet ripe fruits in Wine 4 are noticeable immediately when you swirl it around your palate. It then becomes drier.

Finish: Think about the sensation you feel once you take a sip and swallow to see the wine's finish – and the length of time you can still taste it after you have swallowed. Remember that higher-quality wines linger longer on the palate than less expensive wines.

Conclusion: You have learned to distinguish between four thick-skinned red grapes – all with high alcohol levels but with varying flavours and acidity; also that tannin textures in full-bodied reds can vary widely, as can their overall structure.

Now check the crib sheet on the next page, and consider trying the tasting again using the alternative wines suggested.

CRIB SHEET: FULL RICH REDS

1. SYRAH

REGION: **NORTHERN RHÔNE**

COUNTRY: **FRANCE**

GRAPE: **SYRAH**

PRICE: **££**

ALCOHOL: **14%**

SIGHT: **Moderately deep red, with ruby rim**

SMELL: **Aromatic, violets, wild raspberries; hints of black pepper**

TASTE: **Dry, high acidity**

FRUIT INTENSITY: **Moderate fruit, touch of spice and black pepper**

TEXTURE: **High tannins; fine-grained, powdery**

CONCLUSION: **Acidity obvious throughout; well structured, marked tannin; French oak not noticeable; savoury edge**

COMMON BLIND TASTING MIX-UPS: **Ribera del Duero, cool-climate Cabernet Sauvignon**

ALTERNATIVES TO TRY

Syrah from South Africa or California; South African Pinotage; Portuguese Baga or Touriga Nacional

2. PRIMITIVO

REGION: **PUGLIA**

COUNTRY: **ITALY**

GRAPE: **PRIMITIVO**

PRICE: **££**

ALCOHOL: **14.5%**

SIGHT: **Deep, dark, inky black/red**

SMELL: **Raisiny, sweet, licorice; dark-chocolate notes**

TASTE: **Moderate acidity, raisiny sweetness**

FRUIT INTENSITY: **Full, fleshy, sweet prunes and dark cherry**

TEXTURE: **Moderate tannins; soft, velvety**

CONCLUSION: **Sweet notes, luscious mouthfeel, soft overall; vanilla hints from French and American oak**

COMMON BLIND TASTING MIX-UPS: **Zinfandel, Merlot, Negroamaro**

ALTERNATIVES TO TRY

California Zinfandel; Italian Negroamaro (Puglia) or Nero d'Avola (Sicily)

3. CARMENÈRE

REGION: **COLCHAGUA**

COUNTRY: **CHILE**

GRAPE: **CARMENÈRE**

PRICE: **££**

ALCOHOL: **13%**

SIGHT: **Dark ruby red**

SMELL: **Green herbaceous notes; fennel; blackcurrant fruit**

TASTE: **High acidity; sweet fruit**

FRUIT INTENSITY: **Moderate to full; herbs, black fruit, balsamic**

TEXTURE: **Moderate to high tannin, grainy**

CONCLUSION: **Herbaceous, graphite notes; light cedar from large oak ageing; acid is more marked than the Malbec, but texture is softer**

COMMON BLIND TASTING MIX-UPS: **Cabernet Sauvignon, Malbec**

ALTERNATIVES TO TRY

Chilean Merlot; Italian Aglianico

4. MALBEC

REGION: **MENDOZA**

COUNTRY: **ARGENTINA**

GRAPE: **MALBEC**

PRICE: **££**

ALCOHOL: **14.5%**

SIGHT: **Dark ruby red, purple hint**

SMELL: **Damsons, blackberries, dark-red plums**

TASTE: **Moderate to low acidity; initially sweet, finishing dry**

FRUIT INTENSITY: **Full, concentrated; rich blackberry**

TEXTURE: **Firm, rustic tannin; supple fruit softens**

CONCLUSION: **Starts with plush dark fruits, but tannins are chunky and firm; cedary notes from French oak; finish is earthy and dry**

COMMON BLIND TASTING MIX-UPS: **Carmenère, warm-climate Cabernet Sauvignon**

ALTERNATIVES TO TRY

Uruguay Tannat; Argentinian Cabernet Sauvignon

PACKAGING FOR THE FUTURE

Winemakers keen to reduce their carbon footprint are rethinking their packaging, trying to find more sustainable options. Cans, pouches, kegs, recyclable plastic bottles and bag-in-box are becoming more commonplace, while some producers switch to lighter-weight glass.

It is a well-known fact that up to 60 per cent of the carbon footprint of a wine is the glass bottle; plus glass recycling is also carbon-intensive. The problem is that glass is deeply immersed in our wine culture as the vessel of choice, and it will take time to change that. It remains the viable format for cellaring wine too. However, if you care about sustainable issues, there are alternatives to try for wines to be enjoyed within a few months of purchase – as most wines are.

LIGHTER-WEIGHT GLASS BOTTLES

Next time you reach for a bottle of wine, think about the weight of the glass. Some producers persist in using ridiculously heavy bottles (up to 1kg empty) for their luxury cuvées – like some sort of status symbol.

It has been clearly shown by environmental-activist winemakers like Miguel Torres (Spain) and Nigel Greening (Felton Road, New Zealand) that lighter-weight glass has a lower carbon footprint. The answer lies in reducing the weight of all glass bottles, not just for less expensive wines. The only caveat is sparkling wines, which have greater pressure inside so require slightly heavier bottles (800 to 900g).

A recent initiative by Sustainable Wine Roundtable (swroundtable.org) has brought key supermarkets, major wine retailers and producers on board – representing 1.5 billion bottles (five per cent of global wine). The aim is to reduce the weight of 75cl glass bottles to 420g (empty) by 2026. (At the time of writing, the average is 550g.)

Dr Laura Catena, managing director of Catena Zapata in Argentina, is part of this initiative and has an innovative take on the matter. Her approach is through education, and she cleverly compares the need for action to the luxury-goods market. 'It's like suitcases; no one buys a heavy one anymore. That industry, using technology and better packaging materials, has convinced consumers that lighter suitcases are more valuable. That is what we need to do for wine. Heavy bottles might look fancy, but people need to know that they have a higher carbon footprint.'

POUCHES ①

Some of the wine put into pouches has not been of a high quality. Le Grappin is offering a good-quality product and has cleverly named its magnum bags of wine 'bagnums'. The carbon footprint is ten times lower than for glass, and pouches are easily transported and stored.

BAG-IN-BOX (BIB) ②

It's now possible to find interesting BIB wines as some smaller-scale artisan growers turn to this format – so BIBs are enjoying a renaissance as the quality improves. These are said to be ten times lower in carbon footprint than glass, but the main issue is that the plastic taps and bags present a recycling challenge.

CANS ③

Many wine-lovers baulk at the idea of a 'tinny', even though it is fine for beer and cider. However, these are ideal for outdoor festivals and beach parties, suited to young wine styles that don't need airing or ageing. There is an environmental complication as manufacturers use mined bauxite to convert to aluminium, but cans have 35 per cent less weight than glass and are easier to recycle, overall requiring 90 per cent less energy than glass.

PAPER BOTTLES ④

Wine in paper might sound like a mushy disaster, but new technology has created a paper bottle that has a 94 per cent recycled paperboard outer and inner food-grade plastic pouch. This is five times lighter than a standard glass bottle, is easier to carry and is unbreakable – making it a truly sustainable option.

POSTABLE PET ⑤

You might have noticed flat bottles appearing on wine shelves and online recently. These are polyethylene terephthalate (rPET) bottles, made from Prevented Ocean Plastic™ – the 'r' stands for recycled. Ten times lighter than a standard glass bottle, easier to recycle than glass and made from a stable inert material (just like glass), they have a significantly lower carbon footprint than single-use glass bottles. They are useful on trains or planes, requiring less storage space, and are ideal for wines to be drunk within 12 months.

One leading Provence producer used this format for its higher-priced rosé but found consumer resistance at home; France is now developing alternatives using rPET.

WINE KEGS

Wine on tap is popular in the US, UK, Scandinavia and Australia. Kegs allow 20 litres (27 bottles) of wine to be kept fresh for six to eight weeks after opening (12 months after filling). Quality has improved, but these suit early-consumption wines. Kegs are either in reusable (but heavy) stainless steel (as beer) or in single-use plastic with a foil inner bag that collapses in on itself (similar to BIB). While kegs do have a reduced carbon footprint in comparison to glass bottles and are cost-effective for selling wine by the glass, there is a question over how many actually get recycled.

EXPLORING TASTE

ROSÉ WINE

Once a simple holiday glugger, rosé wine is now being taken much more seriously. Winemakers around the globe are experimenting with all things pink, and rosé sales look buoyant in comparison to reds, while celebrity-backed 'lifestyle'-brand prices head into the stratosphere.

What began as a fashion trend has now become an important category in wine. Or perhaps it always was? Rosé might be one of the world's oldest wines: *clairet* was popular until the 19th century for its delicacy and colour, then big reds took over. After that, through to the 21st century, rosé was considered a red by-product, a pale red (*saignée*) that was run off vats just after fermentation began. When I started to learn about wine, rosé was barely mentioned; it was considered inferior and simple compared to more serious white and red.

PALE & DRY

Provence lit the rosé flame. After careful research from mid-1990s onwards, producers focused on pale-dry rosé as their quintessential ideal, a style that suits their light-skinned grapes (Grenache and Cinsault). This model of 'pale and dry' proved popular. Now all rosé worldwide seemingly has to be pale, which I have a bit of a problem with. My other issue is with luxury-cuvée, status-symbol rosés, which are rarely worth the money.

CHANGE OF ATTITUDE

Winemakers from Chile, New Zealand, Spain and Greece have started to take rosé seriously, searching for the most suited grapes (Cinsault, Carignan, Grenache, Xinomavro and Blaufränkisch are better than thick-skinned Cabernet Sauvignon and Nebbiolo), the right terroir and picking at the right time for freshness and acidity. Thanks to an influx of well-made wines, wine-lovers now realize how super-adaptable and versatile rosé can be.

HOW ROSÉ IS MADE

There is no legal definition for rosé worldwide; it's made from any grapes in any style (dry to sweet), depending on local traditions and appellation laws. The pink/rosé colour comes from red grape skins, but white grapes can be used in the mix.

The method used widely today is to direct press (pre-maceration), with a short maceration (up to 24 hours) of the juice with the red grape skins after crushing. The juice is then separated off and fermented as if it was white. The other method, used in Rhône's Tavel and Spain's Navarra, is a longer maceration with extended skin contact to add colour, fruit and structure before the juice is run off.

European appellations have their own laws. In Champagne, blending is allowed – a little red wine is blended into the white cuvée. Producers use a variety of methods: some use traditional maceration (*saignée*) and/or co-fermentation depending on the house style, rather than just having a coloured version of their white. Now that the climate is better for ripening red grapes in Champagne, their rosé has improved.

Rosé can come from anywhere. Provence and Languedoc like to think they are the rosé heartland, searching for the perfect quality with lees contact, oak and terroir focus. However today, my money is on Spain and Greece for value rosé picks. Countries often use different names for light or dark styles: *rosado* or blend of red/white grapes *clarete* (Spain), *rosato* or *chiaretto* (Italy), blush (California), *Weissherbst* or co-fermented white/red grapes *Schillerwein* (Germany).

WHAT'S IN A COLOUR?

This brings me back to colour. For me, colours should range from pale pink, damask pink, Barbie pink and onion-skin pink, to very pale red. However some are too water-white, almost white wines, but labelled rosé. Dark rosés like Cerasuolo d'Abruzzo and some Tavel rosés, with more texture and structure, have sadly become a rarity.

LIGHTSTRIKE

With so many rosés bottled in light-coloured glass, lightstrike (*see page* 26) is a major issue that rosé-lovers need to be aware of. According to rosé expert Elizabeth Gabay MW, at least one-third of rosés she encounters have been tainted by this. Some premium rosé-makers are now moving to darker glass bottles: Provençal Château Galoupet uses lightweight amber glass made from 85-per-cent recycled glass, distinguishing it with a pink wax capsule (as the rosé indicator).

Lightstrike affects white and sparkling wines too. To protect their wines, some Champagne producers, such as Louis Roederer, use cellophane wrapping; others, such as Ruinart, use a paper shell – but that just adds to the packaging.

SERVING

Most rosé is best drunk young, although serious avant-garde producers are experimenting with ageing. Darker rosés with more structure can benefit from bottle-age.

Serving temperature: pale dry at 7 to 10°C (45 to 50°F); richer darker styles at 11 to 13°C (52 to 55°F).

RECOMMENDED ROSÉS TO TRY

Pale pink:

① *Fleuriet Sancerre Rosé* (Loire, France)
② *Domaine de Montrosé Rosé* (Provence, France)
Baudry Chinon Rosé (Loire, France)

Darker rosé:

③ *Señorío de Sarría Rosado* (Spain)
④ *Tardieu-Laurent Tavel VV* (Rhône, France)
Thymiopoulos Rosé de Xinomavro (Greece)

Rosé fizz:

⑤ *Vadio Rosé* (Portugal)
⑥ *Roebuck Blanc de Noirs Rosé* (England)
Billecart-Salmon Rosé, Charles Heidsieck Rosé, Laurent-Perrier Rosé (Champagne, France)

ORANGE WINE

It's all the rage now, with a kaleidoscope of colours and diverse styles to explore, but orange wine is far from new – it is, in fact, one of the most ancient styles in the world.

So, firstly, what is an orange wine? It is like a halfway house between a white and red wine. Although made from white grapes, it is treated as if it was red – with fermentation on its skins. This skin-contact method can last from a few days, to weeks and even months; the longer the juice is in contact with the skins, the darker and more tannic the resulting wine.

DIVERSITY OF COLOUR & TASTE

One thing to note is that orange wines are not always orange in colour. They come in an eye-catching array of tones – from pale gold (short maceration time or less ripe grapes), electric orange (ripe grapes with two weeks' skin contact), and blood orange (from pink-tinged white grapes), to orange-amber (very ripe grapes macerated for weeks or months). In all cases, the colour comes from the skins and not from oxidation.

Taste-wise, expect zesty textural wines, with the vibrant acidity of a white wine but more body, texture and flavour than you would normally expect in a white – and with the tannic structure of a red wine. Flavours vary from more conventional floral, honey, grassy and tangerine to slightly funkier exotic tea, orange peel, marmalade, ginger, dried apricots, herbs and spice, and even more unexpected and weird bruised apple, rhubarb and resin.

WINEMAKING HISTORY

The popularity of crunchy vibrant orange wines has slowly gathered pace since around 2000, rather like the renewed interest in rosé (*see page* 132), but the concept is very old. Skin-contact wines have been around for thousands of years – 8,000 years, in fact. The early pioneers were in Georgia and Armenia ('the cradle of wine'), where it was normal (and still is) to put whole bunches – stems and all – into underground clay *qvevri* pots (*karas* in Armenia), seal them up and leave them untouched for at least six months.

The modern era of orange wines began in a corner of Eastern Europe in the 1990s on the border of Italian Fruili Collio and Slovenian Goriška Brda and gradually began to spread. It was not until the 21st century that the real impetus began, but until recently the wines were wildly inconsistent. Some were superb, with tension and power; others had unconventional earthy flavours, with volatile acidity or bitterness. Now winemakers everywhere are experimenting, there is more consistency and exploration of styles. The best examples are made with natural yeasts.

Orange wines are often confused with natural wines. While some orange wines are made in a natural manner with minimal intervention, the term natural wine refers to all wine styles – not just to orange (*see page* 136).

GRAPES (NOT ORANGES)

Orange wines are made from any white grapes. Popular choices include Sauvignon Blanc, Chardonnay, Muscat, Gewurztraminer, Grenache Blanc, Pinot Gris, Albariño, Assyrtiko and Grüner Veltliner. Winemakers experiment with blends too, and many use lesser-known indigenous grapes, such as Spain's Verdil, Italy's Ribolla Gialla, Georgia's Mtsvane or Crete's Vidiano.

The name 'orange wine' was coined in 2004 by a sommelier friend of mine, David Harvey of Scottish wine importer Raeburn Fine Wines, while working at Frank Cornelissen in Etna, Sicily. Harvey described the amber liquid as 'orange' and felt the style needed its own category to be accepted by the trade – and there it stuck.

VERSATILITY WITH FOOD

With their palate-cleansing acid structure and textural element, these wines make versatile food matches to be enjoyed throughout a meal. The robust, dry, baked-fruit flavours of deeper amber wines match with roast vegetables, gnocchi, lamb kebabs, spicy Thai or spaghetti *alle vongole* with clams – anything earthy works well. Charcuterie platters or harder cheeses like Gouda, Comté, Pecorino or Manchego alongside membrillo quince jelly are also a delicious pairing.

SERVING

These wines are easy to order, no decanting required; deeper amber styles can benefit from aeration.

Serving temperature: light styles at 10 to 12°C (50 to 54°F); richer textural styles at 14 to 15°C (57 to 59°F).

WHERE TO BUY

The best place to start is an independent wine merchant; try also natural-wine bars and restaurants (*see page* 137).

RECOMMENDED ORANGE WINES TO TRY

Lighter:

① *Litmus Bacchus* (England)
② *Château Jau Or-ange* (Roussillon, France)
Cramele Recaș Solara (Romania)

Medium:

③ *Gerard Bertrand Orange Gold* (Languedoc, France)
④ *Ancre Hill Orange Wine* (Wales)
⑤ *Calmel & Joseph Ams Tram Gram Pomone* (Languedoc, France)
Lyrarakis Melissaki (Crete)
Baia's Wine Tsolikouri (Georgia)
Niedermayr Souvignier Gris (Italy)
James Rahn Pinot Gris (Oregon, US)

Full:

⑥ *Tiko Estate Orange Kisi* (Georgia)
Casreli Chitistvala (Georgia)
Dakishvili Qvevri Kisi (Georgia)
Gravner Ribolla Gialla (Italy)

NATURAL WINE

The natural-wine movement has been called a philosophy, a phenomenon and a fad – but whatever it is, it appeals to a growing number of wine-lovers who see natural wines as more ethical.

'Natty wines' are often dismissed as funky, weird and just an excuse for faults, but they can be great wines, a real expression of culture and sense of place. Since the 1980s, the movement has gained momentum worldwide as a reaction to 'technologically made wines'.

However, natural wine is an undefined term. This lack of definition has led authentic natural pioneers like Frank Cornelissen in Sicily to avoid the term, as he feels it is unfortunate. 'What is good, however, is that it obviously appeals to those with a sensitivity of what they drink, but artisanal wines might be a better term to use,' he says.

So, natural wines are self-policed, unlike organic or biodynamic viticulture, which has certification bodies. The danger here is that as the movement becomes popular, winemakers jump on the bandwagon saying they are natural.

WHAT IS A NATURAL WINE?

Natural wine refers to wines made from grapes that are farmed organically (with biodynamic and regenerative methods incorporated) but not necessarily certified. The wines are made and bottled using natural ferment (native yeasts), without chemical alteration and additions, except for a small amount of sulphites when necessary. Due to their handcrafted nature, they tend to be made by artisan producers in small batches, often in amphorae or eggs (*see page* 116). These are basically low-intervention wines.

Natural-wine guru Doug Wregg says, 'Natural wines are a vigneron's attempt to express as faithfully as possible the nature of the place (vineyard or region), the terroir, the cycle of the vineyard and to follow the process of transformation from grape into wine with as few interventions as possible, so as not to "denature" the wine with chemicals, with overt technique and over-filtration.

'I don't think they should be defined,' adds Wregg. 'I usually say "more or less natural"... Often associations with manifestos and wine fairs define natural wines with checklists, including total sulphites permissible. These wines appeal to anyone looking for authenticity, and the ethical aspect of organic, chemical-free farming and all-round sustainability. But, most of all, the taste – they tend to be delicious, digestible and free of artifice... A non-intervention wine is alive and energetic.'

NATURAL CURIOSITIES

High-toned and characterful they might be; they will also possibly be harmlessly cloudy (as the natural yeast is not removed by filtration or fining). Occasionally they might have a cider smell, the whiff of a cow pat or mouse cage (due to a bacterial infection caused by *Lactobacillus*, which can disappear with time if not suppressed by sulphur). There may be a slight palate spritz (again, no sulphur), with wild yeasts and bacteria left to do their own thing for months, occasionally years. However, a natural wine should never be an excuse for faults.

A label offers no guide as to whether a wine is natural, but it does encourage curiosity and research into provenance. Specialist and online retailers can help with this. The best regions and countries to watch are Burgenland in Austria, Rheinhessen in Germany, Georgia, Catalonia in Spain, and Loire, Jura and Beaujolais in France. French associations include AVN (Association for Natural Wines), Vins SAINS and Vin Méthode Nature (the only one allowed to use 'natural method' on its labels). Italy has Triple A.

NATURAL-WINE BARS

One of the best ways to try a wide selection of these wines is to visit a natural-wine bar. Here are some to try: Made from Grapes (Glasgow); Remedy, Sager & Wilde (London); Brutal, Contracorrent, Garage (Barcelona); Denicheur, Quincave, Septimo (Paris); Normal (Berlin); Den Vandrette, Ved Stranden (Copenhagen); Weinskandal (Vienna); Bottlestop, Glou Glou (Amsterdam); L'Angolo Divino (Rome); Bunon, Verre Vole (Tokyo); Vino Underground (Tbilisi); Four Horsemen (New York); Love Tilly Devine (Sydney). Or attend Real Wine or RAW wine fairs.

RECOMMENDED NATURAL WINES TO TRY

Orange:
① *Alonso y Pedrajo Pequeñita Maturana* (Spain)
Mersel Phoenix Merwah Skin-Contact (Lebanon)

White:
② *Clos Lapeyre Mantoulan* (Jurançon, France)
Krásná Hora La Blanca (Czechia)

Rosé:
Frank Cornelissen Susucaru Rosato (Sicily, Italy)

Red:
③ *Vino di Anna Jeudi 15 Rosso* (Sicily, Italy)
Woodfine Lost Vagus Red (England)
Wirth Ranch Zinfandel Broc (California, US)

PÉT-NAT WINE

With names like I Wish I Was a Ninja, Astro Bunny, Flower Girl and Lost in a Field, and bottles that are decorated with hip psychedelic labels and topped with a crown cap, pét-nat might look like a frivolous fizzy drink.

Pét-nat (*pétillant naturel*) is in fact a serious fruity sparkling-wine style and one of the oldest sparklers, predating Champagne. Currently, it's the hippest drink in the bar and, with its minimal-intervention winemaking processes, popular with natural-winemakers.

AGE-OLD METHODS

According to pét-nat specialist Tim Wildman MW, the style is made using either the interruption or intermission technique. The first is the oldest, dating back 500 years, called *méthode ancestrale* or *méthode rurale*. It involves one single-harvest wine, and the alcoholic fermentation is interrupted by bottling; if bottled early, the resulting alcohol level, fizz pressure and residual sugar will depend on sugar and yeast activity left in the bottle, so it can be risky.

The second method, called *entr'acte*, or Col Fondo in Italy, is when fresh juice is added to a base wine from the current vintage or a previous one. It has two alcoholic fermentations, separated by a period of stabilization, and the second is preceded by bottling. Some winemakers choose to disgorge from the natural sediment to ensure clarity. Both methods use the crown cap (or beer cap), which is more effective than a cork as a closure for sparkling wines.

CAREFUL TIMING

'It's like a bottle of our vineyard, as we have done nothing to it,' says Will Davenport, a pét-nat winemaker in Sussex, England, who uses the interruption method. 'We just press organic grapes and bottle at the right time, it's as simple as that. It's technically challenging as the grapes must have perfect acid-sugar balance and the right flavours; we try different grapes each vintage, from Auxerrois to Meunier, to get floral and citrus notes in a fruit-driven style, with yeast developing over time.'

As Davenport explains, 'The timing of bottling is about how fizzy the eventual wine is; earlier bottling gives a fizzier wine. Alcohol and sugar in the final wine is beyond my control [apart from deciding harvest dates] and depends on the yeast and the wine's ability to complete fermentation. One of the more interesting things about the interruption method is the lack of control that the winemaker has over the process. Personally, I love the way that, without disgorging, the wine continues to develop a more yeasty complexity in the bottle for a couple of years.'

NO RULES

There are no rules on style, region or grape. Pét-nats can be dry or sweet, white, rosé, red or orange. They are genuinely authentic and natural, with no additives or dosage and zero sulphur; they are made in small quantities by artisans around the world from Austria to Australia. (There are now 45 pét-nat producers in the UK alone.)

Pét-nats have a soft, frothy, floaty mousse and pure fruit character – not unlike authentic cider. Some are cloudy (not a fault), but if the fizz is clear, the winemaker has disgorged the wine, taking it off its lees (*see page* 102).

SERVING

Best enjoyed in their youth (they are not for long maturing) and served alongside salads or light desserts, pét-nats make a perfect food match. Alcohol levels are moderate, varying from 7.5 to 12.5%.

Serving temperature: 5 to 8°C (41 to 46°F).

RECOMMENDED PÉT-NATS TO TRY

White:

① *Davenport Pét-Nat* (England)
Fuchs und Hase Volume 2 Pét-Nat (Austria)
Mylonas Savatiano Pét-Nat (Greece)
③ *Celler de les Aus Pét-Nat* (Spain)

Orange:

Orsogna Ancestrale Malvasia Pét-Nat (Italy)

Rosé:

② *Tim Wildman Astro Bunny Pét-Nat* (Australia)
Ancre Hill Pét-Nat Pink (Wales)
Jan-Philipp Bleeke Cosmonat Pét-Nat (Germany)
Bodegas Gratias Comboi Vino Ancestral Rosado Pét-Nat (Spain)
Botanica Flower Girl Pét-Nat (South Africa)

LOWER, LOW OR NO

The race is on to find the best way to make a low- or no-alcohol wine that is able to deliver the same sensory experience as a normal wine. While techniques have advanced and there are ever more eye-catching wine labels with quirky names (like Noughty or Zero Regrets), there is still nothing on the market that is able to compare with the real thing.

WHY NO ALCOHOL?

There are a growing number of people becoming more conscious about what they consume and cutting down on their alcohol intake, but who still want a product that tastes the same. This is where the problem lies, because alcohol is crucial to a wine's weight and mouthfeel, spreading and prolonging the flavour.

HOW LOW DO I GO?

There is a difference between Lower, Low and No. Lower-alcohol wine has alcohol levels between 5.5 and 10%; this is not an official term. It is the category offering the best alternative to standard wine (11 to 14.5%), but these wines can be sweet – for example, Moscato d'Asti (5%).

In the UK, the government sets official guidelines (*see also* wsta.co.uk).

Low alcohol: This is a wine with 1.2% alcohol or less.

De-alcoholized: As alcohol free (below), but it contains no more than 0.5%.

Alcohol free: This term should only be applied to a drink from which alcohol has been extracted if it contains no more than 0.05%.

In the EU, at the time of writing, a new group of sensible classifications look set to be agreed.

Alcohol light: with alcohol content above 0.5% (but at least 30 per cent lower than the minimum strength of the category before dealcoholization).

Alcohol free: not exceeding 0.5%.

0.0%: with alcohol not exceeding 0.05%.

HOW LOW- & NO-ALCOHOL WINES ARE MADE

Lower-alcohol wines do not have alcohol removed. Some wines are made using a special fermentation yeast and some by interrupting fermentation before all the sugar has been converted to alcohol. Other producers – for example, Dr John Forrest in New Zealand – use natural viticultural techniques. Forrest, who currently makes the best naturally made lower-alcohol dry wine, *The Doctors' Sauvignon Blanc* at 9.5%, says, 'We divide our canopy into three. To naturally lower the alcohol, we remove the top third of the canopy halfway through grape ripening, forcing the middle section to take over. It produces less sugar so ultimately lower alcohol in the final wine, but still with full flavour development. Timing is crucial.'

Many low-alcohol, de-alcoholized and alcohol-free wines (*Torres Natureo,* 0.0%) are made by starting with quality base wine, then techniques such as vacuum distillation, spinning cone or reverse osmosis remove the alcohol, while keeping the original flavours and aromas. Some fizz producers then add carbon dioxide and possibly glycerine (to give a sweet impression without sugar).

A relatively new method has been developed by *Bolle* to make alcohol-free fizz, through the removal of alcohol by vacuum distillation, then carrying out a second fermentation by adding juice, a little carbon dioxide and a special yeast strain that ensures only trace alcohol of 0.5% is achieved. The second fermentation here is key, as it creates flavour, aroma, mouthfeel, finish and more carbon dioxide.

Other 'wine alternatives' like *Wild Idol* are not wines; they are not fermented or de-alcoholized but are just given a wine-like flavour using water, grape juice, fruit vinegar and carbon dioxide.

RECOMMENDED LOW- & NO-ALCOHOL WINES TO TRY

Wine alternative:

② *Wild Idol* sparkling (0.0%)

White:

③ *Torres Natureo De-alcoholised Muscat* (0.0%)

④ *The Doctors' Marlborough Sauvignon Blanc* (9.5%)

Concha y Toro Be Light Casillero del Diablo Sauvignon Blanc (8.5%)

Zonin Spumante Cuvée Zero (0.0%)

Rosé:

① *Bolle Rosé* sparkling (<0.5%)

Thompson & Scott Noughty sparkling rosé (0.0%)

Red:

Niepoort Nat Cool Primata (10.4%)

Moderato Cuvée Revolutionnaire Merlot Tannat (<0.5%)

TASTING PRACTICE
TASTE TRENDS

Rosé wine is popular again, and sales are booming in many markets. Natural wine, made using non-interventionist methods, is becoming widely accepted as wine-lovers look for more authentic styles. Orange wine, made by the ancient skin-contact method, is available in a diverse range of styles around the world.

You might well have seen these wine styles emerging in store or online and wondered how they taste. This tasting offers the chance to find out more, comparing the distinctive characteristics of rosé, natural and orange wines, as well as a new variety. The final wine is made from one of the up-and-coming fungus-resistant and sustainable Piwi grapes (*see page* 62), which offers us a sneak taste of the future.

WINES TO BUY (IN ORDER OF SERVING):
① Rosé: Loire Rosé (France) **££**
② Natural: Merwah (Lebanon) **££**
③ Orange: *Qvevri* Rkatsiteli (Georgia) **££**
④ Piwi: Bordeaux Cabernet Cortis (France) **£**

Preparation: *See page* 32.

Buying & alternatives: Replace the dry rosé with another from Loire, Rhône or Provence and the Lebanese with a Central European natural wine. Try to find another Georgian orange wine, and for the Piwi, choose an alternative German or Austrian, or Rondo from England or Wales.

Serving temperature: Wines 1 and 2 should be served at 8 to 12°C (46 to 54°F); chill wines in the fridge for 2 hours or in an ice bucket with ice and water for 20 minutes. Wines 3 and 4 should be served at 14 to 16°C (57 to 61°F).

Method: Pour the same amount into each of your four glasses, and sample them side by side.

Look: Examine the colour and clarity of the wines against the white background. Wine 1 has a pale onion-skin colour and is clear and bright, compared to the yellow gold and slight cloudiness of Wine 2. (Natural wines can be cloudy, it is not a fault, *see page* 136.) Wine 3 is dark amber, with bright clarity, and Wine 4 is deep crimson, almost inky in colour.

Smell: Wine 1 has bright, red fruits, whereas Wine 2 is less fruity and more subdued. Wine 3 has a wide spectrum of aromas – from candied fruit to vanilla pod – with the layers of secondary aromas often found in *qvevri*-fermented and aged wines (*see page* 192). Wine 4 is highly perfumed, dominated by primary fruit, with blackcurrants, violet and lavender.

Taste: A typical example of cool-climate dry rosé, Wine 1 has high natural acidity and light red-fruit intensity; it's all about freshness and juicy fruits, with an appealing creamy texture.

Wine 2 is from a high-altitude site in a warm climate and has moderate to good acidity. Part of the blend was aged for three weeks on skins, tasting less bright and fresh but offering more texture. Its rich exotic-fruit palate, with luscious apricot, guava and a honeyed, almost figgy tone, is gained from its old-vine heritage.

Wine 3 has had six months' skin-contact in *qvevri* – it's more textural, almost grainy and oily, with a phenolic grip, rather than fruity. It is the most structured of all the wines in this tasting, with a palate layered with toasted nuts, herbs and caramelized fruits.

Wine 4 has good fruit intensity, soft tannins and good balancing acidity, with earth and chocolate; its approachable smooth structure is similar in taste to Merlot and Gamay wines.

Finish: Take a sip of each wine; swallow and think about the finish of these different styles. You will notice that all the wines are dry, particularly Wine 3, which is the driest, with a bitter grippy length. Wine 1 is fresh and vibrant to finish; Wine 2 has a light, honeyed sweetness. Whereas Wine 4 is lush on the palate, it is dry to finish.

Conclusion: You have compared four quite different wine styles, noting differences in flavour and texture, giving you the chance to explore and understand skin-contact styles, as well as a modern Piwi example.

Repetition is the best way of learning these tastes – especially for these less conventional styles – so, now check the crib sheet on the next page, and consider trying the tasting again using the alternative wines suggested.

CRIB SHEET: **TASTE TRENDS**

1. ROSÉ

REGION: **LOIRE**

COUNTRY: **FRANCE**

GRAPE: **CABERNET FRANC**

PRICE: **££**

ALCOHOL: **12.5%**

SIGHT: **Pale onion skin**

SMELL: **Light redcurrants**

TASTE: **High acidity**

FRUIT INTENSITY: **Attractive red fruit**

TEXTURE: **Mouthwatering acidity gives freshness; light creamy mouthfeel**

CONCLUSION: **Good example of cool-climate, dry, pale rosé style**

COMMON BLIND TASTING MIX-UPS: **Lirac Rosé; Provençal Rosé**

ALTERNATIVES TO TRY
French Rosé (Sancerre, Lirac, Bandol); Spanish Rosé (Navarra)

2. NATURAL WINE

REGION: **BEKAA VALLEY**

COUNTRY: **LEBANON**

GRAPE: **MERWAH**

PRICE: **££**

ALCOHOL: **12.5%**

SIGHT: **Pale yellow gold**

SMELL: **Toffee, herbs, apricot**

TASTE: **Moderate to good acidity**

FRUIT INTENSITY: **Ripe, exotic fruits**

TEXTURE: **Soft, luscious palate, smooth structure**

CONCLUSION: **Short skin-contact natural wine; subdued fruit with rich, powerful structure and grip**

COMMON BLIND TASTING MIX-UPS: **White Rhône blend**

ALTERNATIVES TO TRY
Old-vine Cypriot (Troodos) Xynisteri or Sicilian (Etna) Carricante; Slovakian, Slovenian or Croatian natural wines

3. ORANGE WINE

REGION: **KAKHETI**

COUNTRY: **GEORGIA**

GRAPE: **RKATSITELI**

PRICE: **££**

ALCOHOL: **13%**

SIGHT: **Amber gold**

SMELL: **Candied fruits, melon, burnt sugar, baked apples**

TASTE: **Moderate acidity**

FRUIT INTENSITY: **Less fruit, more layered toasted nuts, fenugreek, honey, herbs**

TEXTURE: **Dry and textural, with earthy, oily notes and a touch of bitterness**

CONCLUSION: **Typical *qvevri* style; less fruit, but elegant; layers of secondary flavours**

COMMON BLIND TASTING MIX-UPS: **Orange wine from Slovenia or Italy's Friuli**

ALTERNATIVES TO TRY
Georgian Kisi or Khivhki (Kakheti) *qvevri* wines

4. PIWI

REGION: **BORDEAUX**

COUNTRY: **FRANCE**

GRAPE: **CABERNET CORTIS**

PRICE: **£**

ALCOHOL: **12.5%**

SIGHT: **Deep crimson, with inky depth**

SMELL: **Rich blackcurrant, violets, lavender**

TASTE: **High acidity**

FRUIT INTENSITY: **Good fruit balance, with earthy, chocolate undertones**

TEXTURE: **Soft tannins, velvety mouthfeel**

CONCLUSION: **Good example of a Piwi grape; plenty of fruit, soft and approachable, with bone-dry finish**

COMMON BLIND TASTING MIX-UPS: **Merlot**

ALTERNATIVES TO TRY
German or Austrian Cabernet Cortis; Rondo (England, Wales)

PAIRING WINE AT HOME

Discovering different wine and food matches is a very personal journey – one that you will definitely enjoy.

In your own home, my advice would be to experiment and be flexible as a way of discovering your own preferences – and make it a fun adventure. There should be no hard-and-fast rules for pairing food and wine; it is such a personal experience and there are very few unpalatable combinations, but there are common-sense guidelines to follow.

Balance is the key – the food should not overpower the wine, or vice versa. The most perfect culinary combinations are about enhancement, and with experimentation you can find the perfect dish to flatter a wine. The best wines for matching with food are often those from cooler climates with high natural acidity – they can keep the mouth fresh and cut through any fat in the dish.

ACHIEVE THE RIGHT BALANCE

Here are my prompts and suggestions for getting the most out of food-and-wine matching.

- **Match weight and flavour intensity:** Think about the weight of the food and its flavour intensity – lighter dishes with ingredients like eggs or fish match better with lighter wines; heavier dishes with offal, smoked fish or strong cheeses welcome heavier richer wines.

- **Match texture:** Some meats are fattier than others (pork belly, lamb shoulder, goose, bacon), so they need richer, higher-alcohol white and red wines, but with good acidity to cut through the fat. The least fatty meats (wild game) match well with lighter wines like Pinot Noir or Gamay.

- **Check the sauce and seasoning:** This is very important when considering a wine match; the strongest flavour in the dish might well be the sauce or seasoning, rather than the main ingredient. Spiciness can bring out tannins and bitterness in wines. Spicy sauces with fish work best with spicy wines like Grüner Veltliner or soft reds like Garnacha; herby sauces match with the herbaceous notes of Vermentino or Cabernet Franc. A salty sauce is particularly wine-friendly, as it can enhance the wine's fruit.

- **Use a bridge ingredient:** Include fruit, vegetable or spicy preserves (tomato salsa, citrus preserve), or just the squeeze of a lemon – these can match with an element in the wine, such as a citrus sauce with Catarratto or Silvaner.

- **Contrast elements:** This will enhance the sweetness in the wine. Try a sweet wine matched with salty food, such as Tokaji Aszú and blue cheese.

- **Consider the cultural theme:** If you are creating a specific cuisine from a region or country, try matching the dish with a local wine. For example, if you are cooking a Greek dish that uses specific herbs (thyme), try to find a Greek wine from the same place as the recipe, and you will most likely find the flavours complement each other perfectly.

- **Think beyond the season:** Although popular in summer, rosés are not just for outdoor apéritifs; with their refreshing vibrancy, they can work throughout a meal. The only criteria is for the rosé to be dry and full-bodied, with enough textural richness to match with, for example, crab, spicy kebabs, game or wild-boar sausage, sheep's milk cheese, or fruit desserts.

- **Eschew tradition:** Try red as well as white with fish.

TOP CHARCUTERIE MATCHES

Pork Rillettes and Vouvray; Speck Ham and Lagrein; Ibérico Bellota Jamón and Fino Sherry*; Saucisson de Marin and Picpoul de Pinet; Gordal Olives and Txakolí; Salchichón Ibérico and Szekszárd Kadarka*; Basque Pâté and Palo Cortado Sherry; Prosciutto di Parma and Pinot Bianco; Spianata Calabra Salami and Ciro Rosso; Jambon de Corse and Provençal Rosé; Terrine de Campagne and mature Beaujolais Cru; Chourico and Touriga Nacional; Prosciutto di Parma and Pinot Bianco. [*pictured]

WINE MATCHES FOR MAIN INGREDIENTS

MAIN INGREDIENT	WHITE	RED	ROSÉ	ORANGE
Vegetarian	Fiano, Viognier, Falanghina	Grenache/Syrah Rhône blend, Garnacha, Tempranillo	Provençal or Languedoc dry rosé	Any orange wine
Vegan	Sauvignon Blanc, Verdejo	Pinot Noir, Cabernet Franc	Provençal or Languedoc dry rosé	Light and medium orange wines
Shellfish	Muscadet, Aligoté, Sancerre, Chablis		Rhône or Languedoc dry rosé	
Rich textured seafood	Albariño, Pinot Gris, Moschofilero, white Bordeaux	Pinot Noir	Xinomavro rosé	Light orange wines
Lean flaky fish (sole, haddock)	Vinho Verde, Verdejo, Albariño, Fruilano	Pinot Noir	Sancerre rosé	
Fuller-flavoured fish (salmon, monkfish)	Assyrtiko, Chenin Blanc, Encruzado, Sémillon, dry Riesling or Furmint	Gamay, Pinot Noir	Garnacha rosé	Light orange wines
Oily fish (mackerel, smoked salmon, red mullet)	White Rioja, Grenache Blanc, white Rhône, Cava, Sancerre	Pinot Noir, Gamay	Garnacha rosé	Medium orange wines
Chicken, turkey	Godello, Verdelho	Pinot Noir, Gamay		Medium orange wines
Duck	Chenin Blanc, Savagnin	Pinot Noir, Gamay, Kadarka	Kékfrankos rosé	Savagnin-based orange wine
Pork	Viognier, dry Riesling, Chardonnay	Pinot Noir, Gamay, Grenache, Tempranillo	Bordeaux dry rosé	Light to medium orange wines
Goose	Grüner Veltliner, Chenin Blanc	Pinot Noir, Barbera		Medium orange wines
Game	Alsace Riesling or Pinot Gris	Blaufränkisch, Gamay, Merlot, Shiraz/Syrah	Blaufränkisch rosé	Medium orange wines
Sausages	White Rhône, Alsace Riesling, Pecorino	Barbera, Carmenère, Sangiovese, Aglianico	Tavel, Zinfandel or Negroamaro rosé	Rkatsiteli or Kisi-based orange wine
Beef	Chenin Blanc, oaked Chardonnay	Cabernet Sauvignon		Medium to full orange wine (with beef kebabs)

MAIN INGREDIENT	WHITE	RED	ROSÉ	ORANGE
Lamb	Sauvignon Blanc, unfortified Palomino, Viognier, Pinot Gris	Pinot Noir, Tempranillo, Garnacha, Cabernet Franc, Sangiovese	Tavel, Rioja or Australian Grenache rosés	Medium to full orange wines
Offal	Viognier, Savagnin	Grenache/Syrah Rhône blend, Zinfandel		Rkatsiteli or Kisi-based orange wine
Thai	Riesling	Zweigelt, Pinot Noir, Merlot		Pinot Gris or Muscat-based orange wine
Chinese	Champagne, Gewurztraminer, German Riesling	Pinot Noir, Gamay, Cabernet Franc	Provençal dry rosé	Light skin-contact wine (Bacchus or Tsolikouri-based)
Indian	German Riesling Kabinett, New Zealand Sauvignon Blanc	Tempranillo, Garnacha, Malbec	Garnacha rosé	Medium to full orange wine
Fruit dessert	Sweet Chenin Blanc, Sweet Oloroso, Muscat de Beaumes-de-Venise			Muscat orange wine
Chocolate dessert	Malmsey Madeira, Liqueur Muscat, Amontillado Sherry	Banyuls, Tawny Port, Zinfandel, Amarone		Darker amber wines

VEGAN & VEGETARIAN WINES – WHAT ARE THEY?

Easy to understand, these wines are made without the use of animal-derived fining and stabilizing agents.

In winemaking, animal products can be used to remove organic matter and cloudy deposits, which might affect the colour, taste and flavour of the wine. The most commonly used include fish bladder membrane (isinglass), proteins from animal body parts (gelatin), casein, bone marrow or egg albumen (egg white). These are only for clarifying the wine; they are not additives.

When a fining agent is added, it sticks to the microscopic particles (by electrolyte attraction), creating very small clusters that drop to the bottom of the tank as sediment.

Now that more people are converting to vegan and vegetarian diets, winemakers are focusing on using only plant- and mineral-based methods for fining – such as silica gel, activated charcoal, pea protein or bentonite clay.

For vegetarians: Wines are only fined with egg albumen, casein, charcoal, pea protein, silica gel or bentonite clay.

For vegans: Wines are only fined with silica gel or bentonite clay.

Supermarkets and wine merchants often include vegan/vegetarian symbols on labels and websites, so it is now much simpler to search for wines that suit these diets.

WINE MATCHES FOR HERBS AND SPICES – SAUCES AND SEASONING

SAUCE, HERB OR SPICE	WHITE	RED
Creamy butter sauce	Godello, Marsanne, Roussanne, Chardonnay, Alsace Pinot Blanc, Riesling, Viognier, Champagne	
Basil, mint	Riesling, Cortese, Trebbiano, Verdicchio, skin-contact Moscato	Cabernet Sauvignon, Carmenère
Coriander	Chenin Blanc, Grüner Veltliner, Clare Valley Riesling, Viognier	Merlot
Dill	Sauvignon Blanc	Frappato, Gamay
Rosemary, thyme	Vermentino, white Rhône, Malagousia	Grenache, Syrah, Mourvèdre, Cabernet Sauvignon
Cinnamon	Riesling	Zinfandel, Carmenère, Grenache, Syrah
Tarragon	Sauvignon Blanc, Grüner Veltliner, Godello	Carmenère, Cabernet Franc
Tomato-based sauce	Loire Sauvignon Blanc, Pinot Grigio, Vernaccia	Tempranillo, Barbera, Corvina, Sangiovese, Cinsault
Paprika	Dry Furmint, Grüner Veltliner	Kékfrankos/Blaufränkisch, Tempranillo
Pepper	Grüner Veltliner	Syrah, Garnacha
Clove	Off-dry Riesling	Pinot Noir
Ginger	Dry Furmint, Grüner Veltliner, Hárslevelű, Gewurztraminer, Viognier	Grenache, Corvina
Garlic	Grüner Veltliner, skin-contact Rkatsiteli	Syrah
Star anise	Riesling	Barbera, Teroldego
Teriyaki	Riesling, Chenin Blanc	Gamay, Pinot Noir
Spicy, peppery barbecue sauce	Oaked Chardonnay, Pinot Gris	Zinfandel, Shiraz, Malbec, Grenache

TOP CHEESE MATCHES

Soft: Tomme de Chambrouze and Cape Chenin Blanc*; Valençay and aged Alsace Riesling; Époisses and Rully; St-Félicien and Pouilly-Fumé; Taleggio and Cortese.
Hard: Gruyère and Saumur Champigny*; Tomme de Savoie and Gringet de Savoie; Manchego and Garnacha; Orkney Grimbister and Godello; Comté and Vin Jaune.
Blue: Stilton and Banyuls*; Valdeón and Sweet Oloroso; Fourme d'Ambert and Tokaji Aszú. [*pictured]

CHOOSING WINE IN A RESTAURANT

A meal out in a restaurant can be both an enjoyable and an educational experience, offering a chance to discover new wines as well as food pairings – particularly when you have an expert sommelier on hand to guide you.

CHOOSING WINE WHEN EATING OUT

A restaurant wine list is there to enhance the dining experience, not to intimidate the customer. A good list should reflect the menu and ethos of the place – and the philosophy of the cooking. The sommelier should be adept at reading the customer, helping them understand the list and working out how they can help.

One of the best tips if you are going out with a group of friends, business colleagues or celebrating a special occasion – and you know the restaurant you are going to and that you will be the one choosing the wine – is to do a bit of prep beforehand. Browse the menu and wine list online, so that you have some idea of what is on offer, as well as the prices.

If it is a more casual impromptu restaurant visit, that's when the skills of a good sommelier come into play, helping you feel confident and relaxed so that you can enjoy the moment.

START AT THE BACK

My own advice is to order your dishes, then take time to read the wine list when you know what everyone is eating. I often start at the back of the list as the geeky stuff is often there – and I always ask the sommelier questions, because they compiled the list and know the chef's food style. Remember, sauces and seasoning are often more important than the main ingredient when choosing a wine to match.

Seafood-led Lyla Restaurant in Edinburgh, Scotland, gained its first Michelin star in 2025.

WINE ORDERING Q&A

Here I have enlisted help from two leading sommeliers from Michelin-starred restaurants in Edinburgh, Scotland: Alsace-born Joel Bastian, head sommelier of The Kitchin, and Scots-born Stuart Skea, head sommelier of Lyla.

SHOULD I AVOID THE HOUSE WINE?

This is one of the most frequently asked questions, because some house wines can be a bit lacklustre. If it is a good restaurant, the house wine should have been well chosen, but it might not be the most exciting wine on the list.

'A house wine should be representative of the restaurant's values and philosophy, so one should put faith in the house wine,' says Skea.

Bastian agrees: 'You can judge a fair bit of the place's approach by trying their house wine, but it might be better to look at the wine-by-the-glass selection instead.'

DO I CONSIDER A WINE-BY-THE-GLASS OPTION?

Rather than choosing a bottle of house wine, you could try this option – it is also a good way of experimenting with different wines.

'We offer 15 whites and 15 reds by the glass, including recognizable varietals and more obscure offerings at all price points. Half are classics like Albariño, Rioja, St-Émilion; others are more obscure wines like Rkatsiteli, Timorasso, Barbera and Pais,' comments Bastian.

DO I JUST CHOOSE THE CLASSICS?

What a good sommelier looks for is balance, freshness, fruit purity and a sense of place.

'It is easier to choose familiar names, but I suggest going off-piste and making a new discovery; as wonderful as Chablis is, you can get it anywhere, whereas Galician Godello or Santorini Assyrtiko might become your new favourite grape,' says Skea.

CAN I SEND A WINE BACK?

Don't be afraid to say if you think a wine is faulty – remember, the customer is always right.

'For a sommelier, it is best to start a conversation with the guest and let them explain what they think is wrong with the wine, so you can maybe advise another wine more suited to their taste,' Bastian recommends.

WHERE DO I START?

Ask questions, and be guided.

According to Bastian, 'A good sommelier should read the customer, find out what they like, what they normally spend and their taste. More often than not, it's not about price.'

Skea agrees: 'Don't feel nervous: ask questions and don't worry about pronunciation – no one knows the proper way to pronounce Xinomavro.'

CAN I CHOOSE ONE WINE FOR ALL DISHES?

If everyone has ordered different dishes and you're picking one wine, it needs to be versatile.

'Avoid anything too alcoholic, oaky, tannic or acidic,' suggests Skea. 'My go-to versatile wine is the rich-textured, minerally white blend Aristargos from David and Nadia in Swartland... Remember, white wine can sometimes be a better pairing than red with meat.'

Bastian says, 'Alsace Pinot Gris works with seafood, but equally with meat – for example, Martin Schaetzel's Roche Granitique Pinot Gris.'

HOW DO I CHOOSE A GOOD-VALUE WINE?

For best value, Skea suggests Spain, South Africa and Portugal, while Bastian recommends Portugal, Romania and Moldova.

Skea adds, 'Explore beyond everyday names; typically, more unfamiliar grapes and regions are the ones that overdeliver in quality and are a product of passion and discovery. Someone has listed these out of love and enthusiasm.'

ORIGINS OF TASTE

WINE COUNTRIES OF THE WORLD

We have learned how to taste wine, how its grapes are grown in the vineyard, how it is made and about the range of styles; now it is time to focus on the origin of the wine. Here, we look in detail at the classic regions around the world, as well as highlighting the expanding number of countries now producing wine.

Wine strongly reflects the environment where its grapes are grown, and location is one of the key drivers to quality and style in a wine. Careful site selection will become even more important as our climate changes – and our wine world's horizons are continually changing.

To help the wine-lover dig deep into this ever-expanding wine world, 51 countries are detailed here, covering key facts, indigenous grapes of note and recommended producers. There is also a directory of the best wineries to visit in each region (*see* opposite). As the late Professor Emile Peynaud once said, 'Wine is a reflection of the people who make it and the region that produces it.'

For the wine traveller, reading about wine regions with glass in hand, and even better visiting the vineyard to see where the wine is made, are the most rewarding experiences.

WORLD WINE PRODUCTION

Global wine production: 226 million hectolitres.

WHO MAKES THE MOST WINE?

Top three countries that make the most wine:
1. Italy: 44 million hectolitres
2. France: 36 million hectolitres
3. Spain: 31 million hectolitres.

SIZE OF THE WORLD'S VINEYARD

Global vineyard area: 7.1 million hectares.

WHO HAS THE MOST VINES?

Top three countries with the largest vineyard area:
1. Spain: 930,000 hectares
2. France: 783,000 hectares
3. China: 753,000 hectares.

[OIV data 2024]

Sauska's stylish new winery in Tokaj, Hungary, looks like two flying saucers have landed in the middle of the volcanic vineyard landscape.

DIRECTORY OF WINERIES TO VISIT

This is my pick of the best wineries to visit. For more on wine tourism, *see page* 160.

FRANCE

CHAMPAGNE

Ruinart, Taittinger (Reims); Alfred Gratien, Gosset, Moet & Chandon, (Épernay); Ayala, Henri Giraud (Aÿ); Vilmart (Rilly-La-Montagne); André Clouet, Pierre Paillard (Bouzy); Pierre Gimonnet (Cuis); Larmandier-Bernier (Vertus); Drappier (Aube).

BURGUNDY

Christian Moreau, Daniel Dampt, La Chablisienne, William Fèvre (Chablis); Faiveley, Hudelot-Noëllat (Nuits); Barolet Pernot, Bouchard Père & Fils, Joseph Drouhin, Lejeune, Louis Jadot, Moulin aux Moines (Beaune); Alain Hasard, Dureuil-Janthial, Michel Briday (Chalonnaise); Beauregard (Mâconnais); Thivin (Beaujolais).

BORDEAUX

Left Bank: Cos d'Estournel (St-Estèphe); Lynch-Bages, Pichon-Longueville Baron (Pauillac); Beychevelle (St-Julien); d'Arsac (Margaux); Haut-Bailly, Smith Haut Lafitte (Pessac-Léognan); Suduiraut, Yquem (Sauternes). **Right Bank:** Gazin (Pomerol); Fleur de Boüard (Lalande de Pomerol); Rivière (Fronsac); Dominique, Montlabert, Pavie, Canon-la-Gaffelière (St-Émilion).

LOIRE

Bruno Cormerais, Cléray, Luneau-Papin (Muscadet); Baumard, Coulée de Serrant (Savennières); Forges (Coteaux du Layon); Filliatreau, Gratien & Meyer (Saumur); Thibaud Boudignon (Anjou); Bernard Baudry, Charles Joguet, Couly-Dutheil (Chinon); Yannick Amirault (Bourgueil); Frédéric Malibeau (St Nicolas de Bourgueil); Nicolas Paget (Touraine); François Chidaine, Taille-aux-Loups (Montlouis); Huet, Vincent Carême (Vouvray); Henri Bourgeois, Mellot, Pinard (Sancerre); Tracy, Ladoucette (Pouilly-Fumé).

RHÔNE & PROVENCE

Northern Rhône: Guigal (Côte-Rôtie); Cuilleron (Condrieu); Chapoutier (Hermitage). **Southern Rhône:** Beaucastel, Caillou, Pegau, Vieux Télégraphe (Châteauneuf-du-Pape); Santa Duc (Gigondas); Bernardins (Venise); Aqueria (Tavel). **Provence:** Bégude, Tempier (Bandol); Leoube, Richeaume, Rimauresq (Provence).

SOUTHERN FRANCE

Southwest: Chambert (Cahors); Montus, Plaimont (Madiran). **Languedoc:** Calmel & Joseph, Ollieux Romanis (Corbières); Jonquières (Larzac); d'Anglès (La Clape). **Roussillon:** Jonquères d'Oriola, Gauby, Soula **Jurançon:** Clos Lapeyre.

ALSACE, JURA & SAVOIE

Alsace: Barmes-Buècher, Bott-Geyl, Dopff au Moulin, Emile Beyer, Hugel, Marcel Deiss, Meyer-Fonne, Rolly Gassmann, Trimbach, Weinbach, Zind-Humbrecht. **Jura:** A&M Tissot, Berthet-Bondet, Fumey Chatelain, Montbourgeau, Pignier. **Savoie:** Berthollier, Claude Quenard, J-C Masson, Ripaille.

ITALY

NORTHWEST ITALY

Piedmont: Aldo Conterno, Cascina Fontana, Chiara Boschis, Ettore Germano, Fontanafredda, Marchesi di Barolo, Michele Chiarlo (Barolo); Bruno Giacosa, Cascina delle Rose, Gaja (Barbaresco); Cornarea (Roero); La Mesma (Gavi); La Colombera, Massa (Colli Tortonesi); Nervi (Gattinara). **Lombardy:** Bellavista, Ca' del Bosco (Franciacorta); Ar Pe Pe, Barbacan, Nino Negri (Valtellina); Conte Vistarino, Fiamberti, Mazzolino (Oltrepò Pavese); Ca' dei Frati, Zenato (Lugana).

NORTHEAST ITALY

Alto Adige: Franz Haas, Lageder, Tiefenbrunner. **Trentino:** Ferrari Trento, Foradori, San Leonardo. **Veneto:** Allegrini, Masi (Valpolicella); Anselmi, Pieropan (Soave). **Friuli Venezia Giulia:** Jermann, Lis Neris, Vignai da Duline.

CENTRAL ITALY

Tuscany: Ama, Antinori, Cecione, Coltibuono, Fontodi, Isola e Olena, Ricasoli, Vicchiomaggio, Volpaia (Chianti); Potentino (Maremma); Banfi, Barbi, Biondi-Santi, Poggio Antico (Montalcino); Avignonesi (Montepulciano); Capezzana (Carmignano); Ornellaia, San Guido, Sette Cieli (Bolgheri). **Emilia-Romagna:** Baldini, Moretto, Rinaldini. **Umbria:** Neri (Orvieto); Lungarotti (Torgiano); Carini, Madrevite (Perugia), Arnaldo Caprai (Montefalco). **Latium:** Fiorano, Volpi. **Marches:** Bruscia, Pievalta. **Abruzzo:** Emidio Pepe.

SOUTH ITALY

Campania: Feudi di San Gregorio, Mastroberardino. **Basilicata:** Basilisco, D'Angelo, Elena Fucci. **Puglia:** A Mano, Morella, Mottura, Pastini, Polvanera, San Marzano. **Calabria:** Librandi, Vita, Arcuri. **Sicily:** Bartoli, Benanti, Cornelissen, Cos, Donnafugata, Graci, Occhipinti, Planeta. **Sardinia:** Contini.

SPAIN

NORTHWEST SPAIN

Rías Baixas: Fefiñanes, Galegas, Maior de Mendoza, Pazo Señorans, Zárate. **Ribeiro:** Arman, Gomariz. **Ribeira**

Sacra: Bibei, Guimaro. **Valdeorras:** Valdesil. **Monterrei:** Muradella. **Bierzo:** Palacios. **Asturias:** Vidas, Urogallo. **Getaria:** Txomin Etxaníz. **Toro:** Valbusenda. **Rueda:** Naia.

NORTHEAST SPAIN

Rioja: La Rioja Alta, López de Heredia, Muga, Murrieta, Remelluri, Riscal, Ysios. **Ribera del Duero:** Abadía Retuerta, Emilio Moro, Hacienda Monasterio. **Aragón:** Arinzano, Artazu, Otazu (Navarra). El Escocés Volante (Calatayud); Frontonio (Valdejalon). **Alella:** Alta Alella, Celler les Aus. **Penedès:** Gramona, Juvé y Camps, Torres. **Priorat:** Mogador, Martinet. **Montsant:** Acustic, Domenech. **Terra Alta:** Edetària, Pinol.

CENTRAL SPAIN

Cebreros/Sierra de Gredos: Comando G, Maranones, Rico Neuvo, Soto Manrique. **Salamanca:** Cambrico. **Valdepenas:** Estrellas, Los Llanos. **Manchuela:** Altolandon, Gratias. **Utiel-Requena:** Chozas Carrascal, Murviedro, Mustiguillo. **Valencia:** Celler del Roure. **Jumilla:** Carchelo, Juan Gil. **Yecla:** Castano.

SOUTH & ISLANDS SPAIN

Jerez: Alonso, Barbadillo, Fernando de Castilla, González Byass, Gutierrez Colosia, Luis Pérez, Ximénez-Spínola, Tradición. **Montilla-Moriles:** Alvear, Toro Albala. **Málaga:** Bentomiz, Malaga Virgen. **Mallorca:** 4 Kilos, Anima Negra, Can Majoral, Can Xanet. **Canary Islands:** Arautava, Suertes del Marques, Tajinaste (Tenerife); Bermejos, Titerok-Akaet (Lanzarote); Bentayga, Bien de Altura, Tameran (Gran Canaria).

PORTUGAL

Vinho Verde: Anselmo Mendes, Soalheiro. **Douro:** Fonseca Panascal, Graham's Bomfim, Nápoles, Noval, Rosa, Wine & Soul. **Dao:** Carvalhais, Roques. **Bairrada:** Filipa Pato, Luis Pato, Vadio. **Lisbon:** AdegaMãe, Chocapalha, Pancas, Sant'Ana. **Colares:** Adega de Colares. **Alentejo:** Cartuxa, Cortes de Cima, Esporão, Mouchão. **Algarve:** Barranco Longo, Morgado de Quintão, Miradouro, Vales. **Madeira:** Barbeito, Henriques & Henriques, Pereira d'Oliveira.

GERMANY

Ahr: Bertram-Baltes, Fiebrich, Meyer-Nakel, Stodden. **Mosel:** Dr Loosen, JJ Prüm, Maximin Grunhaus, Volxem. **Nahe:** Donnhoff, Schafer-Frolich, Schonleber. **Rheinhessen:** Dreissigacker, Kühling-Gillot, Raumland, Wittmann. **Pfalz:** Bürklin-Wolf, Knipser, Müller-Catoir. **Rheingau:** Kesseler, Kloster Eberbach, PJ Kühn, Schloss Johannisberg, Weil. **Baden:** Bernhard Huber, Dr Heger. **Württemberg:** Aldinger. **Franken:** Horst Sauer.

AUSTRIA

Wachau: Domäne Wachau, Emmerich Knoll, Pichler-Krutzler, Prager. **Kamptal:** Bründlmayer, Hirsch, Loimer, Schloss Gobelsburg. **Kremstal:** Nikolaihof. **Wienviertel, Wagram, Traisental & Vienna:** Bauer, Ebner-Ebenauer, Ehmoser, Huber, Weininger, Zillinger. **Thermenregion & Carnuntum:** Artner, Muhr, Reinisch. **Burgenland:** Feiling-Artinger, Beck, Igler, Lentsch, Moric, Kracher, Pittnauer, Prieler, Schiefer, Schrock, Tschida. **Styria:** Polz, Sattlerhof.

SWITZERLAND

Valais: Chanton, Domaine des Muses, Jean-René Germanier, McCulloch Wines, Simon Maye. **Vaud:** Blaise Duboux, Domaine Dufaux. **Trois Lacs:** Chambleau, Krebs & Steiner, Montmollin. **Deutschschweiz:** Besson-Strasser, Meier, Pircher. **Ticino:** Gialdi, Luigi Zanini.

ENGLAND & WALES

Bucks: Harrow & Hope. **Essex:** Danbury Ridge, New Hall. **East Anglia:** Flint. **Kent:** Balfour, Evremond, Gusbourne, Herbert Hall, Simpsons. **Sussex:** Ashling, Bolney, Breaky Bottom, Nyetimber, Ridgeview, Sugrue South Downs, Wiston. **Hampshire:** Black Chalk, Exton Park, Hambledon, Hattingley, The Grange. **Wiltshire:** Domaine Hugo. **Dorset, Devon & Cornwall:** Bride Valley, Camel Valley, Furleigh, Langham. **Wales:** Ancre Hill, Montgomery.

GREECE

North Greece: Alpha Estate (Amyndeon); Gerovassiliou (Epanomi); Boutari, Dalamara, Kir Yianni (Naoussa); Biblia Chora (Kavala); Pavlidis (Drama). **Peloponnese:** Skouras (Argos). **Islands:** Lyrarakis (Crete); Argyros, Karamolegos, Sigalas (Santorini).

BULGARIA

Danube Plain: Bononia, Borovitza, Burgozone, Haralambievi, Tipchenitza. **North Thracian Lowlands:** Bessa Valley, Chateau Copsa, Eduardo Miroglio, Minkov. **Struma Valley:** Aya Estate, Libera, Orbelia, Villa Melnik, Damianitza. **South Sakar:** Bratanov, Castra Rubra, Terra Tangra.

HUNGARY

Balaton: Figula, Gilvesy, Homola, Palffy, Zelna. **Somló:** Kofejto, Kolonics, Kreinbacher, Spiegelberg. **Upper Pannonia:** Csetvei, Etyeki Kuria, Pannonhalma Archabbey, Steigler. **Eger:** Bolyki, St Andrea, Tibor Gál. **Tokaj:** Demeter Zoltán, Disznókő, Kikelet, Oremus, Patricius, Sauska, Szepsy. **Szekszárd:** Heimann, Lajver, Takler, Vida Peter. **Villány:** Gere Attila, Heumann, Sauska, Vylyan.

ROMANIA

Transylvania: Darabont, Villa Vinèa. **Moldovan Hills:** Cotnari, Girboiu. **Muntenia & Oltenia Hills:** Avincis, Budureasca, Ceptura, Davino, Metamorfosis, Prince Ştirbey. **Dobrogea:** Dropia, Rasova. **Banat:** Cramele Recaş, Petro Vaselo.

ARMENIA, MOLDOVA & UKRAINE

Armenia: Hin Areni, Karas, Trinity Canyon, Noa, Van Ardi, Voskevaz, Zorah. **Moldova:** Cricova, Fautor, Purcari, Salcuta, Vartely. **Ukraine:** Beyrush, Chizay, Shabo, Villa Tinta.

GEORGIA

Kakheti: Alaverdi, Mildiani, Orgo Teleda, Pheasant's Tears, Twins Wine House. **Kartli:** Mukhrani, Ori Marani. **Imereti:** Baia's Wine. **Samegrelo:** Oda Martvili.

CENTRAL & NORTHERN EUROPE

Slovakia: Slobodne, Pivnica Brhlovce, Bott Frigyes, Belá, Ostrožovič. **Czechia:** Cibulka, Krásná Hora, Vican.

CROATIA & SLOVENIA

Croatia: Cattunar, Kozlović, Matošević, Clai (Istria), Matusko (Dalmatia); Tomac (Croatian Uplands). **Slovenia:** Batic, Edi Simčič, Marjan Simčič, Movia (Primorje); Istenič (Posavje); Dveri-Pax, Marof (Podravje).

WESTERN BALKANS

Serbia: Aleksandrovic, Despotika, Deurić, Jeremić, Matalj, Radovanović, Tarpos, Tonkovic, Zvonko Bogdan. **Bosnia & Herzegovina:** Tvrdos, Vukoje. **Kosovo:** Stone Castle. **Montenegro:** Kopitovic, Lipovac, Markovic. **Albania:** Alpeta, Cobo, Kokomani, Uka. **N Macedonia:** Kamnik, Tikveš, Stobi.

EASTERN MEDITERRANEAN

Turkey: Chamlija, Kavaklidere, Suvla, Urla. **Cyprus:** Tsiakkas, Marathatra, Argyrides, Kyperounda, Makarounas, Zambartas. **Lebanon:** Ixsir, Kefraya, Massaya, Musar, Tourelles. **Israel:** Castel, Golan Heights, Tzora.

THE US – CALIFORNIA

Mendocino: Drew, Pennyroyal, Roederer Estate. **Sonoma:** Buena Vista, Hirsch, Marimar Torres, Ramey, Ridge (Lytton Springs). **Napa:** Corison, Far Niente, Frog's Leap, Montelena, Shafer, Shramsberg, Spottswoode, Stags' Leap. **North Central Coast:** Birichino, Ridge (Monte Bello). **South Central Coast:** A Tribute to Grace, Scar of the Sea, Stolo, Talley. **Lodi, Sierra Foothills:** Harney Lane, M2, Michael David, Terra Rouge/Easton.

REST OF THE US

Oregon: Adelsheim, Bergstrom, Domaine Drouhin, Domaine Serene, Eyrie, Nicolas-Jay. **Washington State:** Gramercy, Kiona, L'Ecole, Syncline. **New York State:** Bloomer Creek, Dr Konstantin Frank, Hermann J Wiemer, Ravines. **Virginia:** Barboursville, Early Mountain, King, RdV.

CANADA

Ontario: Bachelder, Henry of Pelham, Inniskillin, Hidden Bench, Malivoire. **British Columbia:** Mission Hill, Phantom Creek, Quails' Gate. **Nova Scotia:** Benjamin Bridge, Luckett, Lightfoot & Wolfville.

CHILE

Elqui, Limarí & Aconcagua: Alcohuaz, Errázuriz, Falernia, Seña, Tabalí. **Casablanca, San Antonio & Leyda:** Casablanca, Casa Marín, Garces Silva, Matetic. **Maipo:** Antiyal, De Martino, Odfjell, Undurraga, Santa Rita. **Rapel:** Casa Silva, Emiliana, Lapostelle, Maturana, Montes, Vik. **Curico, Maule & Itata:** Bouchon, Echeverria, Torres.

ARGENTINA

Salta: Colome, Esteco, Piattelli. **Mendoza:** Catena, Durigutti, Mendel, Monteviejo, Salentein, Zuccardi. **Patagonia:** Chacra, Humberto Canale.

URUGUAY

Canelones & Montevideo: Bouza, Deicas, Pisano. **Atlantida:** Bracco Bosca, Pablo Fallabrino. **Maldonado:** Cerro del Toro, Garzon, Viña Edén.

REST OF SOUTH AMERICA

Brazil: Casa Valduga, Cave Geisse, Pizzato, Salton. **Peru:** Intipalka, Tacama. **Bolivia:** Campos de Solana, Cepas de Fuego, La Concepcion.

AUSTRALIA

Western Australia: Cullen, Cherubino, Frankland River, Leeuwin, Vasse Felix. **South Australia:** Ashton Hills, d'Arenberg, Grosset, Henschke, Jim Barry, Shaw & Smith. **Victoria:** Campbells, Château Tahbilk, Giant Steps, Giaconda, Ten Minutes by Tractor, Yarra Yering. **Tasmania:** Domaine A, Derwent Estate, Freycinet, Holm Oak, House of Arras. **New South Wales:** Brokenwood, Clonakilla, Tyrrell's. **Queensland:** Hidden Creek, Sirromet.

NEW ZEALAND

Waiheke Island/Auckland: Kumeu River, Man O' War, Stonyridge. **Hawke's Bay:** Craggy Range, Te Mata. **Martinborough:** Ata Rangi, Dry River, Palliser. **Marlborough:** Cloudy Bay, Dog Point, Giesen, Greywacke, Hunter's, Te Whare Ra. **Nelson:** Neudorf, Seifried. **Canterbury:** Greystone, Pegasus Bay. **Central Otago:** Burn Cottage, Felton Road, Rippon.

SOUTH AFRICA

Constantia: Buitenverwachting, Klein Constantia. **Stellenbosch:** Kanonkop, Rustenberg, Rust-en-Vrede, Tokara, Waterford. **Elgin:** Almenkerk, Iona, Paul Cluver, Richard Kershaw. **Walker Bay:** Creation, Hamilton Russell, Newton Johnson. **Robertson:** De Wetshof, Springfield. **Swartland:** AA Badenhorst, Mullineux. **Cape South Coast:** Sijnn, Strandveld.

ASIA

China: Changyu Tinlot, Grace Vineyards, Silver Heights, Xige, Longyu. **Japan:** Grace Wine, Kumamoto, Mercian, Takahata. **India:** Chandon India, Grover Zampa, Sula, Vallonne.

VISITING WINERIES

Wine tourism is now big business. Many new wineries today are built with the visitor in mind – with a restaurant, tasting room, café, picnic and concert area and even accommodation – and wine regions all around the world are promoting their own wine routes.

In the 21st century, wine tourism has become a phenomenon, and wineries are now much more welcoming to wine-lovers. Before this, if you weren't working in the trade, it was difficult to gain entrance. I have personal experience of this, having organized tours for wine-lovers around the world for over 25 years. Visitor experiences are now a thriving and innovative part of the wine business, as wineries realize that attracting people to visit their vineyard and cellar door to taste (and hopefully buy) their wine is an essential part of the brand connection.

THE WINE EXPERIENCE

The wine tourist experience really first began in New World countries. California, Australia, New Zealand, South Africa, Chile and Argentina didn't just have wine labels named by grape variety that were accessible; their young wine regions were inviting and welcoming to visitors too.

Wine tourism was becoming a concept just at the time of the major expansion of their wineries, so they were built with the visitor experience in mind, with food and tasting facilities included, with vistas out across the vineyards, and cellars with special walkways for their guests. They realized that wine tourism was about entertainment – and there was money to be made.

FROM CELLAR TO WINE MARATHONS

In France, Spain, Italy, Portugal, Austria and Germany, a cellar-door policy of selling direct from the vineyard existed (called Heurige in Austria), but the wines were drunk there in the regions, and few wineries had sophisticated visitor facilities.

The quirky d'Arenberg Cube set in the vineyards in McLaren Vale, South Australia, has a tasting room and art exhibits.

Marqués de Riscal's hotel, designed by Frank Gehry, adjoins its winery near medieval Elciego village in Rioja Alavesa, Spain.

Interestingly, the Champagne houses first spotted the potential and began offering cellar tours. Other regions followed suit, but it has taken a long time for things to change, even though Europe has great wine festivals, charity wine auctions, wine museums, vineyard cycling routes, balloon trips and marathon races. There are now ever larger and more sophisticated food-and-wine festivals globally, from Oregon to Marlborough.

Even today, some regions are difficult to access, due to the small size of their businesses and cellars. For example, in Burgundy, leading producers are often not open to the public, and Bordeaux has been slow to change, as imposing-looking châteaux lock their gates at the weekend, a time when many wine-lovers would choose to visit. Things are changing however, and some châteaux are now very welcoming. The price of a visit can vary considerably too: in California, Napa wineries charge eye-wateringly high prices for tastings.

Now we are seeing wineries in emerging countries like China, Georgia, Bulgaria, Hungary and Greece with ever more sophisticated tasting rooms and restaurants.

For the wine-lover, there is nothing better than enjoying a wine in its location, where it was made – and it is now possible to do this all over the world.

PLANNING YOUR VISIT

You might prefer a self-guided holiday, driving (or cycling) around different wineries at your own pace, but that can be tricky when it comes to tasting. That is why so many people prefer to be in a group led by an expert who knows the best wineries to visit. For more information on the tours I run, visit rosemurraybrown.com.

FOLLOW THE ETIQUETTE

Make a reservation, as some wineries are only available by appointment. If you need to cancel or are running late, remember to contact them. Small family wineries are often busy in their vineyards; visiting during the harvest can be interesting, but some wineries do not allow visitors at that time.

Choose a maximum of two to three wineries per day to visit – and leave enough time to get from place to place. Before you go, read up about the wineries and region, so that you can ask questions at the visit; the winemaker will also appreciate it if you take notes on their wines.

Avoid wearing perfumes, colognes and high heels – and eat beforehand unless you are eating at the winery; and of course, when you are sampling, don't forget to spit.

FRANCE

France is the world's second-largest wine-producing country by volume, with a long wine history dating back to the 6th century BCE. Today it is considered the birthplace of the modern wine industry, as the classic French regions of Champagne, Burgundy and Bordeaux have influenced winemakers worldwide, and top French grapes are now so well travelled that they are known as 'international grapes'. This famous wine country is also known for its strict appellation regulations and diversity across its regions.

KEY FACTS

Size: 783,000 hectares
Styles: white, red, rosé, sparkling, sweet, fortified
Wine laws: AOP, IGP, Vin de France

CHAMPAGNE

Home of the world's best sparkling wines. Although there are many imitators today, only sparkling wines made here, in this legally defined area across 319 villages, can be called Champagne.

The traditional method (*see page* 102), with second fermentation in bottle, is used exclusively here but is not unique to the region. There are four subzones: Montagne de Reims (Pinot Noir); Vallée de la Marne (frost-resistant Pinot Meunier); sunnier Côte des Blancs (Chardonnay); and 170km southeast of Reims with 23% of the region, Côte des Bar (Aube), which is closer to Chablis than Reims (Pinot Noir on Kimmeridgian limestone). With thousands of growers, an increasing number now make and sell their own fizz (over 3,000), focusing on highlighting their own terroir – the polar opposite of the big brands' subzone blending.
Producers to try: *Charles Heidsieck, Drappier, Jacques Lassaigne, Pierre Paillard, Pol Roger*

The gently undulating landscape of the Champagne region in France has an average gradient of 12 per cent. The steepest slopes reach 60 per cent.

KEY FACTS
White grapes: Chardonnay (31%), Pinot Gris, Pinot Blanc, Petit Meslier, Arbane
Red grapes: Pinot Noir (38%), Pinot Meunier (31%)
Size: 34,000 hectares
Styles: mostly sparkling; white, red
Main soil: chalk

KEY STYLES
NV: blend of vintages
Vintage: single year
Rosé: macerated red grapes or red Pinot Noir added at blending
Blanc de Blancs: white fizz from white grapes
Blanc de Noirs: white fizz from red grapes

CHANGES IN PRODUCTION
Current challenges: spring frost (prune later), humidity, heatwaves (riper grapes, lower acid)
Future positive: disease-resistant Piwi grape Voltis now authorized in five per cent of total vineyard

BURGUNDY

Once considered rustic, this bucolic region is now the height of elegance and finesse, and with insatiable demand, its prices are skyrocketing. Most of its wines are varietals, and terroir is key here, with 96 appellations, including Beaujolais. Burgundy's geology is incredibly diverse – from northerly Chablis and its firm, steely Chardonnay, to the Côte d'Or's floral, spicy Côte de Nuits Pinot Noir and Côte de Beaune's softer Pinot and intense Chardonnay. Bourgogne is renowned for artisanal, soft, aromatic reds and crisp, minerally whites. Côte Chalonnaise and Mâconnais now offer better value, as does southerly Beaujolais from its ten crus.

There are no producer classifications here and quality varies dramatically even within a vineyard, where multiple growers own rows of vines; a 'monopole' vineyard has just one owner. It is the vineyard that is classified within Burgundy's pyramid – referred to as the *climat*, a parcel of vines carefully delimited with particular geological and climatic conditions.

Producers to try: *Armand Rousseau, de Montille, Eleni & Edouard Vocoret, Genot Boulanger, Joseph Drouhin, Méo-Camuzet, Robert Chevillon*

The 15th-century Hospices de Beaune, a former charitable almshouse, in Beaune, France, holds an annual charity wine auction and dinner.

KEY FACTS
White grapes: Aligoté, Chardonnay
Red grapes: Pinot Noir; Gamay (in Beaujolais)
Size: 32,000 hectares, plus 13,500 in Beaujolais
Styles: white, red, rosé, sparkling
Main soil: Clay-limestone

VINEYARD CLASSIFICATION PYRAMID
Grands Crus: 33
Premiers Crus: 684
Village: 44
Regional / subregional: 8

CHANGES IN PRODUCTION
Current challenges: spring frost, humidity, summer drought, heat stress (early bud-burst/harvest, high sugars, low acid), sky-high prices
Future positives: growers adapting canopies, correcting grape-to-leaf ratio, raising vine rows to increase shade and avoid sunburned grapes.

A new generation is experimenting with natural wines and zero sulphur, while established domaines also now use inert containers (large *foudres*, clay amphorae, concrete eggs and glass globes) alongside traditional oak barrels to enhance subtlety and complexity.

BORDEAUX

Renowned worldwide for its red wines and glamorous châteaux, Bordeaux is the largest fine-wine region in the world. In its diversity, scope and size, Bordeaux is unrivalled.

The Gironde estuary and rivers Dordogne and Garonne influence the region. On the left bank (left of the estuary and Garonne), later-ripening Cabernet Sauvignon is king of the deep-gravel soils of Médoc and Graves, making structured tannic reds. Merlot and Cabernet Franc thrive on the clay and limestone soils in St-Émilion and Pomerol in Libournais on the right bank, known for more supple reds. Bordeaux whites range from oaked dry Pessac-Léognan blends to famous Sauternes and Barsac botrytis-affected sweet wines.

There are 65 appellations in six categories: Médoc, Blaye and Bourg, Libournais, Entre-Deux-Mers, Sauternes and Barsac, and the catch-all Bordeaux and Bordeaux Supérieur.

Bordeaux blending tradition is unique, and there are no rules; blends depend on terroir, structure, ageing potential and fruit, alongside the personality of the vintage and château. Classification is given to the property in Bordeaux, not to the terroir as it is in Burgundy. The 1855 'Cru Classe' ranking of 58 châteaux in communes St-Éstephe, Pauillac, St-Julien, Margaux and Graves still stands today.

Classed Growth châteaux tend to grab the headlines, but many small family-owned vineyards off the beaten track offer great value.
Producers to try: *Fourcas-Dupre* (Listrac); *Dutruch Grand Poujeaux* (Moulis); *Dauzac* (Margaux); *Sociando-Mallet* (Haut-Médoc); *Roc de Cambes* (Bourg); *Thieuley* (Entre-Deux-Mers); *Guillot Clauzel* (Pomerol); *Annereaux* (Lalande de Pomerol); *Jean Faure and L'If* (St-Émilion); *Puygueraud* (Francs); *L'Aurage* (Castillon)

KEY FACTS

White grapes: Sémillon, Sauvignon Blanc, Muscadelle
Red grapes: Cabernet Sauvignon, Cabernet Franc, Merlot
Size: 110,000 hectares
Styles: white, red, rosé, sparkling, sweet
Main soils: gravel, clay, limestone

CHANGES IN PRODUCTION

Current challenges: overproduction, extreme weather
Future positive: experimentation with new grapes; first French region to authorize new grapes to help combat climate change: Alvarinho, Liliorila; Arinarnoa, Castets, Marselan, Touriga Nacional.

As world demand for red wine decreases, this traditional region must appeal to new consumers with dry whites, rosé and Crémant, and visits.

RHÔNE

France's oldest region is now second-largest after Bordeaux. The valley divides north from south; its long-lived reds are most famous, but other styles tempt too. The northern climate is continental, with steep-sloped vineyards and only five per cent of Rhône's output. Côte-Rôtie, Cornas and Hermitage make dark, peppery Syrah, while Crozes-Hermitage and St-Joseph offer lighter, value reds. Condrieu's whites are from Viognier. Heading south, a warmer, windier Mediterranean climate prevails, with drought and heat-stress concerns. Heading south, Grenache and friends make hearty reds in Côtes du Rhône and its villages. Vast Châteauneuf-du-Pape hosts many organic growers, making powerful reds, but lesser-known Gigondas, Vacqueyras, Duché d'Uzès, Costières de Nîmes, Cairanne, Puyméras and Ventoux offer value. Whites tend to be blends down here; Tavel has outstanding rosé, and Beaumes-de-Venise makes famous sweet VDN.
Producers to try: *André Perret, Chapoutier, Guigal* (North); *Clos du Caillou, Montirius, Mordorée, Santa Duc, Vieux Telégraphe* (South)

KEY FACTS

White grapes: Grenache Blanc, Viognier, Muscat, Roussanne, Marsanne
Red grapes: Grenache, Syrah, Mourvèdre, Cinsault
Size: 70,000 hectares
Styles: white, red, rosé, sparkling, sweet, fortified
Main soils: granite (North); limestone, alluvium, sand, gravel, galets/cobblestones (South)

CHANGES IN PRODUCTION

Current challenges: hail, drought, heat stress
Future positive: planting at higher altitude

This Cabernet Franc vineyard is near Chinon in Touraine, France, the heartland of the Loire's red wine area.

LOIRE

France's largest white-wine region and longest wine route, Loire has 69 appellations that hug the banks north and south of its beautiful languid river. Diversity here is key; it is also a hotbed of experimentation in organic and biodynamic viticulture and natural winemaking. Once on the edge of ripeness, Loire has benefited more than any other region from warming temperatures. Chiselled whites and lush velvety reds are riper and more approachable – although spring frosts and fungal diseases are still major concerns.

In the west, citrusy dry Muscadet from Pays Nantais brings great value; Chenin Blanc shines in Anjou as Savennières and Anjou Blanc, both dry, and botrytis-affected sweet Bonnezeaux, Coteaux du Layon and Quarts de Chaume. Saumur is the home of sparkling Chenin in Crémant de Loire, but Saumur-Champigny (its Cabernet Franc-based red), is improving. Heading east into Touraine, Loire's red-wine quarter continues, with Chinon, Bourgueil and St Nicolas de Bourgueil showing early-drinking, fruit-driven Cabernet Franc (Breton). Chenin works its magic here with invigorating taut whites, sparkling and sweet in Vouvray and Montlouis.

Central Loire is a different world, where Sauvignon Blanc reigns supreme, alongside Pinot Noir. Sancerre grows both on its diverse soils; Pouilly-Fumé makes perfumed styles; and lighter whites are found in Menetou-Salon, Quincy and Reuilly.

Producers to try: *Bernard Baudry, Cleray, Lucien Crochet, Nicolas Paget, Taille aux Loups, Vacheron, Vincent Careme, Yannick Amirault*

KEY FACTS

White grapes: Melon de Bourgogne, Chenin Blanc, Sauvignon Blanc
Red grapes: Cabernet Franc, Gamay, Pinot Noir
Size: 42,000 hectares
Styles: white, red, rosé, sparkling, sweet
Main soils: schist, slate, limestone, clay, flint

CHANGES IN PRODUCTION

Current challenges: spring frosts, disease
Future positive: organic focus; revival of lesser-known grapes

PROVENCE & CORSICA

Provence is renowned for its pale, dry, fruity rosés, with the majority coming from Côtes de Provence and Coteaux d'Aix-en-Provence. Spicy reds from the coastal slopes of Bandol and aromatic whites from the bay of Cassis are also be found here.

Off the Mediterranean coast, the island of Corsica is mostly planted with red Nielluccio (aka Sangiovese).

Producers to try: *Montrose, Richeaume, Tempier* (Provence); *Saparale, Torraccia* (Corsica)

LANGUEDOC-ROUSSILLON

Languedoc lies in a vast arc of vineyards around the Mediterranean's north shore. It is a progressive region dominated by reds, with large co-ops churning out good-value IGP and single estates producing characterful old-vine wines in Terrasses du Larzac, Pic St-Loup, La Clape, Minervois-La-Livinière, Faugères, St-Chinian, Corbières and Fitou.

Roussillon is a beautiful windswept region with a Catalan heritage and lots of old vines set in an amphitheatre beneath the Pyrenees. It is shedding its old sweet-wine image in favour of *vin sec* table wines as fortified VDNs Rivesaltes, Maury and Banyuls diminish. With 80 per cent of its vineyards on slopes (up to 1000m), high altitude offers future potential.

Producers to try: *Calmel & Joseph, Jonquières, Ollieux Romanis* (Languedoc); *Gauby, Jonquères d'Oriola, Soula, Terres Fidele* (Roussillon)

SOUTHWEST FRANCE

This is a huge disparate area stretching from Bergerac, home to sweet Monbazillac, on the outskirts of Bordeaux, across to Cahors in the Lot, with wild, tannic Malbecs, and heading south to Gaillac. Gascony, to the west, is Tannat's homeland, with sturdy Madiran and sweet Pacherenc du Vic-Bilh. It finally moves through Basque Irouléguy to Jurançon in the Pyrenees foothills, home to thrillingly delicate whites from Petit Manseng.

Producers to try: *Tirecul La Gravière* (Monbazillac); *Cèdre, Chambert, Triguedina* (Cahors); *Barrejat, Barthoumieu, d'Aydie* (Madiran); *Cauhape, Clos Lapeyre, Hours* (Jurançon)

PROVENCE & CORSICA, LANGUEDOC-ROUSSILLON, SOUTHWEST FRANCE: KEY FACTS

White grapes: Vermentino (Rolle), Grenache Blanc, Grenache Gris, Petit Manseng, Gros Manseng
Red grapes: Grenache, Syrah, Mourvèdre, Carignan, Cinsault, Cabernet Sauvignon, Tibouren, Nielluccio, Tannat, Malbec
Size: 27,300 hectares (Provence); 70,000 (Languedoc); 18,000 (Roussillon); 7,400 (Southwest)
Styles: mostly rosé; white, red (Provence); mostly red; white, rosé, sparkling, sweet (Languedoc); white, red, rosé, fortified (Roussillon); white, red, rosé, sweet (SW France)
Main soils: limestone, clay, sand, schist, granite

CHANGES IN PRODUCTION

Current challenges: hail, drought, heat stress
Future positive: planting at higher altitude

ALSACE

Hugging the picturesque eastern slopes of the Vosges Mountains, this region is distinctly different and the only one to use single-variety names. Majoring on aromatic whites, it's the only part of France producing Riesling and Gewurztraminer – bottled in distinctive flutes. It has had a turbulent history and has a unique terroir as one of the driest areas in France, with plentiful sunshine and cool nights retaining acidity in the grapes.

Alsace growers have successfully pioneered organic and biodynamic viticulture, and 51 Grand Crus (three per cent of vineyards) highlight the best of its thrilling dry, zesty, rich, spicy, aromatic wines. In recent years, there has been a Pinot Noir renaissance here, with a tenfold increase in plantings since 1960.

There has also been a dynamic increase in the volume of Crémant d'Alsace – now one-third of the region's production – as well as in its quality, making it France's most popular Crémant.

Producers to try: *Albert Mann, Barmes Buecher, Bott-Geyl, Emile Beyer, Hugel, Meyer-Fonne, Rolly Gassmann, Trimbach, Weinbach, Zind-Humbrecht*

JURA

This is an enchantingly small historic region, where resilient artisans tend a mosaic of soils. Chardonnay rules, but Crémant production is growing; tough-skinned aromatic Savagnin is used to make natural Vin Jaune, and its distinctive oxidative style has put Jura on the map.

Reds are planted on lower, warmer soils. Vignerons do not specialize in one grape or style; everyone makes all styles, experimenting with *ouillé*, amphorae, *foudres* and concrete eggs.
Producers to try: *A&M Tissot, Fumey Chatelain, Pélican, Pignier*

SAVOIE

This spectacularly beautiful sub-Alpine region stretches over 110km, from east of Geneva (Lac Leman) to south of Chambéry. It is home to crisp sparkling, glacial mountain-fresh whites – the indigenous Jacquère grape is most planted – and light reds from steep limestone slopes.
Producers to try: *Berthollier, Quenard (A&M, J-F, P&A and Claude), Ripaille*

ALSACE, JURA, SAVOIE: KEY FACTS

White grapes: Riesling, Gewurztraminer, Pinot Gris, Muscat, Sylvaner, Pinot Blanc, Auxerrois (Alsace); Savagnin, Chardonnay (Jura); Jacquère, Altesse, Chardonnay, Roussanne, Chasselas (Savoie)
Red grapes: Pinot Noir (Alsace); Poulsard, Trousseau, Pinot Noir (Jura); Mondeuse, Pinot Noir, Gamay, Persan (Savoie)
Size: 15,500 hectares (Alsace); 2,150 (Jura); 2,130 (Savoie)
Styles: mostly white; red, sparkling, sweet
Main soils: granite, limestone, slate, clay

CHANGES IN PRODUCTION

Current challenges: spring frosts, drought, heat stress
Future positive: consistent ripeness for reds, organic/biodynamic producers are higher than the French average; cooler higher slopes in Savoie

Alsace has a unique terroir in the foothills of the Vosges Mountains and is one of the driest areas in France; shown here is Hunawihr church in the vineyards.

Jura winemaker Stéphane Tissot uses amphorae for ageing Savagnin and Trousseau.

ITALY

Italy is the world's largest wine producer, with a 4,000-year wine history. Vines are grown in all of the 20 regions, from the high Alps to volcanic slopes and coastal peninsulas; many are planted with indigenous grapes only grown in their locality. Italy might be best known for its red wines Barolo and Chianti, but it has an incredible diversity of regional styles. Organic viticulture is also on the rise, making up almost 20 per cent of its total vineyard.

KEY FACTS
Size: 728,000 hectares
Styles: white, red, rosé, sparkling, sweet, fortified
Wine laws: DOCG, DOC, IGT, Vino da Tavola

NORTHWEST ITALY

Piedmont is a vast hilly region of 60 denominations, sheltered by the Alps and Apennines. An impressive 80 per cent of its wines are DOC or DOCG; its gastronomic reds are world-famous, but it is also home to whites, rosato, sparkling, sweet passito, fortified vermouth and aromatized Barolo Chinato.

Nebbiolo is known as Chiavennasca in Italy's Alpine Valtellina region, making elegant reds from steep terraced vineyards up to 700m high.

Barolo and Barbaresco in the Langhe hills produce long-ageing, complex, tannic Nebbiolo. Gattinara, Ghemme and Carema make characterful, earlier-drinking styles. Piedmont's most planted red grape, Barbera, is now being taken seriously. Roero, Colli Tortonesi and Gavi make crisp whites, while tank-fermented Asti Spumante and semi-sparkling Moscato d'Asti dominate fizz – but emerging Alta Langa DOCG is now making traditional-method styles. Piedmont is one of Italy's most beautiful wine regions, but there is less experimentation here.

Lombardy, around Milan, is best known for Franciacorta sparkling from glacial soils, while long, thin Alpine Valtellina makes elegant reds. Oltrepò Pavese is Italy's Pinot Nero capital, with fizz and fresh whites. Further east, benefiting from Lake Garda's influence, are Lugana's creamy citrus whites. Valle d'Aosta is Italy's smallest and most mountainous region, making light reds. Finally, coastal Liguria makes zippy, lively whites.
Producers to try: *Aldo Conterno, Ca' del Bosco, Ca' dei Frati, Chiara Boschis, Gaja, La Mesma, Marchesi di Barolo, Mazzolino, Nervi, Nino Negri*

KEY FACTS
White grapes: Arneis, Timorasso, Cortese, Moscato Bianco, Chardonnay, Erbaluce, Pinot Bianco
Red grapes: Nebbiolo, Barbera, Dolcetto, Grignolino, Pinot Nero, Freisa, Brachetto (Piedmont); Croatina (Lombardy)
Size: 43,500 hectares (Piedmont); 23,400 (Lombardy); 1,500 (Liguria); 450 (Valle d'Aosta)
Styles: white, red, rosé, sparkling, sweet
Main soils: limestone, clay, marl (lime and clay), sandstone, quartz, slate

CHANGES IN PRODUCTION
Current challenges: frost, hail, floods, heat spikes creating high alcohol
Future positive: high-altitude plantings

Altitude is very important in Alto Adige, Italy; vines are planted at altitudes up to 1,000m, with added risks of hail and frost.

NORTHEAST ITALY

The home of Prosecco, Valpolicella, Soave and Pinot Grigio, this is Italy's most prolific wine area, but within its four wine regions there are hidden gems.

Alto Adige's stunning Alpine landscape is one of Italy's smallest and most northerly regions. Yet the climate is Mediterranean, and altitude is all important, with vineyards to 1,000m and creeping higher with climate change. Grapes and styles are Austrian- and German-influenced, and 12 co-ops dominate 70 per cent of production.

Neighbour Trentino also makes mountain wines – 70 per cent of its land is above 1,000m, with vineyards cultivated up to 900m – and its traditional-method sparkling is some of Italy's finest fizz.

Centred around Verona, the huge Veneto region is renowned for red Valpolicella and white Soave, with the best from the volcanic Classico area; serious dry Amarone and sweeter Recioto are made in these cooler northern hills. Prosecco's best is from superior Conegliano Valdobbiadene on Cartizze hill.

Overlooking the Adriatic, Friuli Venezia Giulia makes Italy's finest whites. There is a hub of natural-wine experimentation in Colli Orientali and Collio Goriziano, and the local speciality grapes are especially interesting.

Producers to try: *Allegrini, Duline, Foradori, Gravner, Lageder, Pieropan, Radikon*

KEY FACTS

White grapes: Pinot Grigio, Gewurztraminer, Pinot Blanc, Chardonnay, Sauvignon Blanc, Müller-Thurgau, Kerner, Riesling (Trentino-Alto Adige); Trebbiano, Glera, Garganega (Veneto); Ribolla Gialla, Sauvignonasse, Picolit (Friuli)
Red grapes: Schiava, Lagrein, Pinot Nero, Merlot, Cabernet Sauvignon, Marzemino, Teroldego (Trentino-Alto Adige); Corvina, Molinara, Rondinella (Veneto); Refosco, Pignolo (Friuli)
Size: 5,700 hectares (Alto Adige); 10,000 (Trentino); 90,000 (Veneto); 23,000 (Friuli)
Styles: white, red, rosé, sparkling, sweet
Main soils: limestone, clay, marl, volcanic

CHANGES IN PRODUCTION

Current challenges: frost, hail, overproduction
Future positive: high-altitude plantings

Set on a Tuscan hillside, Castello Banfi in Montalcino, Italy, has a hotel, restaurants and a glass museum.

CENTRAL ITALY

Tuscany is Italy's oldest wine region – a beautiful, unspoiled, historic landscape with a temperate climate and an infinite number of slopes, altitudes and aspects. It is home to Italy's finest reds, nutty whites and sweet Vin Santo, and it is also an important organic hub. Sangiovese is planted in 60 per cent of the region; it is the main grape of Chianti, making elegant oaked reds in its Classico heartland between Florence and Siena. South of Siena, Brunello di Montalcino makes deeper-coloured, structured, long-lived wines; and in the east, Vino Nobile di Montepulciano uses the same grape from a different strain called Prugnolo.

Coastal Tuscany, notably Bolgheri, produces world-renowned Super Tuscans from international red grapes. There is also much experimentation in southern Maremma, around Suvereto, Monte Amiata and Scansano, where Sangiovese is known as Morellino.

Emilia-Romagna is Italy's culinary capital around lively historic Bologna; it is the home of semi-sparkling red and white Lambrusco – at best refreshingly dry (string-tied cork, not screwcap) in Sorbara and Grasparossa. One-quarter of vineyards are planted with Sangiovese. Landlocked Umbria with its pretty hilltop villages is best known for Orvieto white from Procanico (aka Trebbiano) and Grechetto; also burly reds from Sagrantino in Montefalco and Sangiovese. Perugia's Lake Trasimeno makes interesting Gamay. Between the Apennines and Tyrrhenian sea, Lazio is home to Est! Est!! Est!!! di Montefiascone from Grechetto and Trebbiano and dry white Malvasia-based Frascati from Colli Albani's volcanic soils southeast of Rome.

On rolling hills near Ancona on Italy's east coast, Marches is best known for Montepulciano-based reds and brisk lively Verdicchio dei Castelli di Jesi and Verdicchio di Matelica whites. The majority of Abruzzo's vineyards are on mountainous terrain, making robust fruity Montepulciano d'Abruzzo and vibrant rosé Cerasuolo. Among its whites, citrus-fruited Pecorino has potential. Two-thirds of Abruzzo's wine is from co-ops or négociants.
Producers to try: *Barbi, Capezzana, Carini, Cecione, Isola e Olena, Neri, Sette Cieli*

KEY FACTS
White grapes: Vernaccia, Trebbiano (Tuscany); Trebbiano, Grechetto, Malvasia (Umbria, Latium); Pecorino, Verdicchio (Marches, Abruzzo)
Red grapes: Sangiovese, Merlot, Cabernet Sauvignon, Syrah (Tuscany); Lambrusco (Emilia-Romagna); Sagrantino, Montepulciano (Umbria, Marches, Abruzzo)
Size: 57,000 hectares (Tuscany); 53,000 (Emilia-Romagna); 12,400 (Umbria); 20,000 (Latium); 16,000 (Marches); 34,000 (Abruzzo)
Styles: white, red, sweet
Main soils: clay, limestone, weathered calcareous sandstone (albarese), shale

CHANGES IN PRODUCTION
Current challenges: drought, heatwaves
Future positive: high-altitude plantings

ISLANDS & SOUTH ITALY

Sicily has the largest vineyard area in Italy but is only fourth largest by volume; it now focuses on quality over quantity. Its impressive organic output is the highest in the country. The volcanic slopes of Mount Etna produce ethereal, minerally bright reds and honeyed citrus whites. Lightly fruity Cerasuolo di Vittoria and other light reds are found in Sicily's southeast. Fortified Marsala is out of fashion (best is Vergine), so the west has turned to zippy table wines, while dense dessert wine on the windy volcanic island of Pantelleria is superb.

Sardinia is Italy's second-largest island; its vines have Spanish origins, producing impressive reds and whites inland and in the northwest.

Campania is a hilly, volcanic region inland from Naples, best known for Taurasi reds, but its thrillingly vibrant whites include floral Fiano di Avellino and nutty Greco di Tufo.

Puglia is still a major bulk supplier to northern blending vats; its best reds are from sacred old Primitivo (aka Zinfandel/Tribidrag) bush vines, making elegant tannic reds on limestone in Manduria and bittersweet Negroamaro in Salento. Further north, Uva di Troia makes velvety reds in Gioia del Colle. In rural, arid mountainous Basilicata, the best wine is Aglianico del Vulture, at its finest on the higher slopes of volcanic Mount Vulture. Molise makes red and white up the coast from Puglia, while in Italy's toe, Calabria's best wines are from Cirò's ancient local grapes.
Producers to try: *A Mano, Benanti, D'Angelo, Donnafugata, Feudi di San Gregorio, Librandi, Morella, Planeta, Polvanera*

KEY FACTS
White grapes: Catarratto, Grillo, Carricante, Zibibbo (Sicily); Vermentino (Sardinia); Fiano, Falanghina, Greco (Campania, Basilicata); Verdeca, Bombino (Puglia); Trebbiano (Molise)
Red grapes: Nerello Mascalese, Frappato, Nero d'Avola (Sicily); Cannonau (Sardinia); Gaglioppo (Calabria); Primitivo, Negroamaro (Puglia); Aglianico (Campania, Basilicata); Montepulciano (Molise)
Size: 98,800 hectares (Sicily); 26,000 (Sardinia); 25,000 (Campania); 2,000 (Basilicata); 95,000 (Puglia); 5,400 (Molise); 8,900 (Calabria)
Styles: white, red, rosé, sweet
Main soils: volcanic, granite, calcareous, limestone, clay

CHANGES IN PRODUCTION
Current challenges: drought, heatwaves
Future positive: focus on organics in Sicily

Trulli houses in Alberobello, Puglia, Italy, which is home to rich reds.

SPAIN

Spain's rapid transformation into one of the most dynamic wine countries in Europe is impressive. Its fine-wine gems of Rioja, Ribera del Duero and Jerez have now been joined by myriad wine styles from new producers in rediscovered regions making the most of their indigenous grapes. Spain has the largest surface area under vine in the world (it is still a major bulk-wine producer) and is mountainous, with climate extremes from the cool, wet northwest to its blazing-hot interior.

KEY FACTS
Size: 930,000 hectares
Styles: white, red, rosé, sparkling, sweet, fortified
Wine laws: Vino de Pago, DOCa, DO(P), Vino de Calidad, Vino de la Tierra

NORTHEAST SPAIN

The northeast is home to some of Spain's best-known wine regions. Rioja is the most iconic and was the first to receive DOCa status; it is now Spain's largest fine-wine region, stretching northwest to southeast across the zones of Alta, Alavesa and Oriental. Terroir is king here; its temperate climate is sheltered by the Sierras de Cantabria and de la Demanda, and soils are diverse at varying altitudes.

Fourteen grapes are authorized – including Tempranillo, with Garnacha, Graciano and Mazuelo (aka Carignan) – but recuperation of pre-phylloxera grapes is under way. Oak and age is all important in its Crianzas, Reservas and Gran Reservas, with different ageing periods in American or French oak. Approachability and longevity here are prized. Whites can be superb; rosado, orange, low-alcohol sweet Supurao and traditional-method sparkling are also made.

Fine-wine production only began in the 1970s, in Ribera del Duero on the banks of the River Duero. Its continental climate is harsh with severe frosts, but there is quality potential in top sites, especially for dark, structured, high-acid reds from Tinto Fino (aka Tempranillo). Navarra is a diverse mix of white, rosado (one-third of production) and red. In Somontano, international varieties replaced local grapes. High-altitude (1,000m) Calatayud, Valdejalón VT and Campo de Borja are undergoing a renaissance, while Cariñena shows potential.

Catalonia is the heartland of traditional-method Cava; Alella and Penedès (Penedès Classic is a sparkling offshoot) are now planting old Catalan grapes at high altitude. Empordà shows promise; and down the coast in Tarragona, Terra Alta is up-and-coming, while Priorat's old-vine reds are renowned. Encircling Priorat is Montsant, with similar grapes but a cooler micro-climate.
Producers to try: *Acustic, El Escocés Volante, Frontonio, Hacienda Monasterio, Juve y Camps, La Rioja Alta, Martinet, Muga, Mogador, Torres*

KEY FACTS
White grapes: Macabeo, Malvasia, Tempranillo Blanco, Garnacha Blanca, Albillo, Parellada, Xarel·lo
Red grapes: Tempranillo, Garnacha, Graciano, Cariñena, Mazuelo, Mando
Size: 66,800 hectares (Rioja); 26,120 (Ribera del Duero); 14,000 (Cariñena); 3,200 (Calatayud); 60,000 (Catalonia); 1,700 (Priorat)
Styles: white, red, rosé, sparkling
Main soils: clay, limestone, alluvial pebbles, sand, red/black slate, quartz, volcanic ash

CHANGES IN PRODUCTION
Current challenges: spring frost, drought, floods
Future positive: higher-altitude plantings

NORTHWEST SPAIN

Galicia is the epicentre of new-era Spain; most famous is coastal Rías Baixas (with some of Spain's highest vineyard prices), while Ribeiro and Ribeira Sacra focus on vibrant wines from alternative grapes. Galicia is highly fragmented, making large-scale viticulture for investors difficult.

Expansion in Rías Baixas has been rapid; Albariño is now 95 per cent of plantings. This thick-skinned grape thrives here in cool damp Atlantic air, grown on parral pergolas. Styles vary from zippy and unoaked to more textured oaked styles for ageing. There is plenty of experimentation with still and sparkling Albariño, and with reviving local red grapes like Caino Tinto, Espadeiro and Mencía.

Historic Ribeiro has varied micro-climates for its almost exclusive whites. In contrast, Ribeira Sacra is red, with most potential on the steep 800m terraces in the beautiful Sil Valley. Valdeorras ('valley of gold') is Galicia's most easterly region; Monterrei in the south is the warmest and driest.

Bierzo's 80 bodegas focus almost exclusively on revived Mencía. In high-altitude Asturias, growers revive local grapes, while to the east of Bilbao, the enchanting high-acid, lightly sparkling Txakolí is made from Hondarribi Zuri.

In western Castilla y León, Rueda and Toro have also become magnets for investors. Rueda has grown rapidly to become Spain's top-selling white-wine region. Smaller Toro focuses on robust old-vine reds with some high-profile investment.

Producers to try: *Bibei, Etxaniz, Fefiñanes, Maior de Mendoza, Palacios, Señorans, Vidas, Zárate.*

KEY FACTS

White grapes: Albariño, Godello, Loureiro, Treixadura, Caino Blanco (Galicia); Verdejo (Castilla y León)

Red grapes: Mencía, Caino Tinto, Espadeiro, Loureiro Tinto, Sousón, Brancellao, Merenzao (Galicia); Mencia, Tempranillo (Castilla y León)

Size: 4,320 hectares (Rías Baixas); 1,300 (Ribeiro); 1,250 (Ribeira Sacra); 1,170 (Valdeorras); 2,980 (Bierzo); 530 (Monterrei); 5,400 (Toro); 13,500 (Rueda); 400 (Getaria); 2,000 (Cigales)

Styles: white, red

Main soils: granite, schist, slate, gneiss, clay, limestone

CHANGES IN PRODUCTION

Current challenges: spring frosts

Future positive: indigenous grape revival

The steep terracing of the Ribeira Sacra region's beautiful Sil Valley in Galicia, Spain, is home to the reds Mencía, Brancellao and Merenzao.

Juanan Martín of Rico Nuevo in Cebreros, Spain, uses artisan methods in reviving Garnacha.

CENTRAL SPAIN

The vast Meseta plateau produces nearly half of all Spanish wines. This is the land of cheap-and-cheerful bulk wine, slowly transforming itself with hives of activity and experimentation in Sierra de Gredos, Utiel-Requena and Jumilla.

The high Castilla-La Mancha plateau is Europe's largest wine region. In this extreme climate of freezing winters and baking summers, the world's most planted white Airén thrives as unirrigated bush vines. Neutral dry whites are labelled VT Castilla, but much is distilled. Local reds are being revived. Valdepeñas, on the royal route between Madrid and Granada, is an extension of La Mancha to the south, growing similar grapes.

The most interesting area is the Sierra de Gredos mountain range, west of Madrid. These wines, sold as Méntrida, Vinos de Madrid or Cebreros, are made by passionate young growers nurturing old vines in small mountain vineyards. Sierra de Salamanca, to the west, is reviving fragrant reds.

Manchuela, on the plateau's eastern border, has plantings at 1,000m making light rosado and unoaked reds. Neighbour Utiel-Requena grows white Tardana and Merseguera and red Bobal and Tempranillo. Heading to southern Castilla-La Mancha and Murcia: Almansa, Jumilla, Yecla, Bullas and Alicante (once home to bulk blenders) now all show promise with Monastrell and Syrah.
Producers to try: *Juan Gil, Mustiguillo, Rico Nuevo, Roure, Soto Manrique*

KEY FACTS

White grapes: Airén, Albillo Real, Tardana, Merseguera, Macabeo
Red grapes: Tempranillo, Garnacha, Monastrell, Bobal, Cabernet Sauvignon, Alicante Bouschet, Rufete
Size: 160,000 hectares (La Mancha); 22,000 (Valdepeñas); 12,000 (Manchuela); 7,200 (Almansa); 34,000 (Utiel-Requena); 21,000 (Jumilla); 500 (Cebreros)
Styles: white, red, rosé
Main soils: granite, clay, limestone, alluvium, sandstone

CHANGES IN PRODUCTION

Current challenges: drought, heat; transforming away from bulk production
Future positive: reviving regions, native grapes

SOUTH SPAIN & ISLANDS

In the south, Andalusia's Jerez, Montilla-Moriles and Málaga are undergoing consolidation and revival. Meanwhile, potential keeps growing in Spain's two archipelagos: the Mediterranean's Balearics, historically influenced by Aragón, and the Atlantic's Canary Islands, by Castile.

Andalusia's jewel is Jerez – home of Sherry, named after the historic Jerez de la Frontera. It includes coastal Sanlúcar de Barrameda, where Manzanilla is produced. New regulation changes mean the original Sherry triangle now includes six additional towns. A small, diverse and dynamic region, its growing band of independent, mainly Spanish family-owned bodegas is focused on making Sherry exciting again, with premium dry styles (*see page* 114).

Palomino Fino is the main grape grown on *albariza* chalk (*see page* 73), with Moscatel and a little Pedro Ximénez. New grapes Vejeriego, Perruno and Beba are being trialled for drought-resistance. Jerez's vineyard *pagos* classification system focuses on terroir, and now that grapes can achieve higher alcohol with increasing temperatures, Sherry's mandatory fortification has been lifted. Outside the DO, there is an important revival of unfortified Vino de Pasto table wines, using white Palomino and red Tintilla de Rota.

To the east, hot, arid Montilla-Moriles grows much of the Pedro Ximénez (to be aged in Jerez) and makes its own heady unfortified Fino and Amontillado styles. Heavy fortified Málaga is out of fashion, but five subzones (including Axarquía) have been revitalized by boutique bodegas.

In the Balearics, the focus in Mallorca, Ibiza and Menorca is moving from international to local grapes; the best wines come from Mallorca's Binissalem DO with Manto Negro (on limestone).

In contrast, the Canaries have a subtropical Atlantic climate, fierce winds and volcanic soils pockmarked by volcanoes; there are ten wine regions across the islands, all untouched by phylloxera. There is most potential for Listán Blanco (aka Palomino) in Tenerife's Orotava, saline Albillo Criollo on Gran Canaria, and floral Malvasia Volcanica on Lanzarote – grown in lunar-landscape vineyards.

Producers to try: *Alvear, Bentomiz, Cota 45, Fernando de Castilla, Tajinaste, Ximénez Spínola*

KEY FACTS

White grapes: Palomino, Pedro Ximénez, Moscatel, Listán Blanco, Prensal Blanc, Malvasia Volcanica
Red grapes: Tintilla, Rome, Manto Negro, Callet, Listán Negro, Cabernet Sauvignon, Merlot
Size: 7,000 hectares (Jerez); 8,000 (Montilla); 1,900 (Málaga); 2,000 (Mallorca); 6,500 (Tenerife); 2,000 (Lanzarote); 200 (Gran Canaria)
Styles: white, red, rosé, sweet, fortified
Main soils: limestone, clay, sand, slate, volcanic rock

CHANGES IN PRODUCTION

Current challenges: drought
Future positive: new grapes as well as unfortified table wines in Jerez; Canaries' native grape revival

Manzanilla maturing in the solera system in Barbadillo's Arboledilla 'cathedral', one of Sanlúcar's most beautiful cellars in Andalusia, Spain.

PORTUGAL

Diversity and value for money are the buzzwords for Portugal today, with a vibrant selection of wines made from local grapes in every region. Home of one of the world's first demarcated wine regions, Portugal's historic wine industry has been transformed for the modern era with EU funds. All the Portuguese need now is more confidence in what they offer: a unique array of styles and flavours from varieties rarely seen elsewhere.

KEY FACTS

Size: 173,000 hectares
Styles: mostly red; white, sparkling, fortified
Wine laws: DOC/DOP, IGP, Vinho (table wine)
Main soils: granite, schist, slate, shale, clay, limestone, sandy clay

LANDSCAPE & GRAPES

Portugal has over 250 native grapes and one of the world's highest densities of indigenous varieties. International grape varieties played a small part in encouraging wine-lovers to explore Portugal, but now growers are renewing efforts to experiment with local grapes. This diverse range also means the country is well placed to cope with the challenges of climate change.

With an equally enviable range of micro-climates and soils, Portugal offers four wine styles: mountain wines from harsh continental climates (Douro, Dão), Atlantic wines from maritime climates influenced by strong westerly winds (Vinho Verde, Bairrada, Lisbon), Mediterranean wines from the warm south (Alentejo, Algarve) and island wines (Madeira, Azores). Mainland Portugal's climate is influenced by its extensive 1,794km coastline, which moderates the summer temperatures.

The dramatic Douro Valley in northern Portugal has narrow schist terraces, home to fine Port and table wine.

NORTH PORTUGAL

Vinho Verde is home to fresh, light whites grown in a verdant landscape – from ripe, fleshy varietal styles in Monção e Melgaço, to blends in the south.

Douro is an arid deep valley with steep schist terraces – one of the world's first regulated wine regions, established in 1756. Today, this is Portugal's leading wine region, producing Port and table wines from Touriga Nacional blends, while embracing old-vine field blends (*see page* 83). No other region has changed as much in modern times, and Douro's table-wine revolution attracts dynamic producers. The best quality comes from its heartland in Cima Corgo and Douro Superior, where north-facing higher altitudes give elegance and freshness for table wines. Douro's challenge is heat and drought, so producers now focus on Touriga Franca, altering canopies to avoid sunburned, stressed grapes and using controlled irrigation.

Trás-os-Montes is a historic region with good-value whites and reds (lighter than Douro); mountainous Beira Interior bordering Spain is similar. In remote Dão, on a granite plateau surrounded by pine forests and the Serra da Estrela, the table-wine revolution continues here, with modern fruit-driven reds and whites.

Bairrada is Portugal's most revived region, with excellent whites and fizz. This flat coastal area, with limestone and sandy soils, is home to experimental growers nurturing red Baga and producing two-thirds of Portugal's traditional-method sparkling wine.

Producers to try: *Filipa Pato, Niepoort, Noval, Pradinhos, Roques, Soalheiro, Vadio, Wine & Soul*

CENTRAL & SOUTH PORTUGAL

The Alentejo is a vast arid inland region and home to large estates; traditional *talha* clay amphorae are being adopted here again. Neighbouring Tejo offers bargains, with large properties keeping prices competitive. Lisbon's boutique producers ramp up quality, while in Colares ungrafted Ramisco and Malvasia grow on sand. In Setúbal, Moscatel grows on higher limestone slopes, and the Algarve is slowly improving quality.

Producers to try: *Chocapalha, Esporão, José Maria da Fonseca, Monteiro, Pancas, Reguinga*

Traditional talha *clay amphorae are being revived in Alentejo, Portugal.*

THE ISLANDS

Madeira is home to the world's most unusual fortified wine, with *estufa* replicating the original tropical sea voyages (*see page* 115). Bual and Malmsey are the best-known Madeira styles, but dry table wines are now starting to emerge. The volcanic island of Pico in the Azores specializes in saline whites from local varieties.

Producers to try: *Azores Wine Company, Barbeito, d'Oliveira, Henriques & Henriques*

KEY STYLES & GRAPES

Crisp delicate whites: Alvarinho, Arinto/Pederna, Loureiro
Full rich whites: Encruzado, Verdelho
Soft juicy reds: Aragonêz/Tinta Roriz, Baga, Castelão, Trincadeira/Tinta Amarela, Tinta Miúda
Full rich reds: Alfrocheiro, Touriga Nacional
Fortified: Touriga Nacional, Touriga Franca, Sercial, Verdelho, Malvasia Fina
Grapes recently revived from extinction: white Cercial (Beira), Douradinha (Dão), Terrantez (Madeira); red Tinta Francisca (Douro), Tinta Pinheira (Lisbon), Tinta Grossa (Alentejo).

CHANGES IN PRODUCTION

Current challenges: hail, frost, drought, heat, wildfires
Future positives: heat-resistant grapes (Touriga Franca), controlled irrigation, rise in boutique producers

ENGLAND & WALES

The British Isles now has more than 1,000 vineyards, 220 wineries and over 4,000 hectares of vines. The progress of this young dynamic wine industry has been dramatic, with a growth rate of 123 per cent in a decade. It is an exciting new addition to the wine world. The quality of the bottle-fermented sparkling wines is world-class, attracting the attention of major Champagne houses – two of which have already invested. The next challenge, already underway, is to refine their still white, rosé and red wines.

KEY FACTS
Size: 4,740 hectares
Styles: mostly sparkling; white, red, rosé
Wine laws: PDO English Wine, PDO Welsh Wine
Main soils: clay, gravelly loam, chalk, green sandstone

CLIMATE-CHANGE POSITIVES

No other wine country has benefited more from our warming climate. Grape ripening is now more consistent in the UK, with a longer growing season and more sunshine; but there are still challenges: weather, disease, poor fruit-set, uneven ripeness and young vines. Crop levels also fluctuate wildly due to the marginal climate (for example, 12.2 million bottles in 2022, 21.6 million in 2023, but just six to seven million projected for 2024). Particularly high acidity is also a concern, but winemakers are now embracing this as their calling card.

The game-changer has been in site selection, better fungicides and earlier-ripening clones, with more understanding of soils and plantings in sheltered frost-free pockets with windbreaks. Unfashionable grapes have been replaced with sparkling-wine grapes; at the time of writing there are 51 varieties planted, including Chardonnay, Pinot Noir, Pinot Meunier, Bacchus and Seyval Blanc as the top five, along with Piwis Solaris, Rondo and Regent (*see page* 62).

SPARKLING SUCCESS

Around 80 per cent of plantings are in England's southeast heartland of Kent, East and West Sussex, Hampshire and Surrey. The modern era of sparkling wine began in 1996, with pioneer Nyetimber in West Sussex – the first to plant Champagne varieties. Since then, there has been an explosion in plantings of these varieties and a focus on sparkling wine, but the vines are still young – most planted since about 2015.

This area has a similar chalk soil to Champagne, as an extension of the Paris Basin. However, not all English sparkling-wine grapes are grown on chalk, as drainage is important with the heavy rain that can be experienced. Some producers plant on green sandstone, limestone or rich clay-loam (green sand can give intense fruit; chalk can give acidity, elegance and a gentler focus). Some use all four; the key is that soils are well drained.

Kent's Weald vineyards are in old apple or hop orchards on a mix of soils, while some believe Sussex's higher South Downs and Hampshire are unique for their type of chalk. The Thames and Chilterns area has fewer vineyards but is drier and warmer with mixed soils; Cornwall is wetter, with slate vineyards moderated by the Gulf stream.

English or Welsh fizz from a good vintage can benefit from a little ageing, it is worth remembering. The best examples are made using the traditional method, while some producers are experimenting with other techniques (such as Charmat; *see page* 103).

Producers to try: *Camel Valley, Domaine Hugo, Evremond, Gusbourne, Harrow & Hope, Langham, Nyetimber, Ridgeview, Sugrue*

THE STILL CHALLENGE

Making still wine in the UK is more challenging, as riper grapes are needed, but vintage variation is great. Essex is a hotspot, with the greatest density of plantings; many are sited on semi-arid London clay and benefit from no spring frosts,

Octagon Block vineyard at Danbury Ridge in Essex, home to England's best Chardonnay and Pinot Noir, grown on London clay and gravelly loam.

early bud-burst, a long growing season and good ripeness. South of the River Crouch, pioneer Danbury Ridge planted Chardonnay and Pinot Noir on smectite clay and gravel, which enjoy sunshine hours similar to Burgundy's Dijon. Northern Crouch Valley is a popular hunting ground for producers buying grapes, and there are also interesting still wines emerging from Suffolk, Norfolk, Kent, Sussex and Wales.

Producers to try: *Danbury Ridge, New Hall, Martin's Lane, Flint, Chapel Down (Kit's Coty), Gusbourne, Sugrue*

WINE TOURISM

English and Welsh wines have a good home market and are also exported to Norway, Sweden, Finland, Netherlands, the US, Japan and Hong Kong. Wineries offer direct sales to consumers and tend to have well set-up visitor facilities.

KEY STYLES & GRAPES

Crisp delicate whites: Bacchus, Seyval Blanc, Solaris, Reichensteiner
Full rich whites: Chardonnay, Pinot Gris
Soft juicy reds: Pinot Noir, Précoce, Rondo
Sparkling: Chardonnay, Pinot Noir, Pinot Meunier

CHANGES IN PRODUCTION

Current challenges: spring frost, rain, disease, high acidity
Future positives: improved ripening, international investment, increasing use of Piwis (*see page* 62)

GERMANY

Modern-era Germany is all about the rise of dry wines, which now make up over half of its production. This is partly due to an increasing demand for red wines, with a dramatic rise in plantings and quality of German Spätburgunder (Pinot Noir). The switch to Trocken (dry) is also due to the change in climate, transforming Germany's wine industry by enabling consistent ripeness across its diverse range of varieties. However climate unpredictability has also brought challenges of frost, hail, disease and drought.

KEY FACTS
Size: 103,000 hectares
Styles: mostly white; red, sparkling, sweet
Wine laws: *see* opposite
Main soils: slate, shale, clay loam, loess, sandstone, basalt

The steep slopes of Zeltinger Himmelreich vineyard in Mosel, Germany, have blue Devonian slate, making elegant Riesling with vibrant acidity.

TWO NOBLE GRAPES

Germany has 13 different regions across four northern latitudes, but many have changed dramatically in the grapes they once planted: 30 years ago, Müller-Thurgau was the most popular, today it's only ten per cent of vineyards. Germany's noble grapes, Riesling and Spätburgunder (23.5 and 11 per cent respectively) make a fascinating diversity of styles. As the world's largest producer of Riesling and the world's third-largest producer of Pinot Noir after France and the US, Germany is also world leader in the breeding and planting of fungus-resistant Piwi grapes (*see page* 62), which now cover 3.5 per cent of its vineyards. Meanwhile, the new generation has gained experience abroad and, with a desire to revive historic vineyard sites, is helping to support Germany's renaissance. There is also change at the premium end of the Sekt sparkling-wine industry, with focus on traditional-method Winzersekt from estate-grown grapes.

NORTHWEST

Dramatic images of the floods in the steep narrow Ahr Valley in 2021 shocked the world (*see page* 68), with entire wineries and lower vineyards devastated. As one of Germany's most northerly and smallest regions, it has shown great resilience resurrecting its wine industry. Mosel's precipitous steep slopes run in loops and bends along its 545km of rivers through the upper/middle/lower Mosel, Ruwer and Saar. Climate change has added body to Trocken wines, particularly in Saar, where growers are reviving abandoned cool sites.
Producers to try: *Bertram-Baltes, Clemens Busch, Fiebrich, Heymann-Löwenstein, JJ Prüm, Loewen, Maximin Grünhaus, Toni Jost, Zilliken*

NORTH, SOUTH & EAST OF THE RHINE

On the River Rhine's northern banks, Rheingau is the spiritual home of Riesling, dominating the region with 76 per cent of plantings. On the southern side is Nahe, cooler in its wooded valleys than even Mosel. Heading east, Rheinhessen has

Pfalz, Germany's second largest and one of its sunniest and driest regions, grows varieties including Riesling, Grauburgunder and Pinot Noir.

switched from mass production to quality wine; and in warmer Pfalz, growers are exploring future varieties, from Marsanne to Tempranillo.

Over the Rhine on its eastern banks, Baden and Württemberg are Germany's warmest and most southerly regions, home to half of Germany's Spätburgunder plantings. To the northeast is Franken, with dry full-bodied wines in *Bocksbeutel*.
Producers to try: *Battenfeld-Spanier, B Huber, Dönnhoff, Dr Heger, Fürst, Gunderloch, Horst Sauer, Knipser, Schäfer-Fröhlich, Wirsching, Wittmann*

LAWS & LABELS

Germany has a range of qualities and styles, with sweet wines specifically labelled according to Prädikat-level ripeness:
Wein (formerly Tafelwein): table wine
ggA (geschützte geografische Angabe): dry (formerly Landwein)
QbA (Qualitätswein bestimmter Anbaugebiete) or gU (geschützte Ursprungsbezeichnung): dry or sweet
QmP (Qualitätswein mit Prädikat): level of ripeness – Kabinett (dry, light, purest), Spätlese (later harvest), Auslese (botrytis; stronger, sweeter), BA/Beerenauslese (very sweet), Eiswein (frozen grapes), TBA/Trockenbeerenauslese (very very sweet).

German wine law neglected vineyard classification, so a private VDP (Verband Deutscher Prädikatsweingüter) organization with member estates created a pyramid structure similar to Burgundy's, classifying top sites and limiting yields.
Grosses Gewachs (GG): best still dry wine
Grosse Lage: Grand Cru
Erste Lage: Premier Cru
Orstwein: Village
Gutswein: Estate

KEY STYLES & GRAPES

Crisp delicate whites: Riesling, Müller-Thurgau
Full rich whites: Grauburgunder (Pinot Gris), Weissburgunder (Pinot Blanc), Silvaner
Soft juicy reds: Spätburgunder (Pinot Noir), Dornfelder, Portugieser, Trollinger, Schwarzriesling (Pinot Meunier), Lemberger
Sweet: Riesling

CHANGES IN PRODUCTION

Current challenges: floods, frosts, disease
Future positives: consistent ripeness; Piwi grapes

AUSTRIA

Austria is primarily a white-wine country – home to Gru-V (Grüner Veltliner), its most planted variety. However, like so many nations, Austria is experiencing change due to warming temperatures. Red-wine plantings have doubled in 20 years, now representing one-third of vineyards, with juicy, tangy Zweigelt most widespread, followed by spicy Blaufränkisch and velvety St-Laurent. International grapes are also popular for blending with native grapes.

KEY FACTS
Size: 44,210 hectares
Styles: mostly white; red, rosé, sparkling, sweet
Wine laws: *see* below
Main soils: gneiss, loess, loam, slate, schist

NATURAL FOCUS, STYLES & LAWS

Austria clearly has an industry that cares, with a serious focus on organic viticulture and biodynamics. Around one-quarter of its vineyards are organic, and of those 14 per cent are biodynamic. A further one-third of plantings are sustainable. Nearly all of its wineries are small family-run concerns, which are easier to convert. Austria is also at the forefront of the natural-wine movement.

The wine styles reflect the country's warm, dry, continental climate – which is of course getting warmer. Whites have fruit purity and good acidity, but warmer summers mean acid levels are dropping, while reds have been transformed with a trend away from heavy extraction towards freshness and delicacy.

Austria has the world's strictest wine laws. In 2001, it introduced the DAC (Districtus Austriae Controllatus) system, defining the typicity of specific areas, similar to France's appellations – there are now 18. Single-vineyard classification, with Erste Lage (Premier Cru) and Grosse Lage (Grand Cru), is the latest development – a bold move, making Austria the first country in the world to introduce this nationally.

NORTH

The most potent, vivid and ripest of Austria's dry whites are found in the most westerly vineyard area of Wachau, on the River Danube's steeply terraced left bank. Kremstal sits north and south of the river, while Kamptal, on the Kamp tributary, is warmer than Wachau, with cool nights.

Wagram and Traisental lie to the west of Vienna, and the city itself is home to vineyards with traditional field blend Gemischter Satz. Wienviertel is a huge region, stretching from the Danube to the border with Czechia.

Producers to try: *Bründlmayer, Hirtzberger, Huber, Knoll, Loimer, Pichler-Krutzler*

Cutting grass between vines improves airflow and reduces disease.

SOUTH

Thermenregion is Austria's Burgundy, with more red grapes in the south; and Carnuntum, once a white-wine region, now makes big reds.

In northern Burgenland, east of Lake Neusiedl, is Neusiedlersee, a dynamic red- and sweet-wine area. Leithaburg to the west is home to superb reds, and Rust is renowned for its historic sweet Ruster Ausbruch. Late-ripening Furmint plantings tripled here in a decade, as the grape copes well with heat and drought.

Mittelburgenland is revered for its Blaufränkisch, which thrives in the heat, and Eisenberg has some interesting whites and reds.

Further south, cooler, wetter Steiermark provides interest with Sauvignon Blanc in Sudsteiermark, Traminer in Vulkanland and Blauer Wildbacher for Schilcher pink in Weststeiermark.

Producers to try: *Feiler-Artinger, Gross, Kracher, Muhr, Polz, Sattlerhof, Schrock, Tement, Tschida*

KEY STYLES & GRAPES

Crisp delicate whites: Rotgipfler, Zierfandler, Muskateller, Welshriesling
Full rich whites: Grüner Veltliner, Furmint, Roter Veltliner
Soft juicy reds: Blauer Wildbacher, Pinot Noir, Sankt Laurent, Zweigelt
Full rich reds: Blaufränkisch
Sweet: Welshriesling

CHANGES IN PRODUCTION

Current challenges: frost, heat, drought
Future positives: natural focus, local grapes and improving reds

In Austria's far south, the beautiful wooded and undulating hills of South Styria are home to vibrant, fresh Sauvignon Blanc.

SWITZERLAND

You would be forgiven for not even knowing that this small Alpine country made wine at all, as it exports less than two per cent. Of course, the Swiss like to do things a little differently. They have their own native grapes (a surprising 252), wine laws and some of Europe's highest vines (at 1,150m), plus high domestic consumption. However they don't seem to be drinking enough of their own wines, so foreign markets are seeing more.

KEY FACTS

Size: 15,660 hectares
Styles: white, red, rosé, sparkling
Wine laws: AOC
Main soils: limestone, clay, Alpine moraine

REVIVING NATIVE GRAPES

A new generation of Swiss growers is showing more interest in native grapes. Chasselas (aka Fendant in Valais) is the white leader, grown at high altitude; many whites are made in a creamy and soft style with malolactic fermentation (*see page* 90), as the Swiss don't like high acidity. However, they now drink twice as much red as white, so white-wine vineyards are being replanted with reds, like fashionable Pinot Noir.

At 1,150m, Visperterminen vineyard in Switzerland is one of the highest in Europe; nets protect grapes from birds prior to harvest and reduce hail impact.

ARTISAN FOCUS

This small mountainous country is exciting to explore, with authentic high-quality wines in a range of styles. Six wine regions are spread across Switzerland's 26 cantons, offering diversity in grapes, landscape and language. There is a real artisan focus here, with many small family-run businesses and a hugely fragmented industry. The other challenge here is the eye-wateringly high price of the wines.

Two large regions dominate in the west – Vaud, close to Lakes Geneva and Neuchâtel, is home to white Chasselas, while neighbour Valais makes one-third of Switzerland's wines in its steep sun-drenched Rhône Valley with Petite Arvine and Cornalin.

To the northwest is the country's smallest region of Trois Lacs, also producing Chasselas. Further north are the German-speaking cantons, growing Blauburgunder, and to the southeast is Italianate Ticino, where Merlot is the star.

Producers to try: *Blaise Duboux, Domaine de la Rochette, Domaine des Muses, JR Germanier*

KEY STYLES & GRAPES

Crisp delicate whites: Humagne Blanche
Full rich whites: Chasselas, Petite Arvine, Heida, Chardonnay, Doral
Soft juicy reds: Pinot Noir, Cornalin, Gamay, Cabernet Jura, Gamaret, Garanoir, Humagne Rouge
Full rich reds: Merlot, Syrah, Blaufränkisch

CHANGES IN PRODUCTION

Current challenges: frost
Future positives: native grapes; plenty of altitude

BULGARIA

Varietal labelling is now popular worldwide, but Bulgaria was one of the first countries in the modern wine world to sell its wines by the name of the grape. Following the fall of communism and land restitution, the Bulgarian wine industry has taken a long time to restructure – but now it is back, with a band of independent, artisanal, family-owned wineries focusing on quality, terroir and local grapes.

International grape Merlot and local Melnik thrive in Bulgaria's warm, continental climate.

KEY FACTS

Size: 29,000 hectares farmed of total 60,000
Styles: white, red, rosé, sparkling, sweet
Wine laws: PGI
Main soils: clay, limestone, marl, granite

LEADING THE WAY

Bulgarian wine might not be as affordable as it once was, but it is now much more exciting, better quality and showing potential. Interestingly, women are part of this dynamism – almost half of Bulgaria's wineries have female winemakers, compared to neighbouring Romania with five per cent; even California has just 14 per cent.

Bulgaria has a long wine history dating back 6,000 years to the time of the Thracians, who considered wine a divine drink. Today, only half of its vineyards are in production, the rest abandoned or neglected, with 99 different grape varieties planted. Local flagship red grapes are thriving in the increasingly warm dry continental climate. However, whites are especially popular for sweet styles, and there is now more experimentation with traditional-method sparkling, orange and pét-nat as winemakers gain confidence.

TIME FOR CHANGE

With new (mainly Bulgarian-owned) wineries burgeoning across its two PGIs – Danubian Plain and Thracian Lowlands – it is time to create further subzones. Two vast regions north and south of the country do not do justice to the diversity of micro-climates and soils. Within Thracian Lowlands alone there are vast differences between hot southern Struma Valley and South Sakar, temperate Nova Zagora and Rose Valley (home of rose oil and Red Misket grapes) and milder Black Sea Coast.
Producers to try: *Bononia, Bratanov, Castra Rubra Edoardo Miroglio*

KEY STYLES & GRAPES

Crisp delicate whites: Tamyanka, Vrachanski Misket, Dimyat, Keratsuda
Full rich whites: Chardonnay, Rkatsiteli
Sweet whites: Muscat Ottonel
Soft juicy reds: Merlot, Gamza, Pamid, Pinot Noir
Full rich reds: Broadleaved Melnik, Melnik 55 (Early Melnik), Mavrud, Rubin, Cabernet Franc, Syrah, Cabernet Sauvignon

CHANGES IN PRODUCTION

Current challenges: disease pressure
Future positives: local grapes, highlighting terroir

GREECE

Greece has one of the richest wine heritages in the world, dating back to the 7th century BCE, and boasts an incredible wealth of over 300 indigenous grapes. As it enters a new era, the dynamic wine industry here offers a diverse range of stellar wines from a treasure trove of ancient local grapes, making it one of the most exciting wine countries in Europe for the wine-lover to explore. The current renaissance was spearheaded by Greece's entry into the European Union in 1981 – it has meant quality Greek wine is now very much a reality, exported all over the world.

KEY FACTS
Size: 63,000 hectares (plus 30,000 for table grapes/raisins)
Style: white, red, rosé, sparkling, sweet
Wine laws: PDO, PGI, VQPRD (Superior Quality, Controlled Quality for dessert wines)
Main soils: limestone and sandstone sedimentary rock

MOUNTAINOUS COUNTRY

It might come as a surprise to learn that Greece – often considered a warm Mediterranean-climate destination – is in fact Europe's third most mountainous country. Its vast mountain ranges extend from the Alps of central Europe, running northwest to southeast through the country on the Pindos range.

With extensive mountainous terrain in its wine regions, vines grow in small plots on slopes of up to 750m altitude. This offers great potential for exploring cool-climate sites as the climate warms, allowing growers to push their indigenous varieties to their coolest limits.

WHITE BIAS

Another surprise is that 60 per cent of Greece's wines are white. Most vineyards are close to the sea – the country has 13,700km of coastland – benefiting from cooling breezes, or are on mountain slopes or high plateaux. Crisp, delicately scented whites that make thrillingly dry apéritifs are very much the norm here, while Greece's flagship Xinomavro red grape makes elegant textural styles.

ISLAND MAGIC

Greece has thousands of islands, and more than 200 are inhabited. They encircle the mainland, and many have been renowned for their wines since ancient times, made from the islands' local grapes. The best known is the Aegean island of Santorini, where the increasingly popular white Assyrtiko grape thrives.

NORTH GREECE

Macedonia and Thrace offer exciting potential with their coolish dry summers. Look for firm oaked reds from Naoussa and Goumenissa, and aromatic whites in Epanomi. Serious sparkling wine is emerging from Zitsa in Epirus, with its rugged steep slopes, and on Mount Vermio's northwestern slopes in Amynteo. Rapsani on the foothills of Mount Olympus makes softer elegant red. Kavala and Drama, in the far northeast near the borders with Bulgaria and Turkey, make impressive reds and whites.
Producers to try: *Alpha Estate, Biblia Chora, Gerovassiliou, Kir-Yianni, Thymiopoulos*

CENTRAL & PELOPONNESE

This area is home to Greece's most affordable wines – including pine-scented Retsina made from Savatiano – and it is now making an astonishing comeback. Nemea near Corinth on Peloponnese's east coast is renowned for perfumed, juicy reds and whites. Mantinia's inland plateau creates vibrant dry whites, and in Monemvasia ancient styles of sweet wine are being revived.
Producers to try: *Aoton, Kokotos, Markou, Monemvasia, Novus, Palivou, Papagiannakos, Papagiannis, Papagiannopoulos, Semeli, Strofilia*

The Cyclades island of Santorini is famous for Assyrtiko and has the oldest continually cultivated vineyards on Earth, dating back 3,500 years.

THE ISLANDS

On the black volcanic island of Santorini, ancient grapevines are trained low in curled wreath-shaped *koulouras* to retain moisture and make the world's finest briny and saline Assyrtikos. Greece's largest island, Crete, makes superb whites from Vidiano and Plyto, and on the mild Ionian Island of Cephalonia, Robola thrives on limestone, giving impressive floral whites.

On Rhodes, quality fizz at high altitude is made from Athiri; while on Samos, Paros and Lemnos, ancient Muscat continues to produce world-beating sweet wines.

Producers to try: *Argyros, Gavalas, Karamolegos (Santorini); Lyrarakis (Crete); Gentilini (Cephalonia); Cair (Rhodes); Nopera (Samos); Chatzigeorgiou (Lemnos); Moraitis (Paros)*

KEY STYLES & GRAPES

Crisp delicate whites: Malagousia, Moschofilero, Athiri, Robola
Full rich whites: Assyrtiko, Savatiano
Soft juicy reds: Agiorgitiko, Limnio, Kotsifali, Mandilaria
Full rich reds: Xinomavro, Mavrotragano
Sparkling: Athiri
Sweet: Muscat, Mavrodaphne
Grapes recently revived from extinction: white Kydonitsa (S Peloponnese), Lagorthi (N Pelop), Vilana (Crete); red Mavrotragano (Santorini)

CHANGES IN PRODUCTION

Current challenges: drought and severe lack of water in the south as Greece has few rivers
Future positives: high-altitude mountainous regions

HUNGARY

In terms of wine quality, Hungary has emerged from communism as the clear frontrunner in Eastern Europe. Once known in the west as a supplier of inexpensive white wines, it has changed its image dramatically in the 21st century . This is largely due to Tokaj – a historic region renowned for its sweet wines. It is now successfully switching to more dry wine, and even sparkling, thanks to the versatility of Furmint – a grape that mirrors the unique volcanic terroir of the region. Meanwhile, post-communism, a proactive second generation – which has worked abroad and is now setting the pace in small family wineries across the country – is focused on quality and rediscovering native grapes.

KEY FACTS
Size: 60,000 hectares
Styles: white, red, rosé, sparkling, sweet
Wine laws: PDO, PGI
Main soil: volcanic, loess, limestone, sand, clay

STYLE RANGE

A mix of Hungarian varieties, native to the Carpathian basin, and international varieties (223, across 22 regions) are grown here. Two-thirds are white (dry and sweet), and native grapes cope better in the country's increasingly hot growing seasons; reds include elegant blends and juicy delicate styles. Growers experiment across regions.

NORTH TO SOUTH

In the far northeast, protected from cold north winds by the Zemplens, Tokaj – the world's

Lengyel-Kapolna in Badascony, nr Lake Balaton, where growers plant grapes, from Olaszrizling to Sangiovese, on volcanic basalt, clay and loess.

first delimited region in 1737 – has a sheltered micro-climate with a distinct diurnal range. At the meeting point of the Tisza and Bodrog rivers, misty autumn mornings and sunny afternoons encourage botrytis, making sweet Tokaji Aszú (*see page* 109), with increasingly good Szamorodni and late-harvest dessert wines. In the past, botrytis was more reliable, in six out of ten years, but now it is only three or four vintages each decade. In 2000, Tokaj changed focus in its hilly landscape of 400 volcanoes, and a new range of intense, minerally, high-acid dry whites has emerged. Neighbouring Eger is home to Hungary's highest vineyard, at 501m, and traditional blends in its flagship red Egri Bikavér and white Egri Csillag.

Hungary's most important red regions are in the south, where Szekszárd creates sophisticated single-vineyard Bikavér, while Villány, close to Croatia, makes flagship Villányi Franc.

Producers to try: *Demeter Zoltán, Heimann, Oremus, Patricius, Peter Vida, Royal Tokaji, St Andrea, Sauska, Sebestyen, Szepsy, Tibor Gál*

WEST

Volcanic Somló and Badascony are key subregions in the large Balaton region; to the east, along the north shore, Balatonfüred-Csopak benefits from Lake Balaton's temperate micro-climate. Etyek-Buda is the heart of the sparkling (*peszgő*) revival.

Producers to try: *Gilvesy, 2HA, Homola, Kolonics, Kreinbacher, Pálffy, Spiegelberg, Zelna*

KEY STYLES & GRAPES

Crisp delicate whites: Ezerjó, Olaszrizling, Kéknyelű, Cserszegi Fűszeres, Irsai Olivér
Full rich whites: Furmint, Hárslevelű, Juhfark
Soft juicy reds: Kadarka, Portugieser, Cabernet Franc
Full rich reds: Kékfrankos, Laska, Cabernet Sauvignon
Sweet: Furmint, Hárslevelű
Grapes recently revived from extinction: white Kéknyelű; red Csókaszőlő, Fekete Járdovány, Purcsin

CHANGES IN PRODUCTION

Current challenges: drought, heat, rain, disease
Future positives: native grapes

The Swabian village of Hercegkút in Tokaj, Hungary, has a unique cellar system, that is a UNESCO World Heritage Site.

ROMANIA

Romania is in a state of flux as its domestic market matures and acquires a taste for drier styles, while its export markets (still small at only five to six per cent of production) start to look beyond international grapes to Romania's multitude of local grapes.

KEY FACTS
Size: 97,000 hectares *Vitis vinifera* (187,000 total, including hybrids popular in domestic market)
Styles: white, red, rosé, sparkling, sweet
Wine laws: PDO, PGI
Main soils: shale, limestone, gravel, clay, volcanic

PLANTING OPPORTUNITIES

European Union funding has changed Romania's wine industry since the turn of the century. There are hundreds of new wineries – from hobbyists and dynamic boutiques, to larger, quality-focused concerns – slowly shifting attention to native grapes with almost 40,000 hectares of new plantings. At the same time, the country has a growing culture of selling its own wine and promoting smaller independent producers.

What makes Romania unique is its plethora of local grapes, not grown anywhere else apart from neighbouring Moldova. The flagships are the Feteascăs, which show great quality potential. Grapes are grown in every corner of the country, in eight regions with a mainly harsh continental climate – from the cooler central Transylvanian plateau to warmer Black Sea-coast Dobrogea, and from southerly Oltenia and Muntenia Hills (with famous Dealu Mare), to cooler southwesterly Banat and northerly Crișana. In the east, regions stretch from southern Danube Terraces north to the Moldovan Hills.
Producers to try: *Budureasca, Cramele Recaș, Davino, Prince Știrbey*

KEY STYLES & GRAPES
Crisp delicate whites: Fetească Albă, Fetească Regală, Francusa, Cramposie, Zghihara
Full rich whites: Furmint, Mustoasa de Maderat
Sweet whites: Tămâioasă Românească
Soft juicy reds: Merlot, Pinot Noir, Băbească Neagră, Cadarca
Full rich reds: Negru de Drăgășani, Fetească Neagră

CHANGES IN PRODUCTION
Current challenges: hybrids; drought, frost
Future positives: local grapes

Prince Știrbey in Drăgășani, Romania, plants Merlot and Sauvignon Blanc and is also the only grower of Novac (Negru Vârtos x Saperavi).

ARMENIA, MOLDOVA & UKRAINE

These three historic wine countries in the Black Sea area are definitely worth watching. Each has its own indigenous grapes and vibrant modern wine culture.

KEY FACTS
Size: 15,390 hectares (Armenia); 115,000 (Moldova); 30,200 (Ukraine 2022)
Styles: white, red
Wine laws: PGI (Moldova); PDO, PGI (Ukraine)
Main soils: limestone, clay, volcanic (Armenia); clay loam, chernozem (Moldova); clay loam, limestone, chernozem (Ukraine)

ARMENIA'S CRADLE OF WINE

Mountainous Armenia is home to the world's oldest winery, Areni-1 (6,100 years old); this area alongside Georgia is the 'cradle of wine'. Over 90 per cent of the vineyards are above 1,000m, all phylloxera-free; 350 indigenous grapes (50 in production) are fermented in underground clay vessels (*karas*; *see page* 134).

During Soviet times, brandy was the focus (85 per cent of grapes are still used for *konyak*). Since independence, Armenia's six wine regions have mushroomed, of which Vayots Dzor, Aragatsotn and Armavir are most important. Some producers focus on international grapes, while others revive ancient local grapes, including jasmine-scented Voskehat and spicy Areni Noir.
Producers to try: *ArmAs, Karas, Keush, Van Ardi, Zorah*

MOLDOVA DRIVES VOLUME

Shaped like a bunch of grapes, this small European country has a vast area under vine (larger than Bulgaria and Hungary) and the highest density of vineyards in the world. Over half of the plantings are to four international grapes, a hangover from Soviet times.

A change in wine law has made it easier for new privatized wineries to emerge, although 70 per cent of production is still sold as bulk wine. Four historic regions (three classified PGI) all have moderate continental climates with Black Sea influence.
Producers to try: *Castel Mimi, Château Vartely, Fautor, Novak, Purcari, Salcuta, Timbrus*

UKRAINE'S WINE RESILIENCE

International grapes dominate here, but Ukraine has 200 varieties of its own. This resilient nation has a long wine history dating back to the 4th century BCE in Crimea, and to the 11th century in Chernihiv and Kyiv. Today, its regions stretch from the temperate Black Sea area to the continental climate of the Carpathians. In 2021, wine laws changed to assist new small ventures, leading to a rise in boutique wineries, a culture of experimentation and a focus on export.
Producers to try: *Beyrush, Bolgrad*

ARMENIA, MOLDOVA & UKRAINE: KEY STYLES & GRAPES
Crisp delicate whites: Aligoté, Riesling, Sauvignon Blanc, Alb de Onitcani, Riton (Moldova); Citron Magarach (Ukraine)
Full rich whites: Voskehat (Armenia); Chardonnay, Viorica (Moldova); Timorasso, Telti-Kuruk (Ukraine)
Soft juicy reds: Pinot Noir, Rară Neagră/Băbească Neagră (Moldova); Tempranillo, Zweigelt (Ukraine)
Full rich reds: Areni Noir (Armenia); Cabernet Sauvignon, Merlot, Malbec, Syrah, Fetească Neagră (Moldova); Saperavi, Odesa Black (Ukraine)
Grapes recently revived from extinction: white Chilar, Lalvari; red Syreni (Armenia)

CHANGES IN PRODUCTION
Current challenges: cold winters, intense heat and water stress in summer
Future positives: native grape revival

GEORGIA

Georgia can offer the wine-lover something completely unique. It has the world's longest winemaking history, dating back 8,000 years, and more indigenous varieties than any other country, with vines planted nowhere else in the world, plus an ancient winemaking tradition still very much in use today.

KEY FACTS
Size: 48,500 hectares
Styles: white, red, rosé, sparkling, sweet
Wine laws: PDO
Main soils: clay, limestone, gravel, sand

MOUNTAINOUS BEAUTY

Best known for its *qvevri*-fermented amber wines (*see pages* 123, 134), Georgia's vibrant wine industry has plenty more to offer. Having cast off its Soviet past, it has transformed itself, offering a vibrant range of innovative and elegant styles. It is intensely mountainous, set in a dramatic position at the foot of the Caucasus Mountains, which offer tempering cold northern air and higher altitudes.

For a small country, Georgia has remarkable variation in climate and topography across seven climatic zones – from the subtropical Black Sea coast, to cool Caucasus, to the warmer east by Azerbaijan's border. Of its 525 indigenous grapes, only 45 are currently grown commercially, and just six per cent of vineyards are planted to international grapes.

UNDERGROUND POTS

The *qvevri* winemaking tradition is uniquely Georgian, and these vast egg-shaped fire-clay vessels (1,500 to 2,000 litres) are still handcrafted and in use today. Buried underground with just their rim showing, they are used for fermenting and maturing white and red wines. Whole-pressed bunches are put in with no additives, and the cap is punched down during fermentation to prevent drying.

Reds are pumped from their lees into another *qvevri* to prevent harsh tannins, but white wines are left on their skins and sealed with a stone or perspex lid that is covered with black sand for six months, resulting in orange natural wine. Today, only five to ten per cent of wines are made this way; most are made using European methods, and

Large egg-shaped clay* qvevri *are buried underground in cellars; UNESCO has protected this unique winemaking method.

Traditional tools including* sartskhi *brushes are still in use in* qvevri *winemaking in Georgia.

Kakheti, Georgia's largest and most famous wine region, is home to ripe, dense Saperavi, shown here in the Alazani Valley.

70 per cent of production is made semi-sweet or sweet for Russia and Eastern markets.

EAST

Kakheti is Georgia's warmest wine region. Back in Soviet times, its flatter, warmer valley floors were easier for the older tractors to mechanize and the region still produces 77 per cent of plantings. Now growers are heading into the hills. Southwest of Tibilisi is historic Kartli, Georgia's aristocratic heartland on a high windy plateau, making traditional-method fizz and elegant still wines.
Producers to try: *Casreli, Dakishvili, Lukasi, Mildiani, Mukhrani, Orgo, Ori Marani*

WEST

Viticulture here is less developed. Imereti is influenced by the Black Sea; local whites are fermented in *churi* (*qvevri*) and styles are lighter. Other regions to explore include Samegrelo, Racha-Lechkhumi, Meskheti and Guria.
Producers to try: *Baia's Wine, Chinebule, Guniava, Nikoladze, Oda Martvili*

KEY STYLES & GRAPES

Crisp delicate whites: Goruli Mtsvane, Chinuri, Khikhvi, Tsolikouri
Full rich whites: Kisi, Rkatsiteli, Tsitska
Soft juicy reds: Shavkapito, Tavkveri
Full rich reds: Saperavi, Otskhanuri Sapere, Jani
Grapes recently revived from extinction: white Kisi, Khikhvi; red Jani, Aladasturi

CHANGES IN PRODUCTION

Current challenges: drought, heat, disease
Future positives: native grapes

CENTRAL & NORTHERN EUROPE

Vines were first planted by the Romans in today's Czechia and Slovakia. Both have a strong family wine culture; quantities are small so little is exported. Further north, Poland, Luxembourg, Belgium, Scandinavia and the Netherlands are experiencing warmer climates, with an increasing number of vineyards. These are all countries to watch.

KEY FACTS

Size: 17,300 hectares (Czechia); 13,000 (Slovakia); 1,215 (Luxembourg); 890 (Belgium); 300 (Netherlands); 200 (Poland); 200 (Denmark); 200 (Sweden)
Styles: white, red, sparkling
Wine laws: PDO, PGI (Czechia, Slovakia)
Main soils: loess, gravel, limestone, clay loam (all); plus volcanic tuff (Slovakia)

CZECHIA – DOMINANT SOUTH

Czechia's wines come from the warmer south (96 per cent), in Moravia, which borders Austria and Slovakia and shares a similar continental climate. Veltlínské Zelené (Grüner Veltliner) and Müller-Thurgau are often made off-dry; Frankovka (Blaufränkisch), Svatovavřinecké (St-Laurent) and Pinot Noir are popular reds. North of Prague, cooler Bohemia (Čechy) makes sparkling Ryzlink Rýnský (Rhine Riesling) and Ryzlink Vlassky (Welshriesling).
Producers to try: *Cibulka, Horák, Krásná Hora, Lobkowicz, Porta Bohemica, Stapleton & Springer, Stávek, Thaya*

SLOVAKIA – NATURAL HUB

Slovakia is reclaiming its status as a renowned wine producer. Lost during communism, it is now a hotbed of experimentation, with a dynamic band of small family producers making natural, skin-contact and organic wines. There is much potential for Riesling, Pinot Blanc, Grüner Veltliner, Blaufränkisch and St-Laurent, while local crosses include white Devin, and red Alibernet and Dunaj offer a point of difference. Its six regions are Small Carpathians, South, Nitra, Central, East and Tokaj; in the warmer south the largest production is in the southwest, while interesting volcanic wines are made in southeast.
Producers to try: *Bott Frigyes, Château Belá, Château Ruban, Magula, Ostrožovič, Pivnica Brhlovce, Pomfy, Shebo, Slobodne, Strekov 1075*

HEADING NORTH

It might seem surprising, but Poland has vineyards – planted with cold-hardy Piwis (*see page* 62) and *Vitis vinifera* (Merlot, Zweigelt), making white, orange and sparkling wines. Belgium, the Netherlands and Luxembourg mainly produce whites with Auxerrois, Riesling and Chardonnay; while Denmark and Sweden continue to expand their production, with Piwis including white Solaris and Souvignier Gris and red Rondo.
Producers to try: *Barczentewicz, Bliskowice, Kojder, Poltorak, Turnau* (Poland); *Kullabergs, Särtshöga, Thora* (Sweden), *Dyrehøj, Skærsøgaard, Vesterhave* (Denmark), *Bioul, Bon Baron, Chenoy* (Belgium); *Pauqué* (Luxembourg)

CENTRAL & NORTHERN EUROPE: KEY STYLES & GRAPES

Crisp delicate whites: Riesling (Czechia); Noria (Slovakia); Solaris, Souvignier Gris (Sweden, Denmark)
Full rich whites: Devin (Slovakia); Auxerrois (Luxembourg)
Soft juicy reds: Pinot Noir (Czechia); Rondo (Sweden, Denmark)
Full rich reds: Dunaj, Andre (Slovakia)

CHANGES IN PRODUCTION

Current challenges: winter cold, summer drought
Future positives: local grape revival, organic focus

CROATIA & SLOVENIA

These neighbouring countries share a border and similar climates but have very different wine cultures. Slovenia is influenced by Italy and Austria, focused on quality for the export market. Croatia seems more self-contained, with millions of undemanding tourists to please. While both countries have resurgent wine industries and a new generation of passionate winemakers, in terms of quality, Slovenia is currently leading the way.

KEY FACTS

Size: 22,145 hectares (Croatia); 14,790 (Slovenia)
Styles: white, red, sparkling
Wine laws: PDO, PGI
Main soils: limestone, clay marl, sandstone, shale

CROATIA – TOURIST HAVEN

Croatia is diverse, with four vineyard areas: Istria, Dalmatia, Croatian Uplands and Slavonia. It has a long history of boutique wineries, now being revived by immigrants returning home to focus on quality and local grapes, and to experiment with natural winemaking. Organic viticulture has not yet been embraced here as much as in Slovenia, although the climate is ideal. Generally, quality has been vastly improved, but some wines are still rustic in style. In Istria, star grapes are white Malvazija Istarska and red Teran. Slavonia's continental climate suits Graševina (Welshriesling), while Riesling and Pinot Gris prefer the cooler Croatian Uplands. Juicy red Plavac Mali dominates the warm Dalmatian coast.

Producers to try: *Benvenuti, Fakin, Kabola, Kozlović, Matošević, Misal, Pilato, Štampar, Tomac*

The southern slopes of the Pelješac Peninsula in Croatia's Dalmatia region, where Plavac Mali is used to make Dingač.

SLOVENIA – MODERN PIONEERS

Slovenia is central Europe's most dynamic wine country. Two-thirds is planted to Laski Rizling, Chardonnay, Sauvignon Blanc and Malvazija; the most planted red is Refošk; and 300-plus growers are organic. Primorje is the best-known region; Europe's modern skin-contact and natural-wine movement began here (*see page* 134). Northerly Podravje, bordering Austria's Styria, is home to the world's oldest vine Zametovka, 400-plus years old. Posavje is small, with traditional-method fizz that deserves to be better known.

Producers to try: *Burja, Dveri-Pax, Edi Simčič, Istenič, Kristančič, Marjan Simčič, Movia, Verus*

CROATIA & SLOVENIA: KEY STYLES & GRAPES

Crisp delicate whites: Graševina, Skrlet (Croatia); Laski Rizling/Welshriesling, Zelen (Slovenia)
Full rich whites: Malvazija Istarska (Croatia, Slovenia); Chardonnay, Sauvignon Blanc, Rebula/Ribolla Gialla, Šipon/Furmint (Slovenia)
Soft juicy reds: Teran (Croatia); Refošk, Žametovka, Modri Pinot/Pinot Noir (Slovenia)
Full rich reds: Plavac Mali (Croatia); Modra Frankinja/Blaufränkisch (Slovenia)
Grapes recently revived from extinction: Crljenak Kaštelanski, Privlačka Bilina (Croatia), Zelen (Slovenia)

CHANGES IN PRODUCTION

Current challenges: highly fragmented wine industries with thousands of growers
Future positives: native grapes

WESTERN BALKANS

This area has plenty of potential, with interesting terroir and local grapes, but recent political upheavals mean it will take time for these countries to re-establish their own wine identities. For the moment, Serbia is the frontrunner in terms of quality.

KEY FACTS

Size: 20,110 hectares (Serbia); 3,000 (Bosnia & Herzegovina); 3,200 (Kosovo); 2,370 (Montenegro); 11,450 (Albania); 28,210 (North Macedonia)
Styles: white, red, rosé, sparkling, sweet
Wine laws: PDO, PGI (Serbia, North Macedonia)
Main soils: chernozem, limestone, loess, clay, sand

THE ONES TO WATCH

Serbia: The pace of change here is the most rapid; small artisan producers make 60 per cent of its whites, but the industry is now fragmented post-communism with over 100,000 growers. International red grapes are popular, but a new generation is reviving some of Serbia's 200 grapes. The most dynamic area is Fruška Gora, near Srem.
Bosnia & Herzegovina: This small country has an Adriatic coastline, high mountains and Mediterranean climate. Its wine industry is reviving slowly, best known for spicy white Žilavka, at best from southerly Herzegovina. Local juicy red Blatina is promising, as is the Balkans' flagship red, Vranac.
Kosovo: With a long wine history, Kosovo is in need of modernization, through boutique family operations to state-owned wineries.
Montenegro: The main Podgorica region is dominated (95 per cent) by the giant Plantaže (2,300 hectares), making good-quality Vranac. There are small family wineries now emerging.
Albania: Local grapes here are being revived by an increasing number of boutique wineries, with considerable Italian influence.
North Macedonia: There is promise here, especially with a range of international and local whites, with most production in the central Vardar River Valley.

Producers to try: *Despotika, Deurić, Matalj, Maurer, Ivanović, Temet, Veritas* (Serbia); *Carski, Citluk, Tvrdos, Vukoje* (Bosnia & Herzegovina); *Stone Castle* (Kosovo); *Buk, Kopitovic, Lipovac, Plantaže* (Montenegro); *Uka* (Albania); *Dalvina, Kamnik, Stobi, Tikveš* (North Macedonia)

SERBIA, BOSNIA & HERZEGOVINA, KOSOVO, MONTENEGRO, ALBANIA, NORTH MACEDONIA: KEY STYLES & GRAPES

Crisp delicate whites: Grašac/Welshriesling, Morava (Serbia); Cëruja, Pulëz, Debina (Albania)
Full rich whites: Smederevka (Serbia, North Macedonia), Žilavka (Bosnia & Herzegovina), Rkatsiteli (North Macedonia)
Soft juicy reds: Prokupac (Serbia)
Full rich reds: Probus (Serbia); Vranac, Kratosija, (Montenegro), Vranec [sic], Kratosija, Stanušina (North Macedonia)

CHANGES IN PRODUCTION

Current challenges: heat, drought
Future positives: local grape revival, investment, new generations experimenting

Serbia, one of the most dynamic wine countries in the Western Balkans.

EASTERN MEDITERRANEAN

This part of the ancient world – one of the earliest centres of winemaking – is now reviving its native grapes, wine industries and wine culture, despite climatic, economic and political challenges.

KEY FACTS
Size: 402,000 hectares (Turkey, including table grapes/raisins); 7,330 (Cyprus); 8,830 (Israel), 6,920 (Lebanon)
Styles: white, red, rosé, sparkling, sweet
Wine laws: PDO, PGI (Cyprus), AO (Israel)
Main soils: limestone, clay loam, gravel sandstone, volcanic tuff

TURKEY – AEGEAN TO ANATOLIA

Turkey has the world's fifth-largest vineyard area – but most of its grapes are used for the table and for drying, with only three per cent used for wine. Despite the fact that no alcohol advertising or promotion is permitted here, an expanding wine scene exists around the Aegean coast (including Tenedos island) and north into Thrace; through central Anatolia and on to the southeast. Climates vary from warm Mediterranean to hot continental, with altitudes (over 1,100m) offering cool sites and a mixed bag of elegant and very rustic wines.
Producers to try: *Chamlija, Corvus, Doluca, Kavaklidere, Kayra, Kuzubağ*

CYPRUS – TROODOS SLOPES

Exciting new artisanal wineries are reviving Cyprus's wine heritage and rescuing native grapes. Cypriot winemakers are searching out old phylloxera-free vines and planting new vineyards on steep terracing at high elevations (up to 1,250m) on the slopes of the Troodos Mountains. Quality is impressive, and legendary sweet dessert Commandaria is still made from sun-dried Xynisteri and Mavro grapes.
Producers to try: *Makarounas, Tsiakkas, Vlassides, Vouni Panayia, Zambartas*

ISRAEL'S NATIVE GRAPE REVIVAL

Israel is rescuing its native grapes, alongside extensive plantings of international grapes. The dynamic wine industry here has innovative boutique wineries across its five regions, making use of cool, high-altitude mountain sites. Quality is good, but prices are too high.
Producers to try: *Carmel, Castel, Dalton*

LEBANON'S ANCIENT LANDS

Resilient boutique wineries work against the odds in the ancient wineland of Lebanon, with heritage grapes (Cinsault, Carignan) alongside international and local reds and whites. Initially renowned for hefty exotic-flavoured reds from Bekaa Valley, now vibrant whites emerge from 1,800m vineyards in northerly Batroun – and experimentation continues with pét-nat, rosé and amphorae. Quality is mixed but shows potential.
Producers to try: *Ixsir, Mersel, Musar, Tourelles*

SYRIA – AGAINST THE ODDS

Syria has a long wine history; the grapevine holds an important place in Syrian symbolism. *Bargylus* continues production in northwestern vineyards near Latakia, with impressive international styles.

TURKEY, CYPRUS, ISRAEL, LEBANON: KEY STYLES & GRAPES
Crisp delicate whites: Narince (Turkey); Jandali (Israel), Merwah, Meksassi (Lebanon)
Full rich whites: Emir (Turkey); Promara, Xynisteri (Cyprus), Marawi (Israel); Obeideh (Lebanon)
Soft juicy reds: Öküzgözü, Kalecik Karasi (Turkey); Yiannoudi (Cyprus), Sabbagheih (Lebanon)
Full rich reds: Boğazkere (Turkey); Maratheftiko (Cyprus)
Grapes recently revived from extinction: Urla Karasi (Turkey); Dabuki, Dumiat (Israel)

CHANGES IN PRODUCTION
Current challenges: heat, drought
Future positives: native grape revival

URBAN WINERIES

When we imagine a winery setting, we immediately think of a countryside property surrounded by vineyards. Now, there is a growing trend for wineries to be based in urban areas, with grapes crushed and processed in the heart of the city – not a vineyard in sight, but close to the market they sell to.

For the wine-lover, urban wineries offer an entirely new concept for enjoying wine – and they are super-convenient for those living or working in a city or visiting on a city break. They are by nature small artisanal businesses due to the constraints of city property prices, so they appeal to those looking for unusual handcrafted wines.

Urban wineries were first set up in California in the early 2000s; the idea then spread to New York and Portland (Oregon), Sydney, Melbourne, Brisbane and Hobart in Australia, and South Africa's Cape Town. Today, as the English wine scene expands, London has four, and Enfield, within London's city limits, has an urban vineyard. Other cities including Vienna, Paris, Barcelona, Rome, Florence, Turin, Venice and Brescia also have urban vineyards that are open to visitors (*see* UVA at urbanvineyards.org).

These wineries are often fun, funky places to visit, housed in former ice factories, railway arches or heritage churches. Portland's Hot Chicks Do Wine also has a nano-brewery, Melbourne's

London Cru opened in 2013 as London's first urban winery, based in an old Victorian warehouse that was once a gin distillery.

Noisy Ritual's winery is a popular music venue, and in London's first urban winery, London Cru, visitors are let loose among the vats. You can be 'a winemaker for a day', creating your own Bordeaux-inspired signature cuvée, or hire the sophisticated dining area in the tank room; London Cru now also owns a vineyard in Sussex.

TWO SIDES OF THE STORY

For the winemaker, owning an urban winery allows them to put their resources into buying the best grapes they can from the surrounding areas and to make the best-possible quality very close to a ready market for their wines.

MODERNIZING TRADITION

American-born winemaker Sergio Verrillo set up Blackbook in 2017, in an old network railway arch in Battersea, London, England.

'I love the city and wanted to bring the English countryside and English wine to the masses,' he says, 'and be near an engaged customer base. I source grapes from within a two-hour radius of London; 50 to 60 per cent come from Essex, the remainder from Oxfordshire, London, Kent and Sussex, so I can buy from a range of different micro-climates, because I love making cool-climate Chardonnay and Pinot Noir. I only make still wines. I certainly dream of owning a vineyard one day, but it doesn't have to be next to the winery.

'Blackbook is a winemaking unit, but we encourage visitors to experience our educational events and wine membership. I think the beauty of an urban winery is the drive of innovation; they are part of a fast-paced, quickly changing environment – conduits for progression – and symbolize modernism of a very traditional industry.'

KEEPING IT SIMPLE

The most recent entrant into the world's urban winery scene in December 2024 is Minimalist Wines in South Africa. Set up by winemaker Sam Lambson in Hope Street, in Cape Town's Gardens suburb, it has a view of Table Mountain.

'As an independent producer, not owning any vines, it did not make sense to me to set up shop in a single wine district,' says Lambson, 'because we source fruit from multiple regions, in cool-climate Cape Agulhas, Elgin and Stellenbosch. Urban wineries can be hubs of innovation and experimentation and give full transparency into the production process. Since we are "minimalists" focusing on just one grape – Syrah – we wanted to connect directly with our customers and make our contribution to the next generation of South African fine-wine culture by doing something unique.'

URBAN WINERIES TO VISIT

FRANCE

Bordeaux: Les Carmes Haut-Brion, La Micro Winerie
Lyon: Chai St Olive
Marseille: Microcosmos Chai Urbain

ITALY

Milan: Cantina Urbana
Venice: San Francesco della Vigna
Rome: Parvus Ager

THE US

New York: Brooklyn Winery, City Winery, Red Hook
Portland: Amaterra, Clay Pigeon, Division Hip Chicks Do Wine
Napa: St Clair Brown
Los Angeles: Angeleno, Byron Blatty, Cavaletti, San Antonio, LA River

AUSTRALIA

Brisbane: City Winery
Sydney: Urban Winery
Melbourne: Noisy Ritual
Adelaide: Oddio
Perth: H&C
Hobart: Glaetzer-Dixon

REST OF THE WORLD

Lisbon, Portugal: Adega Belem
Madrid, Spain: La Matritense
Stuttgart, Germany: Weingut Stuttgart
Würzburg, Germany: Burgerspital, Juliusspital
Vienna, Austria: Schlumberger Kellerwelten
London, UK: London Cru, Renegade, Blackbook, Vagabond
Cambridge, UK: Gutter & Stars
Hong Kong: Urban Project
Cape Town, South Africa: Dorrance, Minimalist

THE US – CALIFORNIA

The Sunshine State produces over 80 per cent of US wine, making it the world's fourth-largest producer. With a dry sunny climate, the wines of California can be big, brash, soft and ripe with exotic fruit. In general, expect high-alcohol jammy Zinfandel, dense graceful Cabernet Sauvignon, rich buttery Chardonnay and plush fragrant Pinot Noir; but with over 100 different grape varieties grown in 49 of its 58 counties, there is plenty to discover.

KEY FACTS
Size: 246,860 hectares/610,000 acres (California), of which 23,585/58,280 (Sonoma), and 18,665/46,125 (Napa)
Styles: white, red, rosé, sparkling, sweet
Wine laws: AVA
Main soils: clay, calcareous, sandy loam, loess, shale, volcanic

DIVERSE MICRO-CLIMATES

With a climate dominated by the Pacific, proximity to ocean and mountains is crucial here for wine quality. Fog acts like an air-conditioner, keeping vines cool as it's drawn inland. California's diverse micro-climates, north to south and west to east, will prove useful for ongoing climate challenges.

GREEN MENDOCINO

Coastal Mendocino, 160km north of San Francisco, with its rugged cliffs and redwood forests, is where the 1970s hippies migrated. In the 1980s, it became home to the first certified organic winery in the US, and its first biodynamic in 1996. It now leads the 'green' way with a third of California's organic vines. Roederer's California outpost is here in cool Anderson Valley; you can also find sleek Chardonnay and hearty Zinfandel.
Producers to try: *Frey Vineyards, Roederer Estate*

SONOMA – FOG ON THE VINE

Sonoma is California's Eden, with diverse micro-climates spread between the Mayacamas Mountains and the Pacific, and more soil types than France. Water is never far away – whether ocean or river; the Russian River pulls fog inland through Healdsburg to Alexander Valley.

California's earliest vines were planted in Sonoma by Russian colonists in 1812. It is much cooler than Napa, and foggier – the elegant wines from Russian River, Green Valley and Carneros confirm this. However, cooler 'real' Sonoma Coast on ridges above the rocky coastline makes the most dynamic, tense and taut Chardonnay and nuanced Pinot Noir.
Producers to try: *DuMOL, Hirsch, Joseph Swan, Kistler, Kutch, Ramey, Ridge (Lytton Springs)*

NAPA – CABERNET HEARTLAND

Napa is just 50km long and 8km wide, stretching from southern Carneros to northern Calistoga. It's a dramatic valley surrounded on both sides by mountains, with vineyards up to 800m on volcanic Mount Veeder and the Spring and Diamond mountains. The west side gives structured 'mountain' Cabernets, while the warmer east makes lusher, textured styles. On the benchland, Rutherford, Oakville and Stags' Leap make world-class, top-dollar Cabernet Sauvignon. This is one of the world's most densely planted wine regions – but it is small, producing only four per cent of California's wine.
Producers to try: *Cain, Cakebread, Corison, Frog's Leap, Outpost, Shafer, Spottswoode, Trefethen*

SOUTH OF THE BAY

North Central Coast is diverse. Santa Cruz Mountains AVA is home to top names, with the vineyards directly influenced by the ocean and fog. Inland is white-wine-focused Livermore amid urban sprawl, while down the coast is southern Monterey, California's largest Chardonnay vineyard. Inland Santa Luisa Highlands, Chalone and Mt Harlan make the best hunting ground for wines.
Producers to try: *Birichino, Chalone, Mt Eden, Ridge (Monte Bello), Rhys*

NORTHERN HEIGHTS

Lodi, the most famous AVA in northern Central Valley, sits up on high ground and is renowned for outstanding Zinfandel. Small boutique wineries experiment with Portuguese, Italian and Rhône grapes here and in old Gold Rush country, Sierra Foothills and Amador County.

Producers to try: *Berghold, Bokisch, Michael David, M2, Terre Rouge/Easton*

RHÔNE RANGERS DOWN SOUTH

South Central Coast is arguably California's most experimental area. From warmer Paso Robles in San Luis Obispo (Zinfandel to Pinot Noir), down through Edna Valley (superb Chardonnay and Viognier), to cooler Santa Maria Valley and Santa Rita Hills in Santa Barbara (Chardonnay).

Producers to try: *Alban, Au Bon Climat, Sanford & Benedict, Scar of the Sea, Tablas Creek*

KEY STYLES & GRAPES

Crisp delicate whites: Albariño, Aligoté, Picpoul, Vermentino
Full rich whites: Chardonnay, Roussanne, Chenin Blanc
Soft juicy reds: Pinot Noir, Cabernet Franc, Barbera, Grenache, Trousseau, Gamay
Full rich reds: Cabernet Sauvignon, Zinfandel, Sangiovese, Carignan, Petit Verdot, Touriga Nacional

CHANGES IN PRODUCTION

Current challenges: wildfires, smoke, heat spikes, prolonged drought, lack of water, Pierce's disease (bacterial vine disease)
Future positives: cooler micro-climates, resistant hybrid grapes (Paseante Noir)

Superb Chardonnay and Viognier are made in Edna Valley on California's south-central coast.

THE REST OF THE US

Almost every state of the US produces wine, but after giant California there are four other important states – all with their own specialities: Oregon, Washington State, New York State and Virginia. While Washington State is currently the largest, with Riesling its flagship grape, Oregon is a close second in size, with world-renowned Pinot Noir.

KEY FACTS

Size: 18,000 hectares/44,480 acres (Oregon); 20,000/49,420 (Washington State); 14,165/35,000 (New York State); 1,720/4250 (Virginia)
Styles: white, red, rosé, sparkling
Wine laws: AVA
Main soils: red Jory volcanic clay, Willakenzie sedimentary, silty loess (Oregon); basalt, gravel, loess (Washington State); sand, shale, limestone (New York State); granite, clay, loam (Virginia)

OREGON'S PINOT CHALLENGE

Oregon is as diverse as California, but it focuses on Pinot Noir (60 per cent of plantings) and Pinot Gris. Heartland Willamette Valley has 90 per cent of Oregon's Pinot Noir; styles vary but are more delicate than California's. In the face of challenges (drought, freezes), growers are altering canopy techniques, and in Van Duzer Corridor, Eola-Amity Hills, Umpqua and Rogue they experiment with high-acid, thick-skinned grapes, such as Albariño, Grüner Veltliner, Godello, Gamay and Mencía.
Producers to try: *Chehalem, Divio, Domaine Drouhin, Evening Land, Kelley Fox, Lingua Franca, The Eyrie, Walter Scott*

WASHINGTON STATE – SWEET SPOT

Columbia Valley is east of the Cascade Mountains and has a short, bright growing season and diurnal shift. Not known for one grape, the key five – 80 per cent of production – are Cabernet Sauvignon, Chardonnay, Riesling, Merlot and Syrah; the best examples are from Walla Walla, Columbia Gorge, Red Mountain and Horse Heaven Hills.
Producers to try: *Eroica, Gramercy, Grosgrain, Kiona, L'Ecole No 41, Syncline*

NEW YORK STATE – LAKE INFLUENCE

New York State is the third-largest wine region in the US, but vinifera grapes are less common here. Riesling is Finger Lakes' flagship, enjoying its long, temperate growing season. Long Island is known for its reds, while Hudson, Niagara and Lake Erie grow Riesling. Increasingly hardy hybrids make good dry styles.
Producers to try: *Bloomer Creek, Channing Daughters, Fjord, Konstantin Frank, Red Newt*

VIRGINIA'S FRANC HEARTLAND

Cabernet Franc is now Virginia's most planted grape, while Chardonnay decreases. Humidity, hurricanes and winter freeze are a challenge.
Producers to try: *Linden, RdV, Veritas*

KEY STYLES & GRAPES

Crisp delicate whites: Arinto, Albariño, Grüner Veltliner (Oregon); Riesling (Washington State, NY State); Petit Manseng, Vermentino (Virginia)
Full rich whites: Pinot Gris, Godello (Oregon); Chardonnay, Roussanne, Furmint, Chenin Blanc, Viognier (Washington State); Chardonnay, Viognier (Virginia)
Soft juicy reds: Pinot Noir, Gamay, Tempranillo, Mencía (Oregon); Merlot, Cabernet Franc, Gamay, Lemberger (Washington State, NY State); Cabernet Franc, Merlot (NY State); Cabernet Franc, Merlot, Refosco (Virginia)
Full rich reds: Cabernet Sauvignon, Syrah (Oregon); Cabernet Sauvignon, Syrah, Aglianico (Washington State); Petit Verdot, Tannat (Virginia)

CHANGES IN PRODUCTION

Current challenges: rain at harvest, heat spikes, wildfires, drought, humidity, winter freeze
Future positives: drought resistant clones, cooler micro-climates, hardy hybrids

CANADA

Renowned for its Icewine (*see page* 108), Canada's wine industry has transformed since the 1990s into a hot spot for exciting wines. There might be some benefit from warming temperatures to assist ripening, but British Columbia in particular has had its fair share of climatic challenges.

KEY FACTS
Size: 7,200 hectares (Ontario), 5,000 hectares (British Columbia)
Styles: white, red, sparkling, sweet
Wine laws: VQA
Main soils: sandy loam, gravel, clay, limestone

ONTARIO INCREASES ITS PORTFOLIO

Canada's Icewine harvests are becoming less predictable, so wineries in Ontario are adapting by either migrating plantings to the north or experimenting with alternative grapes. Recently, Pinot Noir has been successful for table wines (more elegant than in British Columbia). Niagara Peninsula is the most important sizewise; Prince Edward County on the north shore of Lake Ontario is now a hotspot of vineyard development, and Lake Erie North Shore is the warmest region, able to ripen Merlot and Cabernet Franc well.
Producers to try: *Bachelder, Cloudsley, Foxcroft, Henry of Pelham, Hidden Bench, Inniskillin, Malivoire, Peller, Pillitteri, Stanners*

BRITISH COLUMBIA'S EXPANSION

Large bodies of water also have an influence in British Columbia's main region, Okanagan Valley, which has 86 per cent of the province's vineyards. All along Okanagan Lake, expansion of red planting has been rapid, but challenges from winter freeze to wildfires devastated crop levels in the 2020s. The warmer, drier south concentrates on elegant reds with less new oak; the cooler, wetter north suits Riesling, Chardonnay and Pinot Noir. Similkameen Valley, Fraser Island and cool, wet Vancouver Island employ hardy hybrids.

Quails' Gate vineyard, on the west side of Lake Okanagan in Canada's British Columbia, grows Chardonnay, Chenin Blanc and Pinot Noir.

Producers to try: *Haywire, Martin's Lane, Mission Hill, Phantom Creek, Quails' Gate*

NOVA SCOTIA SPARKLES

The rapidly expanding eastern Canadian region of Novia Scotia now has over 20 wineries. Hardy hybrids Maréchal Foch and Baco Noir are popular, but focus is on Chardonnay and Riesling. Icewine and traditional-method sparkling are specialities.
Producers to try: *Benjamin Bridge, Blomidon, Domaine de Grand Pré*

KEY STYLES & GRAPES
Crisp delicate whites: Albariño, Riesling (Ontario, British Columbia, Nova Scotia)
Full rich whites: Chardonnay, Pinot Gris (Ontario, British Columbia, Nova Scotia)
Soft juicy reds: Gamay, Pinot Noir, Merlot, Cabernet Franc (Ontario, British Columbia)
Full rich reds: Cabernet Sauvignon, Syrah (Ontario, British Columbia).
Sweet: Riesling, Vidal (Ontario, British C, N Scotia)

CHANGES IN PRODUCTION
Current challenges: deep winter freeze, drought, heat spikes, wildfires, disease
Future positives: consistent grape ripening

CHILE

Chile is a land of contrasts offering an exciting diversity of terroir. Stretching some 4,800km end-to-end, from the northern Atacama Desert to the southern Patagonian icefields, it encompasses a huge range of micro-climates and soils. The largely benign dry climate is ideal for growing a variety of grapes organically. East to west, from the coast to the Andes, it also offers infinite opportunities to winemakers in search of subtle cool-climate styles, pushing the cool edge of Chilean viticulture.

KEY FACTS
Size: 129,000 hectares
Styles: white, red, sparkling
Wine laws: DO, GI
Main soils: granite, clay, gravel, limestone, volcanic

THE NEW VISION

Chile was once the land of cheap-and-cheerful wine, but new-wave Chile is different. Bulk wine produced on its warm, flat valley floor is a thing of the past. Now the search is on for fresher, minerally, less overtly fruit-driven wines – and a new generation of winemakers is pushing the boundaries north, south, east and west to achieve this. They are discovering what lies beneath the vineyard with new soil-mapping technology, using higher-density plantings to get better fruit concentration and reining back on new oak.

GRAPE DIVERSITY

Many of Chile's vineyards are young, half under 15 years old, so the best is yet to come in this phylloxera-free environment. Today, the prime hunting ground for Cabernet Sauvignon – its most planted red grape – is upper Maipo. Flagship grape Carmenère, suitably drought-resistant for a warming climate, is at its best in Colchagua. Old-vine Carignan and Cinsault from Curicó and Itata, alongside País and Romano in the old heartland of Maule, are being revived. Syrah is superb from Elqui, while Pinot Noir is best from coastal Leyda and Paradones. Chile's top Chardonnays now come from northerly Limarí, and Riesling as far south as Osorno.

FAR NORTH

Elqui, Chile's most northerly wine valley, makes crisp Sauvignon Blanc by the chilly coast and peppery Syrah and spicy Carmenère on the warmer granite hills. There are also experimental plantings up to 2,200m high for Roussanne, Malbec and Touriga Nacional. Chile's excitingly taut, minerally Chardonnays thrive in Limarí. Inland Aconcagua is best for bold reds, and coastal Aconcagua for fresh vibrant Pinot Noir.
Producers to try: *Errázuriz, Falernia, Seña, Tabalí*

COASTAL CLASSICS

Casablanca was the first region to be developed in the 1980s, with Chardonnay and Pinot Noir. Winemakers then pushed further towards the coast to Leyda and San Antonio, now home to Chile's top Sauvignon Blanc, Pinot Noir and Riesling. Lo Abarca region, even closer to the ocean mists, makes sleek Pinot Noir and peppery Syrah.
Producers to try: *Casa Marin, Garces Silva, Matetic, Viña Leyda*

CABERNET HEARTLAND

The alluvial terraces of upper Maipo are home to Chile's richest, most muscular Cabernet Sauvignon, grown on round stones and river gravel. This is pure Cabernet with no Merlot needed in the blend to soften it. In Isla de Maipo, Carmenère grows on gravel banks making good examples. To the south, Rapel's Colchagua and Cachapoal also make top Carmenère. Cabernet Sauvignon is additionally found in Apalta and near Angostura.
Producers to try: *Casa Lapostelle, Casa Silva, Concha y Toro, De Martino, Emiliana, Koyle, Maturana, Montes, Vik*

Errázuriz's Don Maximiano vineyard in Aconcagua, Chile, is home to Cabernet Sauvignon, Carmenère and Petit Verdot.

HEADING SOUTH

Curicó, Maule and Itata – once bulk-wine land – are now hunting grounds for winemakers in search of indigenous old vines (crunchy red-fruited País in Curicó). Unirrigated old bush vines give perfumed, grippy Carignan in Maule. In Itata, old-vine Cinsault, Torontel and Muscat make remarkable artisanal wines, with the granite soils of subzone Guarilihue being explored.
Producers to try: *Bouchon, CoPa, Leo Erazo, Mardones, Pedro Parra, Torres.*

THE COOL SOUTH

Bío-Bío is home to Gewurztaminer, Riesling, Chardonnay and Sauvignon Blanc, while exciting Syrah and Pinot Noir are being made on the volcanic soils of Traiguen in Malleco. There are experimental plantings extending as far south as Osorno and Chile Chico and even out to the island of Mechuque. This is serious marginal viticulture, with a climate akin to Oregon or New Zealand.
Producers to try: *Aquitania, Cono Sur, Montes, Trapi del Bueno, Volcanes*

KEY STYLES & GRAPES

Crisp delicate whites: Torontel, Riesling, Muscat
Full rich whites: Sauvignon Blanc, Semillon
Soft juicy reds: País, Merlot, Pinot Noir, Romano
Full rich reds: Cabernet Sauvignon, Carmenère, Syrah, Carignan, Cinsault, Touriga Nacional

CHANGES IN PRODUCTION

Current challenges: water scarcity, drought, heat spikes, wildfires
Future positives: cooler micro-climates in south or higher into Andes foothills

ARGENTINA

Argentina is a country of extremes, with some of the world's largest, highest and most southerly vineyards. Its wine regions are widely scattered from Jujuy on the northern border to Chubut in southern Patagonia – but almost all hug the eastern foothills of the Andes, making the most of altitude. Like neighbour Chile, Argentina has a long wine history that was focused on quantity but is now transitioning to quality with remarkable success. It might be the world's fifth-largest wine producer, but it has been much slower than its neighbour to export because Argentina has one of the world's highest per capita consumption rates.

KEY FACTS
Size: 200,000 hectares
Styles: white, red, sparkling
Wine laws: GI
Main soils: limestone, alluvial silt, clay, sand, gravel

MOUNTAIN WINES

If any country knows how to do mountain wines, it's Argentina. With altitudes up to 1,600m in its biggest region, Mendoza, it makes the most of its desert mountain climate. Stark, bright, sunny days ripen grapes, while plunging night temperatures retain acidity. Argentina is largely continental in climate and has less vintage variation than Chile, but the real risk is hail – and hail nets are expensive. The towering snowcapped Andes provide essential irrigation water, and many of Argentina's vines are ungrafted (as they are in Chile) because phylloxera has not propagated here.

KING MALBEC

For many years, Argentina churned out quantities of easy-drinking plummy Malbecs that lacked depth and complexity, but research carried out since the mid-1990s is bearing fruit. New investments in precision viticulture, digging soil pits (*see page* 71), identifying 40 different Malbec clones and recognizing that UV-B light increases phenolics and anthocyanins giving dark skins, richer mouthfeel and longevity have sent the quality of Uco Valley Malbec stratospheric. Top-level Malbec can compete with the best reds in the world, but sadly prices are escalating too.

Malbec is king, but Argentina can do Cabernets Franc and Sauvignon, Petit Verdot and Bonarda well. Its heritage grape Criolla Chica (same as Chile's País), first planted in the 16th century, has finally gained quality status. Bizarrely, until the 1980s, Argentina grew more white than red. Whites were previously grown in warm areas; now pungent Torrontés, sleek Chardonnay and honeyed Semillon are made widely, plus cool-climate Riesling and Grüner Veltliner in southern Patagonia.

FAR NORTH

Northern Argentina's remote Calchaquí Valley plantings are expanding. Jujuy has the highest vineyards, over 3,000m, bordering Bolivia, with Malbec and Syrah. Catamarca grows mostly pink-skinned Cereza, plus Syrah and Bonarda. Tucuman majors on Malbec, and Salta's Cafayate region is the home of floral Torrontés.
Producers to try: *Colome, El Esteco, Piattelli*

JOURNEYING SOUTH

San Juan grows Bonarda, Cabernet Sauvignon, Torrontés and Viognier, with the best quality from limestone soils and higher altitudes in the Pedernal subzone. La Rioja is dominated by one giant co-op but has a handful of boutique producers; Torrontés is favoured here.
Producers to try: *Graffigna, Las Moras*

UCO HEROES

Mendoza is home to over 70 per cent of Argentina's vineyards. The three main areas are Maipú, Luján de Cuyo and Uco Valley, with new terroirs being explored in Las Heras and San Rafael. Historic Maipú is on flatter silty land and has precious old

vines, as does neighbour Luján de Cuyo, closer to the mountains, making lush succulent Malbec. However it is Uco Valley and subregions Tupungato (and subzone Gualtallary), Tunuyan and San Carlos that are grabbing attention today. Plantings have rocketed since the early 2000s; Uco is now twice the size of Luján, with 30,000 hectares and a roll call of big names exploring higher into the hills, making the best Malbec on the planet.
Producers to try: *Catena, Cobos, Durigutti, Mendel, Susana Balbo, Weinert, Zuccardi*

SOUTHERN FRONTIER

Remote, windswept, cool Patagonia might seem an unlikely place to grow vines. Río Negro was the first area to be planted, then Neuquén's river valley to the west. Now the new frontier extreme has been extended south to Chubut near the Atlantic Ocean. Pioneers first planted here in 1998, and now a sizeable investment has been made, with Chardonnay, Pinot Noir and Malbec planted on an old cherry farm with substantial windbreaks – the world's southernmost vineyard.
Producers to try: *Chacra, Humberto Canale, Noemia, Otronia*

KEY STYLES & GRAPES

Crisp delicate whites: Torrontés Riojano
Full rich whites: Chardonnay, Semillon, Viognier
Soft juicy reds: Bonarda, Cabernet Franc, Criolla Chica, Pinot Noir
Full rich reds: Malbec, Syrah, Cabernet Sauvignon, Petit Verdot

CHANGES IN PRODUCTION

Current challenges: wind, frost, hail, phylloxera
Future positives: drought-resistant clones, higher altitude

Autumn in Las Compuertas, a cool district in Mendoza's historic Luján de Cuyo, which has some of Argentina's oldest vines.

URUGUAY

The vineyard area of Uruguay is very small, not much larger than St-Émilion in Bordeaux, but it punches well above its weight in wine quality. Low coastal hills heavily influenced by the Atlantic, have a mild maritime climate and lush green landscape similar to northwest Spain's Galicia. It is very different from its warmer neighbours, and the wines are different too. Stylistically, cool coastal Uruguayan wines do not have the power and extract of Chile and Argentina, but they offer superb freshness, delicacy and elegance.

KEY FACTS

Size: 5,990 hectares
Styles: white, red, sweet
Wine laws: no official classification
Main soils: river gravel, sand, schist, chalk, clay, calcareous, limestone, granite

QUIET REVOLUTION

Since the early 21st century, there has been a quiet revolution in the Uruguayan wine scene. Though small, it's now the fourth-largest wine country in South America. Flagship grape Tannat has been important, but it took 200 years to perfect it. One of the keys to Uruguay's success is its soil diversity across Río de la Plata, Canelones and Maldonado.

The new vineyards of Bodega Garzón in Maldonado, eastern Uruguay.

Vintage variation is far greater here than in Chile or Argentina, but there is no scarcity of water. Many small wineries have Italian and Spanish ancestry, encouraging the new generation to plant Nebbiolo, Barbera, Arneis, Freisa and Albariño.

THE HEARTLAND

The gentle undulating hillsides of Canelones near Montevideo form the hub of production (60 per cent of plantings), with Uruguay's oldest vines. It is warm, but humidity is high, which suits Tannat's slower ripening. Its subzones include Juanico, one of the warmest (good for reds), northerly cooler Progresso, higher Las Violetas and coastal Atlantida.
Producers to try: *Artesana, Bracco Bosca, Deicas, Pablo Fallabrino, Pisano, Viña Progreso*

PIONEER COUNTRY

Heading east, the areas of Maldonado, Piriápolis and Pan de Azúcar have attracted experimental plantings with Chardonnay and sparkling wines. In 2000, pioneers were enticed even further east along the temperate coast – with its cool winds, swirling sea mists and granite soils – to farmland inland from Punta del Este. Expansion has been rapid here, with fresher Tannat, remarkably vibrant Albariño and promising Pinot Noir.
Producers to try: *Alto de la Ballena, Bouza, Brisas, Cerro del Toro, Garzón, José Ignacio, Viña Edén*

KEY STYLES & GRAPES

Crisp delicate whites: Albariño, Arneis, Torrontés, Petit Manseng
Full rich whites: Chardonnay, Viognier, Marsanne
Soft juicy reds: Moscatel de Hamburgo, Cabernet Franc, Pinot Noir
Full rich reds: Tannat, Malbec

CHANGES IN PRODUCTION

Current challenges: humidity, disease, high rainfall
Future positives: no water scarcity, diverse soils, cool Atlantic influence

BRAZIL, PERU & BOLIVIA

These three South American countries have diverse cultures, landscapes and climates – but they also have one thing in common. Since the mid-1990s, a new generation of winemakers has been keen to explore their potential. The fastest growing is Brazil, South America's third-largest wine country and largest sparkling-wine producer. Peru is South America's oldest wine country, with a revived modern industry and mix of international and native grapes in coastal vineyards. In high-altitude Bolivia, progress is slow, but its treasure trove of old Criolla vines and artisanal methods are being restored.

KEY FACTS

Size: 83,000 hectares (Brazil); 14,800 (Peru); 4,600 (Bolivia); includes table grapes and Pisco brandy
Styles: mostly red; white, sparkling, sweet
Wine laws: DO, IP (Brazil)
Main soils: granite, limestone, clay, sand

BRAZIL – WINTER HARVESTS

Heat and humidity are Brazil's main challenges; that is why 90 per cent of vineyards are in the cooler drier south, in Rio Grande do Sul. However, this region recently experienced catastrophic floods and landslides in heartland Serra Gaucha (Pinot Noir, Chardonnay) and Vale dos Vinhedos (sparkling and Merlot).

Expansion in other areas includes higher-altitude Serra da Mantiqueira in Minas Gerais, where winter harvests are preferred, and northeasterly Bahia, with semi-arid, tropical São Francisco. In both, Syrah looks promising.
Producers to try: *Eterna, Geisse, Miolo, Pizzato, Salton, Valduga*

PERU – ARTISANAL REVIVAL

South America's first vines were planted in Peru in 1539. Today, vineyards are south of Lima, with Ica Valley its most important region; the rest of Peru is too tropical or extreme. Ica is desert-like, but cooling sea breezes, high altitudes and diurnal temperature shifts enable red grapes to be grown. Pisco dominates here, but the recent focus has been on artisanal wines, with indigenous grapes fermented in old clay *tinajas* *(see page* 123*)*. Pioneers experiment with high-altitude plantings at 3,000m in Sierra del Perú.
Producers to try: *Alegre, Apu, Finca 314, Intipalka, Mimo, Murga, Pachawines, Tacama*

BOLIVIA – LADDER HARVESTS

All Bolivia's vineyards are high altitude, at over 1,600m. Its wine capital is now Tarija, near Argentina, but traditional Cinti Valley to the northwest (up to 2,300m) is being revived. A treasure trove of old vines grow up trees (to 6m), requiring ladders for pruning and harvesting, while ancestral methods are used for fermentation. Bolivia's most popular international grape is Cabernet Sauvignon, although the continental climate is not ideal. Fragrant Moscatel de Alejandria, Bolivia's flagship grape, is best when grown at up to 3,600m altitude.
Producers to try: *Campos de Solana, Cepas de Fuego, Jardin Oculto, Kuhlmann, La Concepcion, San Francisco de la Horca*

BRAZIL, PERU, BOLIVIA: KEY STYLES & GRAPES

Crisp delicate whites: Torontel (Peru); Moscatel de Alejandria (Bolivia)
Full rich whites: Albilla (Peru); Chardonnay (Brazil)
Soft juicy reds: Quebranta, Mollar Cano, Negra Criolla, Cantarilla (Peru); Missionera, Vischoquena (Bolivia)
Full rich reds: Cabernet Sauvignon, Syrah, Merlot (Brazil); Malbec, Cabernet Sauvignon, Tannat (Peru), Cabernet Sauvignon (Bolivia)

CHANGES IN PRODUCTION

Current challenges: humidity, heat, drought, floods
Future positives: high altitude, native-grape revival

AUSTRALIA

Many of Australia's 65 wine regions hug the southern coastline, enjoying a more temperate climate, since this vast island continent is mainly too hot for growing grapes. Today, its wine industry is made up of two diverse parts: branded wines sold in supermarkets, and more site-specific wines made by myriad resourceful, innovative boutique wineries offering quality and diversity. Often considered a country of big, bold, high-alcohol wines, Australia has seen a change of late towards brighter, fresher, approachable styles.

KEY FACTS

Size: 146,245 hectares (Australia total); 10,785 (Western Australia), 76,180 (South Australia), 34,000 (New South Wales), 22,000 (Victoria), 2,420 (Tasmania), 675 (Queensland)
Styles: white, red, rosé, sparkling, sweet, fortified
Wine laws: GI
Main soils: clay, loam, granite, schist, terra rossa, limestone

SOUL SEARCHING

Australia has had its fair share of challenges in recent years – from export problems, to climatic issues with wildfires and drought. There has been a lot of soul searching in its 'engine room' – the warm inland, irrigated regions of Riverland, Murray River and Riverina. Suppliers of everyday value wines, some parts of these areas are becoming unsustainable with heat and drought.

Finer Australian wines tend to come from the coastal areas, benefiting from the cooling influence of ocean or mountains and offering regional diversity.

Tolpuddle Vineyard in Coal River Valley, southern Tasmania, is famous for its world-class Pinot Noir and Chardonnay.

MEDITERRANEAN INFLUENCE

The big six grapes are Chardonnay, Riesling and Semillon for white wines, and Shiraz, Cabernet Sauvignon and Pinot Noir for reds. There is a renewed Grenache focus and signs that Shiraz's star might be on the wane – though the world's oldest Shiraz vines here produce world-class wine. Riesling should be world-renowned but is surprisingly underrated. Growers are pivoting towards Italian, Spanish, Portuguese and Greek varieties able to cope in hot, dry conditions, while traditional winemaking techniques are challenged by inventive natural winemakers.

WESTERN BEAUTY

Western Australia has less than five per cent of Australia's wines, but quality is high. Outstandingly beautiful, with a dramatic coastline, since the late-1960s it has carved a stamp for itself as a classic wine region, thanks to windy, coastal Margaret River. Swan Valley is closer to Perth, while in the far south, Great Southern has subregions Albany, Mount Barker and Frankland River – the most promising.
Producers to try: *Cullen, Domaine Naturaliste, Frankland River, Fraser Gallop, Leeuwin, Vasse Felix*

SOUTHERN CLASSICS

South Australia produces the country's largest volume (including Riverland). It's also home to some of Australia's top wines. Clare and Eden Valley Riesling, Barossa Valley Shiraz, Chardonnay from Adelaide Hills, Grenache from McLaren Vale and Cabernet Sauvignon from Coonawarra are classics. Southern Mediterranean grapes, from Assyrtiko to Nero d'Avola, and a new generation of natural winemakers offer a point of interest.
Producers to try: *Alkina, Alpha Box Dice, Grosset, Henschke, Jim Barry, Majella, Powell, Riddoch, Shaw & Smith, Tapanappa, Thistledown, Yalumba*

VICTORIAN DIVERSITY

Cool southerly Victoria has a great range of styles, especially top Chardonnay and Pinot Noir from Yarra Valley, Mornington Peninsula, Gippsland and Macedon Ranges. Further north, Heathcote's Shiraz, Nagambie Lakes' old-vine Marsanne and King Valley's Italian grapes are renowned. In far northeastern Rutherglen, Australia's greatest sweet fortified Muscat offers brilliant value.
Producers to try: *Bindi, Campbells, Giaconda, Ten Minutes by Tractor, Yabby Lake*

THE APPLE ISLE

Tasmania, in the Southern Ocean's cool waters – once considered too wet and windy for wine – is now a hotspot for Riesling, Chardonnay and Pinot Noir from the north to the southeast. Australia's best fizz is made here.
Producers to try: *Domaine A, Freycinet, House of Arras, Lowestoft, Stargazer, Tolpuddle*

HISTORIC NSW HEARTLAND

New South Wales stretches from inland Murray Darling and Riverina to coastal Sydney. Around Canberra, Hilltops is renowned for Rhône blends, and Tumbarumba for sparkling grapes. Orange is reliable at high elevations, while historic Hunter Valley, first planted in 1823, makes renowned wines.
Producers to try: *De Bortoli, Clonakilla, Craigmoor, Tyrrell's*

TO THE NORTHEAST

In Queensland, near Brisbane, the Granite Belt grows a range of varieties, from Viognier to Tempranillo. There is also some experimenting with *qvevri* wines here (*see page* 123).
Producers to try: *Hidden Creek, Lark Hill*

KEY STYLES & GRAPES

Crisp delicate whites: Riesling, Albariño, Assyrtiko, Grüner Veltliner, Fiano, Vermentino
Full rich whites: Chardonnay, Semillon, Sauvignon Blanc, Grenache Blanc, Verdelho, Viognier, Roussanne
Soft juicy reds: Grenache, Pinot Noir, Tempranillo, Montepulciano
Full rich reds: Shiraz, Cabernet Sauvignon, Touriga Nacional, Nero d'Avola, Sangiovese

CHANGES IN PRODUCTION

Current challenges: heat spikes, wildfires, drought, floods, disease
Future positives: drought resistant clones, cooler micro-climates

NEW ZEALAND

New Zealand is now the sixth-largest exporter of wine in the world by value – a staggering achievement for such a small isolated industry that only started planting vines commercially in the 1970s. In terms of vineyard size, New Zealand is not much larger than Burgundy, around one-third the size of Bordeaux, but it is now a major player in the wine world thanks to its triumph with one grape, Sauvignon Blanc.

KEY FACTS

Size: 42,520 hectares (New Zealand total); 30,445 (Marlborough), 4,575 (Hawke's Bay), 2,160 (Central Otago), 1,500 (North Canterbury), 1,225 (Gisborne), 1,080 (Nelson), 1,015 (Wairarapa), 285 (Auckland)
Styles: mostly white; red, rosé, sparkling, sweet
Wine laws: GI
Main soils: gravel, clay loam, schist, loess, limestone, sandstone

ONE TO RELY ON

This country's success is partly due to its long growing season and cool maritime climate – all its vineyards, on North and South Islands, are within 130km of the sea. Its wines have incredibly lucid, pure fruits, combined with vibrant acidity and pungent aromatics, resulting in mouthwateringly fresh, zesty, textured wines. Added to this is meticulous innovative vineyard and cellar work – and a clean, green lifestyle image – with its focus on sustainability. New Zealand wines are never cheap but are always reliably well made.

NOT JUST SAUVIGNON BLANC

The world knows all about New Zealand Sauvignon Blanc – over 70 per cent of production – but the challenge is to get its other wines noticed. Aromatic Riesling, Pinot Gris and Gewurztraminer grow well here; Chardonnay has improved greatly; and winemakers experiment with Albariño and Grüner Veltliner.

One of New Zealand's most picturesque wineries, Man O' War on Waiheke Island has the country's only beachfront tasting room.

New Zealand Pinot Noir is now world-renowned, offering diversity between regions, while Syrah shows promise in Hawke's Bay and Waiheke Island. A new generation of dry rosé is also emerging.

OUT TO SEA

Back in the 1960s, Auckland had half of New Zealand's vines. Today, its best vineyards are out to sea, on dry sunny Waiheke Island, with its bold reds, but the country's top Chardonnay producer is in Kumeū, on the mainland, north of Auckland.
Producers to try: *Kumeu River, Man O'War.*

THE NORTH'S EAST COAST

Northeasterly Gisborne specializes in whites but suffers from a humid climate. Hawke's Bay near coastal Napier makes red and white. Gimblett Gravels, one of New Zealand's hottest and driest areas, is on the same latitude as Bordeaux but has a similar climate to Sardinia, making ripe reds. Bridge Pa to the west looks promising for Syrah.

Cool, dry, sheltered Martinborough in Wairarapa makes earthy, almost Burgundian Pinot Noir, compared to the fruity styles of the South Island.
Producers to try: *Ata Rangi, Craggy Range, Dry River, Escarpment, Sacred Hill, Te Mata*

THE HEARTLAND

Three-quarters of New Zealand's Sauvignon Blanc is in Marlborough – now *the* centre of the wine industry. Bright sun, diurnal temperature shift and a long, dry autumn develop flavour here like nowhere else. Wairau is the heartland, but windier, chillier Awatere to the south has proved successful. Southern Valley's clays are better for Pinot Noir. Smaller neighbouring Nelson on the north coast makes renowned Chardonnay and Pinot Noir.
Producers to try: *Dog Point, Greywacke, Hunter's, Neudorf, Seifried, Te Whare Ra*

THE SOUTHEAST COAST

Waipara and North Canterbury are both chilly, frost-prone areas. The former is home to New Zealand's best dry and sweet Rieslings, the latter to restrained Burgundian-style Pinot Noir and Chardonnay grown on limestone.
Producers to try: *Pegasus Bay, Pyramid Valley*

DOWN SOUTH

In the Southern Alps' foothills near Queenstown, Central Otago is the only region with a continental climate. Pinot Noir is the big success here; long sunny dry days and very cold nights give opulent bright fruit. Subzones vary from cool Gibbston and warm Bannockburn, to hotter Alexandra in the south. Watch this space for good Chardonnay too.
Producers to try: *Burn Cottage, Felton Road, Prophet's Rock, Quartz Reef, Rippon, Sato, Valli*

KEY STYLES & GRAPES

Crisp delicate whites: Arneis, Albariño, Riesling, Grüner Veltliner
Full rich whites: Sauvignon Blanc, Chardonnay, Pinot Gris, Gewurztraminer
Soft juicy reds: Pinot Noir, Merlot, Cabernet Franc
Full rich reds: Syrah, Cabernet Sauvignon, Tempranillo, Malbec

CHANGES IN PRODUCTION

Current challenges: heat spikes, autumn rain, water scarcity
Future positives: drought-resistant clones, cooler micro-climates, sustainability focus

Scenic vineyards in the Upper Brancott Valley in Marlborough, New Zealand, with snow on the Blairich Range beyond.

SOUTH AFRICA

South Africa has come a long way since the fall of apartheid in 1994. While it was once known as a supplier of cheap co-op wine, a new generation of independent estates has transformed and grown the industry into one of the world's most dynamic and exciting. Superb-quality wines, incredible value and a beautiful welcoming nation make South Africa a must-visit for the wine tourist.

KEY FACTS
Size: 120,000 hectares, including table grapes/raisins
Styles: white, red, rosé, sparkling, sweet
Wine laws: WO
Main soils: gravel, granite, shale, sandstone, alluvial clay, limestone

CAPE TURNAROUND

Not long ago, Cape wines were hefty, overextracted or overoaked, but now the focus is on livelier, fresher styles and terroir. Since the early 2000s, Cape winemakers have been searching for new vineyard sites, rediscovering old vines, increasing organic viticulture, lowering alcohol, reducing oak and minimizing intervention. This has resulted in sleek, sophisticated, elegant wines with a real sense of place. Recent droughts and severe lockdowns on the sale of alcohol during Covid have been challenging, but Cape wineries are bouncing back with wines that are better than ever.

RESILIENT GRAPES

Wines are labelled by grape, with Chenin Blanc, Cabernet Sauvignon and Pinotage the signature varieties. In fact, South Africa has more Chenin Blanc than France – historically a workhorse grape here, now highly prized in Swartland and Citrusdal.

Cabernet Sauvignon is more Bordeaux style here than in Napa, and new approaches in the vineyard and cellar have dramatically improved Pinotage. Beyond the famous grape trio, winemakers are seeking out new varieties to thrive in a hotter, drier future.

CAPE TOWN SURROUNDS

Most renowned of Cape Town's wards is historic Constantia, which also gives its name to the legendary Muscat-based dessert wine (Vin de Constance), now revived. Cool ocean breezes and mountain slopes characterize this stunning southern suburb, chilly enough to make aromatic grassy Sauvignon Blanc, at best blended with Semillon. Heading to Cape Point, there is also a focus on white Bordeaux varieties.

Stellenbosch is home to the Cape's greatest concentration of top estates, with a diversity of grapes and soils. Granites in the east are favoured for Cabernet Sauvignon and Pinotage, and there is now more focus on choosing the right clones and higher-altitude plantings. Polkadraai Hills gives freshness, Simonsberg fine tannins and Helderberg rich bold wines.

Beautiful Franschhoek, engulfed by towering mountains, is home to old Cape farms. Here, the best Chardonnay and Semillon vineyards sit on slopes; Cap Classique is also a speciality. North of Stellenbosch, in warmer Paarl, Rhône grapes and Chenin Blanc do well. Heading east to Breede River, Robertson's limestone soils are ideal for Chardonnay.

Producers to try: *Beeslaar, Boekenhoutskloof, Buitenverwachting, Cape Point, De Trafford, De Wetshof, Glenelly, Jordan, Kanonkop, Klein Constantia, Meerlust, Miles Mossop, Rustenberg, Springfield, Uitsig, Van Loggerenberg*

COASTAL-COOL SOUTH

Winemakers have migrated here in search of cooler micro-climates. Surrounded by mountains, Elgin is the country's coldest wine district, making ever-improving Chardonnay, Pinot Noir and Syrah. However, apple orchards far outweigh vineyards. Walker Bay near Hermanus has the top Cape Chardonnay and Pinot Noir pioneers.

Winemakers are now exploring further south to windy Elim in Cape Agulhas – good for Sauvignon Blanc and Shiraz; also east, to the wild, raw, rocky

The Buitenverwachting (meaning 'beyond expectations') wine estate is based in Constantia near Cape Town, South Africa, and is renowned for its Sauvignon Blanc grown on decomposed granite soils.

terrain of Malgas, which is well suited to Viognier, Trincadeira and Mourvèdre. Meanwhile, some are experimenting with Assyrtiko.
Producers to try: *Alheit, Almenkerk, Creation, Crystallum, Damascene, Hamilton Russell, Newton Johnson, Paul Cluver, Richard Kershaw, Sijnn*

NORTHERN NATURAL HUB

South Africa's most dynamic region is Swartland. Once home to large co-ops and wheat farmers, now single vineyards with old vines are nurtured here, creating distinctive earthy wines – from powerful Syrah and Grenache, to elegant Chenin Blanc. It is also a hub of natural winemaking.

Heading northeast into Tulbagh and Piekenierskloof, these are good hunting grounds for old-vine Chenin Blanc, Syrah and Grenache.
Producers to try: *Badenhorst, David & Nadia, Mullineux, Rall, Sadie Family, Tierhoek*

KEY STYLES & GRAPES
Crisp delicate whites: Colombard, Assyrtiko, Vermentino
Full rich whites: Chardonnay, Chenin Blanc, Grenache Blanc, Roussanne, Viognier, Semillon, Sauvignon Blanc, Palomino
Soft juicy reds: Pinot Noir, Merlot, Cabernet Franc, Grenache
Full rich reds: Cabernet Sauvignon, Pinotage, Syrah, Mourvèdre, Cinsault, Touriga Nacional, Trincadeira, Tinta Roriz, Tinta Barroca

CHANGES IN PRODUCTION
Current challenges: heat spikes, drought
Future positives: drought-resistant clones, cooler micro-climates

ASIA

China, Japan and India are the most important Asian wine countries – but there are also vineyards emerging across the continent in Burma, Thailand, Taiwan, Indonesia, Cambodia, Vietnam and South Korea. The latest newcomer is Bhutan.

KEY FACTS
Size: 753,000 hectares (China, mostly table grapes); 18,000 (Japan); 185,000 (India, mostly table grapes)
Styles: white, red, sparkling, sweet
Wine laws: GI (Japan)
Main soils: Loess, gravel, silt, sand (China); clay, sand, granite, volcanic (Japan); clay, loam, gravel, limestone (India); clay, loam, sand (Bhutan)

CHINA – BURYING VINES

China's modern wine industry began in the 1980s – though wild grapevines grew here 9,000 years ago and *Vitis vinifera* arrived in the 4th century BCE. The first vineyards of the modern age were in southern Shandong, with winemakers challenged by typhoons, humidity and uneven ripening. However, they have quickly learned how to cope – particularly with fungal disease and tannin management.

Shandong is now recognized for its Riesling and Chardonnay, while impressive reds have emerged from Yantai (northern Shandong), Ningxia (southwest of Beijing), Shanxi (near the Loess Plateau) and Xinjiang (far northwest). Marselan and Syrah show potential, but 60 per cent of plantings are Cabernet Sauvignon.

Vidal and Riesling in northeastern Liaoning make Icewine – assisted by Canadian consultants. Freezing winter temperatures here, and in Ningxia and Hebei inland, mean vines have to be buried in winter for protection.

Producers to try: *Changyu, Grace Vineyard, Junding, Long Dai, Rongzi, Silk Road, Silver Heights, Weilong, Yizhu, Zhongfei*

JAPAN'S PAPER HATS

Lightness and precision are highly prized in Japan, so it is hardly surprising that the delicate pink-skinned Koshu is the country's flagship grape – now being made in a new dry style to suit modern tastes. It thrives in Japan's tricky climate, trained high with vertical shoot positioning, or on pergolas for aeration – and grape bunches are adorned with paper hats to protect them from excess sun or rain.

Yamanashi is Japan's wine heartland, with steep mountain vineyards (500 to 700m); 90 per cent of Koshu is grown here. Katsunuma is its warmest heat trap; other up-and-coming areas include Nagano (Merlot, Cabernet Franc), and drier, cooler northern Hokkaido is home to the first foreign venture, with the Burgundian de Montille family making impressive Pinot Noir. Japan's reds are still a work in progress, but some winemakers make Muscat Bailey A in an enchanting Gamay style. Japan's new wine culture includes a burgeoning number of artisanal wineries making sparkling, orange and amphora-aged wines (*see page* 134).

Pink-skinned Koshu grapes are protected from sun and rain with individual paper hats during ripening in Yamanashi, Japan.

GorTshalu vineyard in the warm east side of Bhutan, the world's newest wine country, was planted in 2021.

Producers to try: *Grace Wine, Kurambon, Mercian, de Montille & Hokkaido, Sapporo, Suntory Tomi, Takahata*

INDIA'S VISIONARY

Persian invaders brought vines to India in 1,300 BCE. India's wine culture was reignited in the 1980s when local billionaire Sham Chougule of Indage persuaded Piper-Heidsieck Champagne to help him make fizz in Nashik in Maharashtra state, inland from Mumbai. He was closely followed by Sula Vineyards. Nashik is now the most planted area, good for Chenin Blanc and Syrah. Further south, pioneer Grover headed to the Nandi Hills in Karnataka, north of Bangalore, to make Cabernet Sauvignon blends with French consultants.
Producers to try: *Chandon India, Grover Zampa, Sula Vineyards, Vallonne*

NEWCOMER BHUTAN

The first *Vitis vinifera* vines have recently been planted in the Kingdom of Bhutan, tucked into the Himalayas between China and India. Pockets of vineyards are planted from lower eastern Bhutan with warm summers and mild winters (suited to Cabernet Sauvignon and Syrah) to higher-altitude, cooler western Bhutan (Pinot Noir and Riesling), with plans to scale up plantings of those varieties that thrive. The first commercial harvest took place in 2024.
Producers to try: *Bhutan Wine Company*

CHINA, JAPAN, INDIA: KEY STYLES & GRAPES

Crisp delicate whites: Riesling (China), Koshu (Japan)
Full rich whites: Chardonnay (China, Japan), Chenin Blanc (India)
Soft juicy reds: Marselan (China), Merlot, Pinot Noir, Cabernet Franc, Muscat Bailey A (Japan)
Full rich reds: Cabernet Sauvignon, Syrah (China, Japan, India)
Sweet: Vidal (China)

CHANGES IN PRODUCTION

Current challenges: humidity, heat, rain, drought
Future positives: high altitude

BIBLIOGRAPHY

VITICULTURE
- *Regenerative Viticulture*, Dr Jamie Goode (independently published, 2022)
- *The New Viticulture: The Science of Growing Grapes for Wine*, Dr Jamie Goode (Flavour Press, 2023)
- *The One-Straw Revolution*, Masanobu Fukuoka (New York Review of Books Classics, 2009)
- *Vineyards, Rocks, & Soils: The Wine Lover's Guide to Geology*, Alex Maltman (Oxford University Press, 2018)
- *Volcanic Wines: Salt, Grit & Power*, John Szabo MS (Jacqui Small, 2016)
- *Which Winegrape Varieties are Grown Where? A Global Empirical Picture (revised edition)*, Kym Anderson & Signe Nelgen (University of Adelaide Press, 2020)
- *Wine Grapes: A Complete Guide to 1,368 Vine Varieties, Including Their Origins and Flavours*, Jancis Robinson MW, Julia Harding MW & José Vouillamoz (Allen Lane, 2012)

WINE TASTING
- *Beyond Flavour: Wine Tasting by Structure (2nd edition)*, Nick Jackson MW (independently published, 2022)
- *Flawless: Understanding Faults in Wine*, Dr Jamie Goode (University of California Press, 2018)
- *The Taste of Wine: The Art and Science of Wine Appreciation*, Emile Peynaud (Little Brown, 1987)

ORANGE & NATURAL WINES
- *Amber Revolution: How the World Learned to Love Orange Wine*, Simon J Woolf (Interlink Books, 2021)
- *Natural Wine: An Introduction to Organic and Biodynamic Wines Made Naturally*, Isabelle Legeron MW (Cico Books, 2020)
- *Natural Wine for the People: What It Is, Where to Find It, How to Love It*, Alice Feiring (Ten Speed Press, 2019)

CHAMPAGNE & SPARKLING WINE
- *Christie's World Encyclopedia of Champagne & Sparkling Wine (fourth edition)*, Tom Stevenson & Essi Avellan MW (Bloomsbury, 2019)

REGION/COUNTRY
- *Foot Trodden: Portugal and the Wines that Time Forgot*, Simon J Woolf & Ryan Opaz (Interlink Books, 2021)
- *Inside Burgundy: The Second Edition*, Jasper Morris MW (BB&R Press, 2021)
- *Inside Bordeaux: The Châteaux, Their Wines and the Terroir*, Jane Anson (BB&R Press, 2020)
- *Jura Wine*, Wink Lorch (Wine Travel Media, 2014)
- *Jura Wine Ten Years On*, Wink Lorch (Wine Travel Media, 2024)
- *The New France: A Complete Guide to Contemporary French Wine*, Andrew Jefford (Mitchell Beazley, 2006)
- *The South America Wine Guide: The Definitive Guide to Wine in Argentina, Chile, Uruguay, Brazil, Bolivia & Peru*, Amanda Barnes MW (Independently published, 2021)
- *The Wines of Germany (The Classic Wine Library)*, Anne Krebiehl MW (Academie du Vin Library, 2019)
- *The Wines of Northern Spain: From Galicia to the Pyrenees and Rioja to the Basque Country (The Classic Wine Library)*, Sarah Jane Evans MW (Academie du Vin Library, 2018)
- *Wines of the French Alps: Savoie, Bugey and Beyond with Local Food and Travel Tips*, Wink Lorch (Wine Travel Media, 2019)
- *Wines of the Rhône (The Classic Wine Library)*, Matt Walls (Academie du Vin Library, 2021)

GENERAL REFERENCES
- *Hugh Johnson's Pocket Wine Book 2025*, general editor Margaret Rand (Mitchell Beazley, 2024)
- *One Thousand Vines*, Pascaline Lepeltier (Mitchell Beazley, 2024)
- *The New Sotheby's Wine Encyclopedia (6th edition)*, Tom Stevenson (National Geographic, 2020)
- *The Oxford Companion to Wine (5th edition)*, editors Julia Harding MW & Jancis Robinson MW (Oxford University Press, 2023)
- *The Sommelier's Atlas of Taste*, Rajat Parr & Jordan Mackay (Ten Speed Press, 2018)
- *The World Atlas of Wine (eighth edition)*, Hugh Johnson & Jancis Robinson MW (Mitchell Beazley, 2019)
- *Wine Science: Principles and Applications (4th Edition)*, Ronald S Jackson (Academic Press, 2014)

OTHER REFERENCES
- *Climate, Grapes, and Wine: Terroir and the Importance of Climate to Winegrape Production*, GV Jones (2015) – guildsomm.com/public_content/features/articles/b/gregory_jones/posts/climate-grapes-and-wine
- *Historic Changes and Future Projections in Köppen–Geiger Climate Classifications in Major Wine Regions Worldwide*, C Andrade, A Fonseca, JA Santos, B Bois and GV Jones (2024) – doi.org/10.3390/cli12070094
- *Future Climate and the Impact on Wine: Predictable or Uncertain*, M Summerfield (2023) – worldoffinewine.com/news-features/climate-change-impact-wine
- *Climate Change and How It Is Affecting Vineyards*, IMW Webinar Series (2025) – www.mastersofwine.org/events/webinars
- *The Science of Taste*, C Gilby (2020) – thewinesociety.com/discover/explore/expertise/caroline-gilby-the-science-of-taste/

RECOMMENDED WEBSITES
iwcawine.org
swroundtable.org
regenerativeviticulture.org
oldvineregistry.org
jancisrobinson.com
wineanorak.com
climateofwine.com
winescholarguild.org
wsetglobal.com
mastersofwine.org
insideburgundy.com
noblerot.co.uk
trinkmag.com
decanter.com
ucdavis.edu
rosemurraybrown.com

INDEX

PICTURE CREDITS

All pictures by Steve Ryan except for the following:

Alamy Stock Photo/freeartist 170, Georg Berg 184, Hans Blossey 68, Hugo Martin 72l, James Sturcke 80, Julian Elliott/ robertharding 165, LOOK-foto/Image Professionals GmbH 90, Luciano Mortula 103, MadPhotos 183, Oliver Hoffmann 162, Performance Image 109, Peter Eastland 173, Scott Kemper 201, Sergio Azenha 176, Stuart Black 73l, Stuart Forster Europe 81l, Wineographic 175, wronaphoto.com 185, xeipe/Panther Media GmbH 182, Zoltan Bagosi 75l; Courtesy **Alkina Wine Estate**/ Photo Andy Ellis 96; Archmospheres 156; **Bodega Garzón** 91, 208; **Calum Mackintosh** 16; **Cephas Picture Library Ltd**./© Andy Christodolo 71, © Catherine Illsley 180, © Herbert Lehmann 97, © Jean-Bernard Nadeau 84, © Kevin Judd 203, 207, 213, © Mick Rock 38, 120, 167r, 187, © R & K Muschenetz 205; **Courtesy Cullen Wines** 88l, 88r, 89; **Courtesy Danbury Ridge** 179; **David Eldridge/Two Associates** 2–3, 6–7, 36–7, 130–1, 154–5; **Deutsches Weininstitut** 181; **Dreamstime.com**:/Arenaphotouk 64r, Sohadiszno 177; Getty Images/Raymond Roig/AFP 115; Heymann-Löwenstein/Photo VDP 64l; Inter Rhône/Christophe Grilhe 70; **iStock**/CaronB 73c, Ivica Pavicic 195, Klaas Jan Schraa 82c, luxiangjian4711 65, Maria Elena Cervino Ferrin 81r, Matthew J Thomas 57r, 82b, Nalidsa Sukprasert 57c, Oleg_0 193, phbcz 72c, rusm 74, TokioMarineLife 216; **Josef Engelhart** 62r; **London Cru** 198; Courtesy **Lyla**/Photo: Murray Orr 152; Courtesy **Man O War** 212; **© Miles Willis** 192l, 192r; **Nandor Lang** 188, 189; Courtesy **Olivier Humbrecht MW**/Photo Leif Carlsson 86; **Rico Nuevo**/Photo Alberto Galán 174; **Rose Murray Brown MW** 72r; **Shutterstock Creative**/AerialVision_it 168, Arnold.Petersen 214, Batard Jean Marc 82a, Bruno Pereira da Silva 67, Dimitri Lamour 121, FreeProd33 57l, GP PHOTOTRENDS 45r, gurb101088 161, M. Volk 73r, Majonit 163, Marco Taliani de Marchio 108, Mirko Graul 45, myphotobank.com.au 160, Neda Gavrilovicc 196, Nick Pecker 39l, Paul Thomas Curry 69, Razafimbelo Mika 101br, Ripka Gergely 75r, Tatyana Soares 26, thegrimfandango 171, visionteller 45l; Courtesy **Stirbey** 190; **IDM**/Südtirol Wein/Tiberio Sorvillo 169; **Thomas Niedermayr** 62l; Courtesy **Tolpuddle Vineyard**/ Photo Jessica Clark 210; **Tristan Vuano**/avuedecoucou.com 167l; Courtesy **Vignai Da Duline**/Photo © Lorenzo Mocchiutti 87; Courtesy **Weingut am Stein**/© Stefan Schütz 123; **Sherab Dorji** 217; **Wine and Soul** 66; **Zorah Winery** 122.

First published in Great Britain in 2025 by
Mitchell Beazley, an imprint of
Octopus Publishing Group Ltd
Carmelite House
50 Victoria Embankment
London EC4Y 0DZ
www.octopusbooks.co.uk

An Hachette UK Company
www.hachette.co.uk

The authorized representative in the EEA is Hachette Ireland,
8 Castlecourt Centre, Dublin 15, D15 XTP3, Ireland
(email: info@hbgi.ie)

Distributed in the US by Hachette Book Group
1290 Avenue of the Americas, 4th and 5th Floors
New York, NY 10104

Distributed in Canada by Canadian Manda Group
664 Annette St., Toronto, Ontario, Canada M6S 2C8

ISBN 978-1-84091-898-4
eISBN 978-1-84091-899-1

A CIP catalogue record for this book is available from the British Library.

Printed and bound in Dubai.

10 9 8 7 6 5 4 3 2 1

Commissioning editor: Jeannie Stanley
Senior developmental editor: Pauline Bache
Art director: Yasia Williams
Cover designer and illustrator: David Eldridge at Two Associates
Designer: Geoff Fennell
Picture researchers: Giulia Hetherington and Jennifer Veal
Copyeditor: Hilary Lumsden
Proofreader: David Tombesi-Walton
Assistant production manager: Allison Gonsalves

[Data used throughout the book is correct at the time of writing; numbers are rounded]

ACKNOWLEDGEMENTS

I would like to thank the team at Mitchell Beazley/Octopus Publishing Group: Jeannie Stanley, Pauline Bache and Yasia Williams for having confidence in me to write the book in the first place – and for bringing it to life – and also Hilary Lumsden for all her support and encouragement.

For their specialist knowledge or proofreading – thank you to Dr Gregory Jones, Professor Mike Summerfield, Dr José Vouillamoz, Olivier Humbrecht MW, Vanya Cullen, Doug Wregg, Justin Howard-Sneyd MW, Sebastián Zuccardi, Dr Caroline Gilby MW, Elizabeth Gabay MW, Stephen Skelton MW, Will Davenport, Tim Wildman MW, John Szabo MS, Lorenzo Mocchiutti, Federica Magrini, Dr Laura Catena, Joel Bastian and Stuart Skea.

Thank you also to the many winemakers around the world (not already mentioned above) who have given up their time and whose wines and stories have inspired me over the years: Stéphane Tissot, August Kesseler, Dr Katharina Prüm, Jeffrey Grosset, Stephen Henschke, Rick Kinzbrunner, Michael Hill-Smith MW, Helen Masters, Zoltán Demeter, István Szepsy Jnr, Stéphanie Berecz, Vivien Ujvári, Robert Gilvesy, Dirk Niepoort, Sandra Tavares, Heidi Schrock, Erich Krutzler, Etienne de Montille, Eddy Faller, Charla Bosman, Abrie Beeslaar, Andy Smith, David Ramey, Miguel Torres, Fernando Mora MW, Willy Pérez, Ramiro Ibáñez, Dr Misha Dolidze, Giorgi Dakishvili, Frank Cornelissen, José Ignacio Maturana, Susana Balbo, Pablo Fallabrino and many more.

A big thank you to my family for their immense support and patience, particularly my husband Rob.

ABOUT THE AUTHOR

Rose Murray Brown is a Master of Wine, and one of about 400 MWs in the world. She focuses primarily on consumer and trade education and consumer journalism. After university, she trained at Sotheby's for 12 years as a wine and spirit specialist. In 2000, Rose set up her own wine school (Rose Murray Brown Masterclass) offering her brand of consumer courses, masterclasses, dinners and corporate events, and she personally organizes and hosts consumer group wine tours (most recently to Chile, Argentina, Uruguay, Georgia, Sicily and Hungary).

Rose is an award-winning journalist and has been a weekly columnist at *The Scotsman* for 38 years. She is a contributor to international magazines, broadcaster and international wine competition judge; and is a UK-based member of The Institute of Masters of Wine, Association of Wine Educators and Circle of Wine Writers. Rose is well-known for her down-to-earth approach to wine and lively passionate lecturing style, using stories from the wine world to engage and interest people in exploring and experimenting with different wine styles.

www.rosemurraybrown.com
@rosemurraybrown